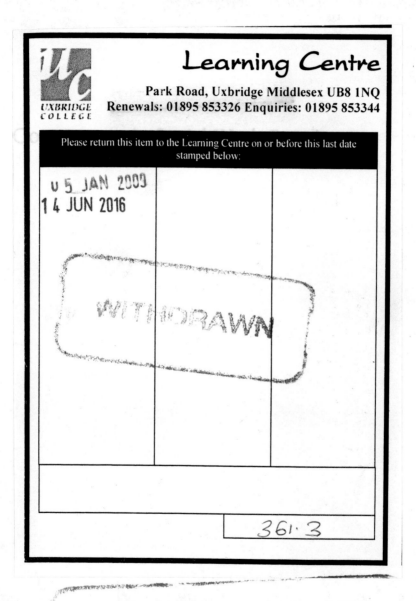

Competence in Social Work Practice

A Practical Guide for Students and Professionals

Second edition

Edited by Kieran O'Hagan

Jessica Kingsley Publishers
London and Philadelphia

First edition published in 1996
This edition published in 2007
by Jessica Kingsley Publishers
116 Pentonville Road
London N1 9JB, UK
and
400 Market Street, Suite 400
Philadelphia, PA 19106, USA

www.jkp.com

Copyright © Jessica Kingsley Publishers 1996, 2007

Library of Congress Cataloging in Publication Data
A CIP catalog record for this book is available from the Library of Congress

British Library Cataloguing in Publication Data
A CIP catalogue record for this book is available from the British Library

ISBN 978 1 84310 485 8

Printed and bound in Great Britain by
Athenaeum Press, Gateshead, Tyne and Wear

Contents

List of Tables

List of Figures

List of Boxes

Acknowledgements

The editor would like to express gratitude to many friends, colleagues, relatives and service users whose contribution towards this book are inestimable. Special thanks are due to Margaret Fawcett for irrepressible humour when it was most needed, to Christine O'Hagan, whose proofreading is increasingly relied upon, to Graham Hunt, for his technical expertise and his calming influence when the computer says it has had enough, and to Jessica Kingsley and Stephen Jones for making both first and second editions possible.

Preface

Being invited to produce a second edition of a text is always a welcome proposition; it suggests some popularity and usefulness in the original, and a sustaining relevance in current practice. In revisiting the whole area of competence in social work practice, two features of the enterprise remain as conspicuous in this edition as they did in the original; first, strict adherence to an entirely new framework (National Occupational Standards) in which all social work training will now take place (a decade ago, that framework was Central Council for Education and Training in Social Work Paper 30). The second feature is that social work students on placement dominate the contents of these pages as much as they did in the first edition. In all but two of the chapters, it is students' aspirations towards professionalism, their enthusiasm to begin practice and serve their clients, to take on complex and demanding challenges, to digest as much relevant research and literature as they can, and to record some of the contrasting emotional highs and lows along the road towards attainment of the new National Occupational Standards now required of them – it is these contents, focusing so much on individual student effort, which convey to readers that social work training is not merely a learning exercise, but a truly multifarious experience, challenging virtually every aspect of self, the emotional, psychological, intellectual, social, cultural and spiritual self.

The task for the editor and contributors has been somewhat different but no less challenging than that facing the students they portray: to scrutinise the National Occupational Standards more methodically than we may have had reason to do before, and to ensure that everything we write, be it about practice, theory or research, or any novel thing we do (e.g. devise a system, construct a framework, draw figures and tables), is compatible with, and will help illuminate, many of the requirements of the National Occupational Standards.

This is an unusual task for social work writers. Like all writers, we want to write freely, lucidly, expansively about our subject areas, without interruption or deviation. We are not often compelled to re-examine our work and repeatedly ask ourselves: is this relevant to the requirements of the Standards, and does it contribute in some small way towards students fulfilling those Standards or practice teachers and examiners upholding them? We know however, that whatever one thinks about such textual features, it is precisely what student social workers require.

It is far too easy for experienced workers and trainers to lose sight of how social work students perceive the challenges they face. These are not the easiest of times for such students. Despite the fact that social work is an immensely rewarding and fulfilling occupation, the intellectual, organisational, societal and professional demands on them are substantially more onerous. New standards, much longer training, and evidence-based practice all contribute to those demands. Social work students justifiably expect that those entrusted with enabling them to attain the new National Occupational Standards are thoroughly familiar with those Standards. They also expect those same people to constantly reassure them (even if the student is already convinced that it is the case) that the students' academic work and their placement practice is in accordance with specific values and ethics, Key Roles, units or elements etc. within the Standards.

The ultimate challenge therefore, in both editions, was to achieve a narrative that combined continuous references to the new Standards with compelling accounts of students striving to attain them. We believe we achieved that objective first time round, and we believe that in this edition, with its new contributors and subject areas rarely written about elsewhere (e.g. competence in social work ethics; competence in protecting adults with learning difficulties), that we have done so again.

CHAPTER 1

Competence: An Enduring Concept?

Kieran O'Hagan

Introduction

The first edition of this book was published in 1996, shortly after major reforms in social work education had been implemented. The Central Council for Education and Training in Social Work (CCETSW 1995) final Paper 30 heralded the new two-year Diploma in Social Work, replacing its predecessor, the Certificate of Qualification in Social Work. Paper 30 required all social work training programmes for the new Diploma to be designed, organised, implemented and resourced by Partnerships. These partnerships would consist of academic institutions and many of the statutory and voluntary social services agencies in which successful students would ultimately work. No less challenging was the requirement that social work training was to be competence-led. Competence in social work practice would be the ultimate goal. There was much resistance, but there could be no turning back. Paper 30 and competence had to be accepted and implemented. It was, in the words of some trainers 'the end of the road' for 'professional social work education...stuck in a cul-de-sac of regulation and conformity that stifles innovation and change' (Committee for Social Work Education and Policy 1995, p.3).

Who could have predicted that only ten years later, this second edition would emerge in response to a similarly hectic period of transformation of training, brought about by:

1. new social policies and legislation relating to various user groups

2. the establishment of numerous regulatory and inspection councils and commissions

3. new codes of practice for both social workers and employers

4. new government guidelines

5. enquiry reports

6. the publication *Every Child Matters* (Department for Education and Skills 2003)

7. the increasing demand for service users' participation in training and in service delivery (Levin 2004)

8. the establishment of National Occupational Standards.

The Standards were developed by the respective 'Care Councils' within the four jurisdictions of the UK, i.e. the Care Council for Wales; the Northern Ireland Social Care Council; the Scottish Social Care Council and, in England, the Training Organisation for the Personal Social Services (TOPSS). These bodies regulate social work training and (together with the General Social Care Council [GSCC] in England) are responsible for the registration of social care and social work staff. The Standards they developed were approved by the Qualification and Curriculum Authority in June 2002. CCETSW was wound up in 2002, having been replaced by the GSCC. This regulatory, organisational and legislative transformation was then sufficiently advanced to bring about the most significant changes: 1. the phasing out of the Diploma in Social Work and replacement by a degree course, internationally recognised; 2. the registration of social workers and social work students, and 3. the protection of the title 'Social Worker'. Although this would imply a good deal of conformity, the fact is that, in the UK as a whole, there remains substantial variation in the educational standards and experience required for entry, the types of degrees awarded (BA Hons, BSc, MSc, etc.) and the means by which they are obtained (college-based, distance learning/employer based routes etc.).

Why was social work subjected to this second root and branch upheaval? There are a number of reasons. First, with regard to the Degree, this change merely completed the realignment of social work education with European education in general in accordance with the Bologna Declaration of June 1999, facilitating easier transfer for social work students from one country to another (Marthinson 2004). Second, the landslide election victory of a Labour government in 1997 heralded major social and welfare reforms. A new government, of whatever political hue, was certain to attempt to make an impact upon many aspects of life after such a long period in the political wilderness. Third, and more pertinent to this text, was that the requirements that brought about the first upheaval in social work training were judged to be unfulfilled. The ultimate goal of all those initial changes was *competence* in social work and social care practice. There was however (and still remains) ample evidence in research and enquiry reports of *incompetent* practice, greatly worsening the service user's situation, and in rare cases, contributing to their deaths in appalling circumstances (e.g. Social Services Inspectorate 1998; Laming 2003). After all the changes in training and preparation therefore, the new Labour government let it be known (particularly after the Victoria Climbié case) that it was singularly unimpressed by the level of competence within social care and social work practice. The government's language was brutally frank. For example, the principal objective of its newly created Commission for Social Care Inspection is to 'stamp out bad practice' (CSCI 2006). In a brief but revealing Foreword to The Department of Health's (DoH) (2002) *Requirements for Social Work Training*, a Minister tells social workers and trainers what they 'must do' four times; what they 'need to do' or 'need to be' twice; what they will be 'required to do' twice; what they 'have to do' once. The Minister's final words are:

> Those providing the teaching and learning opportunities for social work students need to ensure they take on board the implications of these changes… This is not tinkering at the edges of social work training. This is a major shift in *expectations* (*i.e. the government's expectations*) of those providing the training and those undertaking it (p.1) (my italics and parenthesis).

It cannot be a mere coincidence that the National Occupational Standards that followed are headed by six sweeping *expectations* (Training Organisation for Personal Social Services [TOPSS] 2004).

Competence reasserted

Little wonder then, that the concept of competence has endured throughout this second phase of significant change. Even those with strong reservations about it accept that it is now 'embedded in UK government policy' (Trevithick 2005, p.62) and that it occupies a pivotal place in many government publications pertaining to the new social work degree course. More importantly, the National Occupational Standards, which all social work degrees must now ultimately seek to satisfy, 'provide a benchmark of best practice in social work competence across the UK' (TOPSS 2006). The standards actually are, in the words of social work's regulating councils: 'the core competences for every social worker' (TOPSS 2006). They 'form the basis of assessment of competence in practice' and 'social workers will be required to demonstrate competence across the full range of standards before being awarded the degree' (DoH 2002, p.1). The standards are framed within six *key roles*, the last of which requires social work students to *demonstrate professional competence in social work practice*, a role which, along with that of accountability (Key Role 5) should 'underpin all other activity' (Care Council for Wales 2003).

Origins of competence-based education and training

Theoretical origins

Competence-based education and training has its origins in behaviourism and functional analysis, two theoretical orientations which were popular in the 1960s and 1970s. An earlier social worker advocate of functional analysis (Smalley 1967, p.151) wrote 'The use of agency function and function in professional role gives focus, content, and direction to social work processes' and 'assures accountability to society and agency'. The competence-based approach specifically addressed the tasks of assessing and measuring what individuals do in a variety of workplaces. It identified areas of competence and established performance criteria.

Organisational origins

The National Council for Vocational Qualifications (NCVQ) was set up in 1986, with a mandate to develop a competence-based system for defining and assessing standards for all occupations. It created Industrial Lead Bodies (ILB) for each occupational area. Each ILB had representatives from employers and employees. The ILB for the caring professions became known as the Care Sector Consortium (1992). CCETSW was a member of this Consortium. The consortium monitored the development of competence-based occupational standards in Health and Personal Social Services, including statutory, voluntary and private care agencies. All occupational standards development programmes in any of the care agencies had to be approved by the Care Sector Consortium, just as the National Occupational Standards of today were developed and agreed upon by the four respective Care Councils of the UK. (It is fair to say that the Standards have emerged from a much more broadly based forum of participants.)

Key jobs and tasks were identified within care provision generally, e.g. the job of providing hands-on care to patients, residents or clients; the task of enabling and promoting clients' independence. Each task was divided into units (of competence). Each unit was further divided into elements which described precisely what care workers needed to be doing. Examples (i.e. performance criteria) were provided. Probably the most crucial distinction for care provision (in comparison with other occupations) was the importance ascribed to ethics in care work. This was reflected not just in 'values' being given the status of a separate unit of competence but, more importantly, in assessors expecting to see evidence of core values being applied throughout the demonstration of each unit of competence. This emphasis on values was replicated in CCETSW's (1995) Paper 30 and *values* and *ethics* occupy the pivotal place in social work's current National Occupational Standards, around which each of the new six areas of competence revolve: 'Values and ethics are core to competent social work practice' (Care Council for Wales 2003).

Has anything really changed?

If you glance over the principal social work journals and main texts of the last decade, you may be excused for thinking that the dichotomy between the government's and social work trainers' perceptions of competence remains as stark as it was in the preceding decade. You are not likely, for example, to find any author enthusiastically supporting competence-led training, nor any article that would indicate some moderation in the basically hostile, distorted perception of the concept. Many modern social work textbooks don't even mention *competence* or *competent* practice. It's as though some prominent social work writers are either unaware of or have chosen to ignore the pivotal role that the concept plays in the training and in the accreditation of the students, for whom the texts are primarily aimed. Has anything changed, therefore?

The critical voices of the previous decade (1986–95) have not dimmed. Later we will look at more recent criticism of competence-led training. First however, let us consider the origin and historical use of the word competence.

The origin and use of competence

The words 'competence' and 'competent' derive from the Latin word *'competens'*, meaning 'be fit, proper or qualified' (Hoad 1986). This meaning has been sustained more or less intact throughout the centuries. There are, however, two developments worth noting: first, from the fifteenth century, the words were increasingly used in a legal context. The 'fitness, properness and sufficiency of qualification' in the original definitions referred to necessary standards in legal matters and legal processes. Second, in contrast, it was commonly used in a far more personal sense by poets and writers of the eighteenth and nineteenth centuries. Clarendon wrote of 'a competency of discretion and foresight'; Charlotte Bronte spoke of 'References as to character and competency'; Samuel Smiles advised one 'to retire upon a competency'. Wordsworth, believe it or not, was one of the most prolific users of the word. As the most reflective of all the Romantic geniuses, he might be perplexed to hear today's critics of competence talking about its 'mechanistic', 'anti reflective' features, particularly when he was writing lines like 'Heights which the soul is competent to gain...' and 'robbed of competence and her obsequious shadow, peace of mind'. He uses the word seven times in a mere 60 lines of his major poem 'Excursions', a work of 'personal conflicts, sorrows, and consolations' (Moorman 1968, p.77).

Training definitions

NCVQ was the first body to attempt to define competence in the vocational workplace. It produced a rather broad definition that nevertheless included aspects still regarded as central to the social work task: 'transferring skills and knowledge to new situations...planning of work...innovation, coping with non-routine activities...includes those qualities of personal effectiveness that are required in the workplace to deal with co-workers, managers and customers' (NCVQ 1988). CCETSW (1995) attempted to define it specifically within the context of the new social work training that it was bringing into effect through Paper 30:

> Competence is the product of knowledge, skills and values. Students will have to demonstrate that they have met practical requirements, integrated social work values, acquired and applied knowledge, reflected upon and critically analysed their practice, and transferred knowledge, skills and values in practice (p.17).

Trevithick (2005) suggested broadening the concept, by adding 'under-standing' to knowledge, values and skills, an addition that the preamble to today's National Occupational Standards, under the heading Key Core Skills, had already taken on board: 'To know, understand, critically analyse, evaluate and apply the knowledge for each unit' (Care Council for Wales 1993, p.3). More challengingly, Trevithick and other writers (e.g. Neville 2004; Waterson and Morris 2005) believe that competence is not achieved solely by the worker utilising these four attributes within themselves, but also by utilising the same attributes within service users and carers. The National Occupational Standards do precisely what these authors advocate (and what the government sponsored Social Care Institute for Excellence promotes), not just pervasively throughout the competencies, but also, in the *statement of expectations* preceding them: 'Social Workers must recognise the expertise of individuals, carers, groups and communities, about their own situations'…involving them 'in all meetings which affect them…' (TOPSS 2004, p.2)

Knowledge

The knowledge underpinning social work practice derives from many different sources. Competent practice will depend upon knowledge of law, social policy, philosophy (ethics), psychology, sociology, social administration, organisational policy procedures and guidelines, numerous theories, differing social work methods (or disciplines as they may sometimes be called, e.g. behaviourism, family therapy, psychodynamics, mediation, group-work therapy, etc.). Increasingly, social work competence also depends upon knowledge and competence in information technology (Bellefuille and Schmidt 2006; Bolen 2006). All of these components of knowledge are self-explanatory, with the exception of theory, which Mitchell (1975, p.211) refers to as 'one of the most misused and misleading terms'.

Understanding theory

Students are often led to believe that convenient academic tools such as 'definitions', 'concepts', 'frameworks', 'categorisations', 'tables', 'grids' and 'figures' are all theories, and they studiously label them as such in written assignments and practice portfolios. A 'definition' is the descriptive, explanatory and most precise meaning given to any subject. A 'concept' is nothing more or less than an idea or general notion about something; the idea may be original or not; concepts can, however, be the building blocks from which we construct meaning. A 'framework' is a boundary within which one can impose order and sense upon something which otherwise may appear chaotic and unmanageable.

Categorisations, tables and grids and figures are all frameworks; they appear regularly throughout social work texts, performing the same function as frameworks in differing ways. None of these common academic tools, of themselves, constitute theory, yet the exposition and application of theory may depend upon the use of any of them. Figure 1.1 in this chapter may justifiably be referred to as both a framework and a concept, illustrating and emphasising the paramouncy of *values* and *ethics*, around which the six Key Roles revolve. But it is not a theory. The two most important and necessary functions of theory are enhancing understanding and enabling one to predict process and/or outcome. Theory enables us to formulate strategies of intervention and articulate goals. It is obvious therefore, that theory is not (as some practitioners may believe) divorced from reality, rather, it consists of concepts and prepositions about reality. Theory is not rigid or inhibiting, rather, it demands vision and imagination. In approaching the complexities and dilemmas of social work within the framework of a theory, social workers add a dimension to their work which observations, rules and guidelines, policies and procedures cannot themselves provide. Theory often leads to greater insights. It is an instrument by which social workers can construct more comprehensive and effective intervention strategies, and predict outcome with more confidence.

Types and uses of knowledge

The boundless nature of the social work knowledge base has compelled many social work writers to try to categorise it (e.g. Lishman 1991; O'Hagan 1996; Osmond 2005; Trevithick 2005). Publications concentrating on evidence-based practice, data analysis and research are increasingly read (Gilgun 2005; Marsh and Fisher 2005). The Social Care Institute for Excellence (SCIE) was set up in 2001 with the specific aim of developing and promoting knowledge about good practice, and has sponsored many publications towards that aim (SCIE 2006). Correspondingly, researchers maintain their vital role of demonstrating the different consequences of two diametrically opposed perceptions and uses of knowledge:

1. Those professionals who do not feel the need to draw on
    evidence-based knowledge (Rosen 1994; Somerfield and Hughes
    1987) relying instead on their experience, common assumptions
    or convictions.

2. Professionals who are wholly guided by proven knowledge and
    evidence-based practice, thereby achieving much better results
    (Jackson 2002; Nissim and Simm 1994; Sellick and Thoburn
    2002).

Skills

The words *skills, competence, practice,* and *techniques* are often used synony-
mously. Trevithick's (2005) authoritative work is actually entitled *Social
Work Skills,* and distinguishes broadly between generalist skills (of which no
less than 56 are described in the text) and specialist skills. The word skill is
derived from the Old Norse term *skil,* meaning distinction, discernment and
knowledge; the verb *skila* means give reason for, expound, decide. The Middle English word *skilful* meant endowed with reason. In the seventeenth
century the word *skill* meant to have discrimination or knowledge, especially in a specified manner. This intellectual quality is still evident in the
present-day dictionary meaning, though the complete definition is far more
diffuse: practical knowledge in combination with ability... cleverness,
expertise... knowledge or understanding of something...

The National Occupational Standards, regrettably, do not give skills the
status they were accorded in Paper 30, in which they were, both diagram-
matically and content-wise, one of the three towering pillars of social work
competence: *knowledge, values* and *skills.* Nor are skills defined in the scant
mention of them throughout the Standards.

Values and ethics

The centrality and emphasis given to values and ethics in the new standards
may stem in part from the increasing criticism of competence-led training,
and warnings about social work losing its moral base (Bisman 2004). *Values
and Ethics* is the main heading in TOPSS's (2004) publication of the standards. Each unit of competence is accompanied by a 'knowledge base'
which repetitively details the values and ethics challenge that students must
surmount. That challenge has six components (see Figure 1.1), and the first
is probably the most important: 'awareness of your own values, prejudices,

ethical dilemmas and conflicts of interest and their implications on your own practice'. The pivotal location of values and ethics in the illustrative figure adopted by the four UK care jurisdictions at the outset of each of their National Occupational Standards unmistakeably tells the reader that values and ethics permeate every aspect of social work practice.

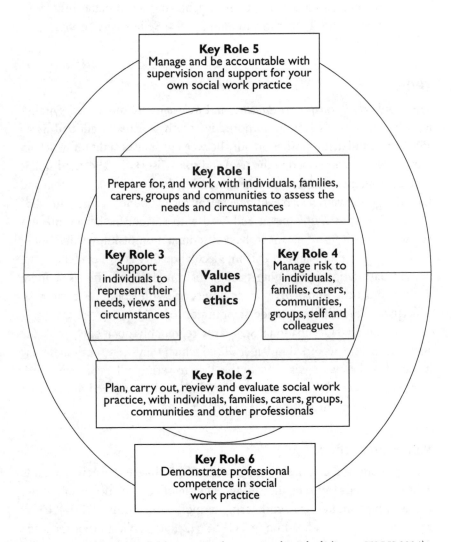

Figure 1.1: The key social work roles in National Occupational Standards (Source: TOPSS 2004)

Competence-led social work training: the main criticisms

Competence-led training provoked many criticisms when the Diploma in Social Work was introduced (O'Hagan 1996). These included the charge that it was racist and lacked an equal opportunities perspective (Issitt 1995; Kemshall 1993). More recent criticisms trawl over much of the same ground. For example:

- It 'is antithetical to depth explanations, professional integrity, creative practice, and tolerance of complexity and uncertainty' (Howe 1996, p.92).

- It narrows the assessment process to a 'tick-box' exercise (Denney 1998).

- It 'separates out different actions or activities into their component parts' (Trevithick 2005, p.63).

- It dilutes social work values, which become subjected to the same reductionist tendencies, and are expressed strictly in measurable, behavioural terms (Bisman 2004; Platt 1994).

- It should 'not be seen as an autonomous "vocational" development but as both the consequence and counterpart of the expansion of corporate management' (Nellis 1996, p.176).

- It 'inadequately describes what occurs in an encounter either between service users and workers, or between workers and those assessing their competence' (Braye and Preston-Shoot 1995, p.66).

- It is not conducive to reflective practice and social work education itself is in danger of leading to 'a practice reduced to technical competence' (Prior 2005, p.13).

Testing the reality

These are obviously deeply held convictions, probably strengthened rather than dissipated by the realities that competence-led training and the achievement of competence are now irrevocably entrenched in every sphere of educational and vocational life. There is little point therefore, in repeating each and every rebuttal of such criticism (O'Hagan 1996). Nevertheless, it is worth considering whether or not the language of competence-led training in general, and of the National Occupational Standards in particular, generate indifference at best, but more commonly a distrust and hostility that precludes objective, incisive assessment. We will therefore address some of the more serious, persistent criticisms, the first of which is that complex tasks are dismantled into component parts, creating a tick box exercise, and ignoring the holistic and dynamic complexity of social work (and also one might add, its risks and dangers).

Figure 1.2 shows a slightly modified illustration of Key Role 1 Unit 2, and the four specified competences, from the National Occupational Standards.

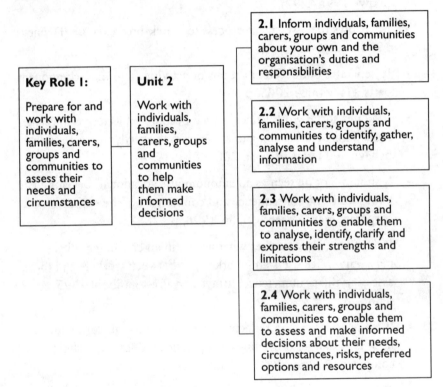

Figure 1.2: Key Role 1 (adapted from TOPSS 2004)

The four elements of competence on the right of Figure 1.2 may appear to be, as Howe (1996) alleges, nothing more than 'routine, standardised practices and predictable tasks' (p.92) that don't really need much *knowledge, understanding, values* and *skills*, and can be quickly 'ticked off' before the student and supervisor get to meatier, more challenging competences. Nothing could be further from the truth, and such perceptions are a dangerous delusion to inflict upon students. The first element for example: *Inform individuals, families, carers, groups and communities about your own and the organisation's duties and responsibilities* may present major, challenging and even dangerous tasks in particular situations. (Therein lies an exercise, for trainers and students alike: give three examples of situations in which informing individuals etc., about your own and the organisation's duties and responsibilities may heighten tension and generate risk to the worker, and what knowledge, understanding, values and skills might the worker utilise to prepare for, and to best exercise control in defusing the heightening tension and risk?) Workers of sufficient experience can probably think of many such situations, particularly in mental health and child protection. Trainers have the responsibility to lead their students to at least think about these unanticipated but harsh realities of practice, which don't conveniently jump out from the pages of the National Occupational Standards.

Aiming for the impossible

Braye and Preston-Shoot (1995) and Trevithick (2005) both highlight what they see as the limitations of 'competences' to describe what occurs in encounters or to capture the 'complex and interrelated nature' of those encounters. There are two contrasting responses to these criticisms. First, 15 years of competence-led training in social work should be able to support or contest the point. Are trainers generally observing more boringly contrived, shallow, mechanistic, soulless recordings made by students bent on nothing more than gaining a competence? Or do trainers occasionally read powerful compelling, psychologically and emotionally realistic recordings of encounters between students and service users? I see no evidence of the former, but have much experience of the latter, both in direct supervision of the student's work and, more importantly, in sharing assessment of that work with colleagues, external examiners and social care agency personnel. Standards vary considerably, but I recall many more occasions when collectively we paused in our deliberations to say how excellent the work was, than when we felt that we had learnt nothing about an encounter.

Some students, however, may need help in conveying the drama, tension, conflict, humour, absurdities, and so on that arise daily in practice, and in accurately recording, for example, conversations, facial expressions, body language and posture, emotional nuances and psychological tensions (O'Hagan 2006). Jones (1995) provides an example of excellent written evidence by a student in a complex child protection case, aptly conveying the nature and 'wholeness' of the student's 'artistry and expertise' and, ulti-mately, the highest level of competence. It is the trainers' and supervisors' responsibility to monitor whatever difficulty students may have in this task, and to help them surmount it. There are numerous additional aids that may be available to help students, supervisors and trainers alike: audio tapes (leading to transcripts), video recordings, interviewing suites, etc. Future training constraints may increase the number of online courses in which trainers could exercise a higher level of scrutiny on this particular issue (Bellefeuille and Schmidt 2006; Quinney 2005).

The second but opposite response to the above criticisms is this: there may well be limitations in the quality of recorded observations a student provides of encounters. How accurate and comprehensive should those recordings be? One asks the question because real perfection and total com-prehensiveness is simply impossible to attain. The great novelists, dramatists and painters readily admit that despite their abilities to describe human interaction and emotion in the most spellbinding, psychologically realistic detail, they still do not really convey the whole process or its long-term impact on the characters involved. Such artists know that human interaction involves myriads of physiological, psychological and emotional phenom-ena, much of which remain hidden or mystifying to most observers. There is therefore, loose talk in the above criticisms, naïve notions of encounters and interactions that have not really been thought through; assessing the whole person in action, 'fully embracing the complex and interrelated nature of many of the situations encountered'(Trevithick 2005, p.61). It is as though hard-pressed students not only have to achieve competence but, in doing so, have also to better the descriptive power of Dickens, the profound insight of Shakespeare, and the spiritual meanderings of Dostoevsky in the hidden depths of the human soul! Students should not be burdened with ostenta-tious, imprecise, unrealistic stipulations about the recording of observation.

Competence and reflective practice

The final criticism to be addressed is that competence-led training is not conducive to 'reflective practice' (Prior 2005; Trevithick 2005). This criti-cism stems in part from Schon's (1983) pioneering text *The Reflective Practitioner*, which had considerable impact in social work education. But even Schon's advocacy of reflectivity is flawed, according to Prior (2005) who raises the debate on reflective practice to an unprecedented level of complexity, dwelling on Aristotle's *Nicomachean Ethics* and Dewey's (1963) moral philosophy. Prior believes that Schon was too preoccupied with 'particular understandings of knowledge' (p.8) and that one of the consequences for social work is a lack of 'moral deliberation'.

It is difficult to reconcile the latter point with the fact that values and ethics remain core components in social work education, and are pivotal – literally and figuratively – within the National Occupational Standards. As for *reflective practice* itself, those standards actually specify it twice as actual elements of competence (Units 19.4 and 20.3, under the Key Role *Demonstrate competence in social work practice*). Additionally, it is an implied and important activity in at least 50 other elements throughout the Units of Competence.

The increasing advocacy of *reflective practice* in social work literature has lacked a rigorous analysis of the concept. Taylor (2006, p.191) begins her perceptive article by exposing the myth that *competence* and *reflective practice* are somehow incompatible. She states that written subjective reflective accounts 'of practice are becoming increasingly important in social work education and training *as a means by which practitioners can achieve competence and demonstrate its accomplishment*' (my italics). 'In essence', she writes, 'the practitioner is performing two closely connected identities, one as competent and caring professional and the other as competent reflector, so that they perform a composite identity as a "reflective practitioner"' (p.195).

Taylor offers a critique of current thinking and use of reflectivity, on both 'reflecting-in-action' and 'reflection-on-action'. She scrutinises 'the performative aspects of narrative rather than its formal properties' (p.193) saying that it is naïve to view reflective accounts as really what happened in a given situation: reflective students 'select, order and report events in particular ways, for particular effects' (p.194). Taylor analyses two lengthy examples of reflective practice and exposes a degree of contrived construction, confession, artfulness and persuasiveness that all social work students would quickly recognise. She nevertheless acknowledges the importance of reflection in social work education, but concludes with the caution:

> Reflective accounts are written to persuade educators and supervisors that the social worker can pass as a competent practitioner. They form part of the cultural resources of the profession and perform particular rhetorical work to accomplish professional identity. There is a need therefore to recognise their artfulness and to examine the devices and conventions they draw on (p.203).

The challenge of competence

The principal objective in this second edition is to give direction and example in responding to the new requirements in social work training, to enable students to fulfil those requirements within the six Key Roles of social work and their Units of Competence. The contents are intentionally less prescriptive than in the first edition, simply because there is greater diversity in the framing of the requirements within the four jurisdictions. Each chapter of the book revolves around a particular case or cases, real or imaginary, within a particular field of practice. The cases and students, where necessary, have been anonymised. In some chapters, the student's work is long term, necessitating numerous face-to-face contacts with clients and other professionals, in others, the work is relatively brief, and/or reflective, based upon minimum encounters with client. Some of the cases enable the worker to partially fulfil requirements and provide evidence indicators for most of the Units of Competence. It is worth emphasising that no single piece of work in any of these chapters would, of itself, constitute the practice requirements of the new degree course, but each certainly can make a contribution to the contents of a successful practice portfolio at the end of that course.

In Chapter 2 Fawcett focuses on mediation between parents in dispute. She meticulously records the activities of a student in the beginning phases of the work. Particular attention is given to the organisational, legal and ethical imperatives involved as the student carefully sets up a process intended to reduce conflict and support disputants in finding their own settlement. Gibson and Taylor focus on residential care in Chapter 3. They provide a comprehensive review of the development of residential care in the aftermath of recent highly publicised scandals. They highlight opportunities for students to considerably enhance the lives of children in care, through competent and imaginative residential practice. Burke and Clifford link competence with ethics in Chapter 4. They review key concepts in contemporary and classic ethics, closely linked to anti-oppressive social work values. They use a case study in which the social worker demonstrates that she has acted (a) ethically in the light of this framework and (b) in accordance with National Occupational Standards. In Chapter 5, O'Hagan begins with a critical analysis of the lack of opportunity for students to acquire competence in child protection work. He describes a brief but challenging child abuse allegation, and how the student coped with the cultural and crisis aspects of the referral. Cambridge in Chapter 6 identifies the competences required in protecting adults with learning difficulties from sexual exploitation and abuse within their homes and community. Such abuses are common, and pose new challenges for assessment and care management. Heery in Chapter 7 provides an account of a criminal justice based student working with a young offender. The chapter explores the student's competence in (a) forming a positive relationship with the young person, (b) assessing his needs in relation to addressing his offending behaviour, and (c) seeking the right balance in the perennial 'care versus control' challenges which invariably arise in these cases. In Chapter 8 Kelly describes a model for analysing and assessing risk. It has been developed in association with child protection services in Northern Ireland. As the student demonstrates, the model is wholly compatible with National Occupational Standards requirements revolving around risk in social work practice. In Chapter 9, McLaughlin explores the process of care management and the single assessment process in a hospital setting. The chapter documents the student social worker's practice with a stroke victim and examines some of the challenges involved in providing a person-centred response to both patient and family at a time of crisis and transition. Iwaniec's student works with a failure to thrive case in Chapter 10. The work is family orientated, and is largely based upon DoH's (2000) Framework of Assessment. The author provides numerous tools for family assessment, underpinned by specific knowledge, values and skills. Campbell's Chapter 11 describes professional and ethical challenges faced by a student working with a family in which a mother has a serious mental health problem. It analyses the way in which the student deals with a range of complex processes, attempting to adhere to the new code of ethics, and demonstrating competence in multi-disciplinary working, assessment, intervention and coping with risk. In Chapter 12 Duffy and Houston demonstrate how the National Occupational Standards are congruent with the changing legal and policy context impacting on child and family social work. The authors explore how a student's critical thinking and extrapolation of theory and research is applied in the case of an alienated Pakistani youth recently settled in the UK.

Conclusion

I began this chapter by reflecting on another major change in social work education, brought about primarily by the Labour party's success in 1997 and 2001. Despite the fact that competence-led training is now embedded in UK government policy, social work literature continues to express its doubts, opposition and trenchant criticism. It is even more evident now, that many of the criticisms are unjustified, and are based upon:

1. unawareness of the meaning and origins of the concept of competence

2. a narrow perception of competence-led training as mechanistic, deductive, anti reflective, anti-imaginative and insufficiently morally based

3. a knee-jerk reaction to the functionalism and behaviourism associated with the origins of competence-based education and training

4. a failure to differentiate between competence-led training in social work and competence-based education and training in general

5. perceiving competence-led training as little more than a manifestation of right-wing economic and ideological dogma.

Perceptions like these may have imperceptibly impeded social work education since the inception of competence-led training. There is a certain incongruity in some influential social work trainers and writers vigorously opposing such training and the National Occupational Standards within which it is framed, and, simultaneously, being responsible for conveying conviction and enthusiasm to students who have 'set their heart' on attaining those standards. Social work has *not* been subjected to the imposition of a singularly ruthless stipulation that 'competence' is the be all and end all of training (as may be the case for many other occupations); on the contrary, social work training, and the National Occupational Standards on which it is now based, repeatedly stress that social work competence can only stem from certain knowledge and skills pivoted around and permeated by core values and ethics, and that the application of these must be demonstrated. It is the knowledge, skills, values and ethics underpinning competence, as much as the achievement of competence itself, which will remain a focal point in assessment for the new social work degree and all subsequent social work qualifications.

References

Bellefeuille, G. and Schmidt, G. (2006) Between a Rock and a Hard Place: Child Welfare Practice and Social Work Education.' *Social Work Education 25*, 1, 3–16.

Bisman, C. (2004) 'Social Work Values: The Moral Code of the Profession.' *British Journal of Social Work 34*, 1, 109–123.

Bolen, R.M. (2006) 'Utilizing Web-based Databases to Introduce Social Work Content in Research Statistics Course.' *Social Work Education 25*, 1, 17–27.

Braye, S. and Preston-Shoot, M. (1995) *Empowering Practice in Social Care.* Buckingham: Open University Press.

Care Council for Wales (2003) National Occupational Standards. Available at: www.ccwales. org.uk

Care Sector Consortium (1992) *National Occupational Standards for Care.* London: Care Sector Consortium.

Central Council for Education and Training in Social Work (1995) *Rules and Requirements for the Diploma in Social Work,* CCETSW Paper 30, rev. edn. London: CCETSW.

Commission for Social Care Inspection (2006) Official Website. Available at: www.csci. org.uk

Committee for Social Work Education and Policy (1995) *Rethinking Social Work Education.* Liverpool: University of Liverpool.

Denney, D. (1998) *Social Policy and Social Work.* Oxford: Clarendon Press.

Department for Education and Skills (2003) *Every Child Matters,* Cm. Paper 5860. London: HMSO.

Department of Health (2002) *Requirements for Social Work Training,* 28150. London: Dott. Available at: www.doh.gov.uk/swqualification.

Dewey, J. (1963) *Experience and Education.* New York: Collier Books.

General Social Care Council (2003) *Training and Learning.* Available at: www.gscc.org.uk/

Gilgun, J.F. (2005) 'The Four Cornerstones of Evidence Based Practice in Social Work.' *Research on Social Work Practice 15*, 1, 52–61.

Hoad, T.F. (ed.) 1986 *The Concise Oxford Dictionary of Word Origins.* Oxford: Oxford University Press.

Howe, D. (1996) 'Surface and Depth in Social Work Practice.' In N. Parton (ed.) *Social Theory, Social Change and Social Work.* London: Routledge.

Issitt, M. (1995) 'Competence, Professionalism and Equal Opportunities.' In P. Hodkinson and M. Issitt (eds) *The Challenge of Competence.* London: Cassell.

Jackson, S. (2002) 'Promoting Stability and Continuity in Care away from Home.' In D. McNeish, T. Newman and H. Roberts (eds) *What Works for Children: Effective Services for Children and Families.* Buckingham: Open University Publications.

Jones, J. (1995) 'Professional Artistry and Child Protection: Towards a Reflective Holistic Practice.' In P. Hodkinson and M. Issitt (eds) *The Challenge of Competence.* London: Cassell.

Kemshall, H. (1993) 'Assessing Competence: Process or Subjective Inference? Do We Really See It?' *Social Work Education 12*, 1, 36–45.

Laming, H. (2003) *The Victoria Climbié Inquiry,* Cm 5730. London, Department of Health and Home Office. Available at: www.victoria-climbié-inquiry.org.uk/finreport/finreport.htm

Levin, E. (2004) *Involving Service Users and Carers in Social Work Education.* London: Social Care Institute for Excellence. Available at: www.scie.org.uk/publications/details.asp?pubID=28

Lishman, J. (ed.) (1991) *Handbook of Theory for Practice Teachers in Social Work.* London: Jessica Kingsley Publishers.

Marsh, P. and Fisher, M. (2005) *Developing the Evidence Base in Social Work and Social Care Practice.* London: Social Care Institute for Excellence. Available at: www.scie.org.uk/publications/reports/10.pdf

Marthinson, E. (2004) 'A Mind for Learning: Merging Education, Practice and Research in Social Work.' *Social Work and Social Sciences Review 11*, 2, 54–66.

Mitchell, G.D. (1975) *A Dictionary of Sociology.* London: Routledge and Kegan Paul.

Moorman, M. (1968) *William Wordsworth, A Biography, The Later Years, 1803–1850.* Oxford: Oxford University Press.

National Council for Vocational Qualifications (1988) *Agency Training Notes (1988).* London: NCVQ.

Nellis, M. (1996) 'Probation Training: The Links with Social Work.' In T. May and A.A. Vass (eds) *Working with Offenders*. London: Sage.

Neville, D. (2004) *Putting Empowerment into Practice: Turning Rhetoric into Reality*. London: Whiting and Birch.

Nissim, R. and Simm, M. (1994) 'Linking Research Evidence in Fostering Work: The Art of the Possible.' *Adoption and Fostering 18*, 4, 10–16.

O'Hagan, K.P. (1996) 'Social Work Competence: An Historical Perspective.' In K. O'Hagan (ed.) *Competence in Social Work Practice*. London: Jessica Kingsley Publishers.

O'Hagan, K.P. (2006) *Identifying Emotional and Psychological Abuse*. Maidstone: Open University Publications.

Osmond, J. (2005) 'The Knowledge Spectrum: A Framework for Teaching Knowledge and its Use in Social Work Practice.' *British Journal of Social Work 35*, 6, 881–900.

Platt, D. (1994) 'Listen and Learn.' *Community Care* (16–23 February).

Prior, J. (2005) 'Some Thoughts on Academic Study if the Proposed New Honours Degree Programme is to Represent a Major Shift in Expectations.' *Social Work Education 24*, 1, 5–18.

Quinney, A. (2005) 'Placement Online: Student Experience of a Website to Support Learning in Practice Settings.' *Social Work Education 24*, 4, 439–450.

Rosen, A. (1994) 'Knowledge Use in Practice.' *Social Services Review* (December), 560–577.

Schon, D. (1983) *The Reflective Practitioner: How Professionals Think in Action*. New York: Basic Books.

Sellick, J. and Thoburn, J. (2002) 'Family Placement Services.' In D. McNeish, T. Newman and H. Roberts (eds) *What Works for Children: Effective Services for Children and Families*. Buckingham: Open University Publications.

Smalley, R.E. (1967) *Theory for Social Work Practice*. New York: Columbia University Press.

Social Care Institute for Excellence (2006) *SCIE's Resources and Publications*. Available at: www. scie.org.uk/

Social Services Inspectorate (1998) *Community Care From Policy to Practice: The Case of Mr Frederick Joseph McLernon*. Belfast: Department of Health and Social Services.

Somerfield, D.P. and Hughes, J.R. (1987) 'Do Health Professionals Agree on the Parenting Potential of Pregnant Women?' *Social Sciences Medicine 24*, 3, 285–288.

Taylor, C. (2006) 'Narrating Significant Experience: Reflective Accounts and the Production of (Self) Knowledge.' *British Journal of Social Work 36*, 2, 189–206.

Training Organisation for Personal Social Services (2004) *National Occupational Standards*. London: TOPSS.

Training Organisation for Personal Social Services (2006) *Social Work*. Available at: www. topssengland.net/view.asp?id=140.

Trevithick, P. (2005) *Social Work Skills: A Practice Handbook*, 2nd edn. Maidenhead: Open University Press.

Waterson, J. and Morris, K. (2005) 'Training in Social Work: Exploring Issues of Involving Users in Teaching on Social Work Degree Courses.' *Social Work Education 24*, 6, 653–675.

Acknowledgements

The author would like to thank Skills for Care and Development (formerly TOPSS) for permission to reproduce Figures 1.1 and 1.2 from the National Occupational Standards.

CHAPTER 2

Competence in Mediation Practice

Margaret Fawcett

Introduction

Mediation is commonly understood as a type of alternative dispute resolution in which the parties involved identify and agree a solution with the support of a neutral third party. It has become an increasingly popular means of resolving disputes in a wide variety of professional contexts: in school settings as a way of addressing bullying, in neighbourhood and community disputes and in the management of industrial relations (Mantle and Critchley 2004). In social work, it is regarded as an important aspect of practice in two key areas – restorative justice and separation/divorce work, which is also known as 'family mediation' – and it is the latter which provides the focus for this chapter.

Family mediation may be defined as:

> a process in which an impartial third person assists those involved in family breakdown, and in particular separating or divorcing couples, to communicate better with one another, and reach their own agreed and informed decisions about some or all of the issues arising from the separation/divorce. (UK College of Family Mediators 1995)

The attractions of family mediation lie in its focus on reducing conflict, improving communication and enhancing parents' decision-making abilities. These goals are compatible with the value base of social work: its emphasis on promoting problem-solving in human relationships, and supporting users' rights to control their own lives. Under the profession's new regulatory framework, UK social workers are now required to demonstrate these principles and values in their daily work (Department of Health, Social Services and Public Safety (DHSSPS) and the Northern Ireland Social Care Council 2003). It is also consistent with the legal framework which courts use to settle issues between estranged parents regarding children. Under the Children (NI) Order 1995, parental rights and responsibilities continue even if the marriage does not. The law also refers to the presumption of 'no order' and states that the range of court orders available to settle disputes between estranged parents (Article 8 orders) should be made only where they are likely to bring real benefits for the children concerned. From a legal perspective mediation is increasingly seen as less costly, less adversarial and more likely to provide a better basis for continuing parental responsibility (Holland 2006; Lord Chancellor's Department 2002).

Despite these endorsements, government initiatives to promote mediation have had a mixed response and social work practice in this area remains diverse. In England and Wales, for example, social workers are involved in child-centred court based mediation as one of a range of services delivered to the courts under the umbrella of the Children and Family Court Advisory and Support Service (CAFCASS) which was set up in 2001. In Northern Ireland, by way of contrast, there has been no overarching strategic approach to court welfare services (Children Order Advisory Committee 2005). Individual trusts have taken their own decisions about how, and what kind of, court welfare services are offered and as a result the arrangements for public sector mediation have been largely 'ad hoc and without any clear planning or direction' (Montgomery 2005, p.7). It is beyond the brief of this chapter to critique the different arrangements in each of these jurisdictions or to discuss mediation services provided by non-social work professionals. For students, the key point is that, wherever they may be on placement, the interface between clients, social workers, mediation and the courts is always likely to be challenging.

The case study which follows has all the ingredients typical of this kind of work – poor parental communication, conflict, children caught in the middle and issues regarding a parent's new partner. The intention is to convey how mediation can be undertaken in a social work setting, and to reflect on some of the complex ethical dilemmas associated with contemporary practice. In the last decade issues regarding residence and contact have moved high up the political agenda: the fathers' rights movement has argued that insufficient weight has been given to the significance of fathers in the lives of children after divorce (Geldorf 2003). Some claim that not enough attention has been given to children's perspectives and rights in the communication, information sharing and decision-making processes following family dissolution (Davey *et al.* 2004; Rodgers and Pryor 1998), and concerns have also been expressed about the appropriateness of mediation where there has been domestic violence, and about the safety of child contact arrangements following divorce and separation (Hester and Radford 1996). These issues of balancing competing needs and rights, and identifying and assessing risk are regarded as fundamental to the standards required of a competent professional social worker (DHSSPS and the Northern Ireland Social Care Council 2003). The case study will illustrate how a student on placement might address these challenges in minimising the potential for harm and maximising the potential benefits of mediation practice.

Work setting

The student is in the third year of a degree course. Her final placement is in a Family Resource Centre run by a voluntary agency. The agency has a service agreement with a local Health and Social Services Trust to provide a number of services including a Court Welfare Officer in attendance at the Family Proceedings Court, and welfare reports under Article 4 of the Children (NI) Order 1995. The student has identified a number of learning needs for this placement including work with families, the use of different methods of intervention, risk assessment and liaising with different networks and agencies. With these learning needs in mind, the practice teacher has asked the student to co-work a referral involving a request for mediation. Co-working is seen as having many advantages, not least the structure it provides for training new mediators (Liebmann 1998). This will be the student's first case on placement and her co-worker will be Merál, one of the other social workers in the Family Centre.

Case study

Mr Niall Brady	41	Telephone engineer	Living in rented accommodation
Mrs Fionnuala Brady	39	Classroom assistant	Living in family home
Connor	12	Living with mother	First year at secondary school
Emer	8	Living with mother	At primary school

Mr and Mrs Brady have been married for 14 years. They separated eight months ago when Mr Brady moved out of the family home following a 'bust up' with his wife about his gambling and credit bills. Initially there was regular contact between the children and their father but these arrangements have since broken down. Communication between the parents has become very acrimonious. While the children have continued to have indirect contact with their father there has been no direct contact in the form of visits or overnight stays for four weeks. Mr Brady has now applied to the Family Proceedings Court for a Contact Order. With the agreement of both parties, the solicitors have approached the Family Centre asking if they could facilitate mediation. If the couple are able to reach agreement, it could be submitted to their solicitors and an application made for a court order. The alternative is an adversarial route in which a welfare or Article 4 report would be formally requested by the court. The couple and their children would be seen separately by a social worker and a full court hearing would follow at which a judge would adjudicate on contact issues.

Competence in mediation practice

The remainder of this chapter will focus on what it is the student needs to know and to do in order to demonstrate competence. The focus will be on the beginning phase of the work when key tasks will include preparation, liaison with other professionals, initial assessment and contracting. It is widely recognised in social work that how a referral is made and received is very important to the person/s needing the service and the agency providing it (Coulshed and Orme 1998). In setting up the mediation process the case study will demonstrate how practice fulfils National Occupational Standards in a number of areas:

1. preparing for social work contact and involvement (Key Role 1 Unit 1)

2. assessing and managing risks to individuals and families (Key Role 4 Unit 12)

3. working in and across multi-disciplinary and multi-organisational teams, networks, systems and agencies (Key Role 5 Unit 17)

4. demonstrating and taking responsibility for professional competence in social work (Key Role 6 Units 19 and 20).

What follows is a brief overview of the relevant knowledge, values and skills underpinning practice in this area.

Knowledge

The knowledge base required in this type of referral may be classified as follows:

1. Contextual, legislative, procedural: Although the student will not be qualified to carry out statutory duties, mediation is conducted in the 'shadow' of the law and they will need to be familiar with court structures and the legislation relevant to their jurisdiction regarding relationship breakdown, domestic violence, mediation and the law relating to children. The Children (NI) Order 1995 (known as the Children Act 1989 in England and Wales) is of particular importance. It provides a set of legal remedies for both private family law and public law and it is essential that the student is conversant with its ethos, principles and the statutory role and responsibilities of social workers.

2. Services and resources: There are significant gaps in information and services available when parents separate (Crockett and Tripp 1994; Fawcett 1999). People are often confused about the role of professionals and this can be compounded by a sense of stigma and shame at the breakdown of relationships. This applies particularly to families whose ethnic or religious background discourages or forbids divorce. The student should be (a) sensitive to such issues, (b) able to provide information on what can be appropriately offered within the Family Centre, (c) able to refer elsewhere if, for example, there is domestic violence, allegations of child sexual abuse or a request for marital counselling.

3. The separation/divorce process: At the point of relationship breakdown there is often a great deal of individual distress, sadness, hurt, anger and confusion as well as very complex family dynamics. Theoretical frameworks are essential to the business of making sense of these dynamics. These may include attachment and mourning theory, the family life cycle and crisis theory. However, the most helpful starting point will be the subject-specific literature which will guide the student to the core concepts underpinning the framework, e.g. separation/divorce as

a process, its stages, the psychosocial tasks for adults and children and factors influencing outcomes (Amato and Keith 1991; Robinson 1991).

4. Research: There is now an extensive body of national and international research evidence in this subject area (Hester and Radford 1996; Rodgers and Pryor 1998). It is readily accessible through some of the major 'research for practice' initiatives such as the National Institute of Social Work Research Unit, The Joseph Rowntree Foundation and the National Children's Bureau and it provides the student with an opportunity to demonstrate their research-mindedness throughout the case.

5. Self-knowledge: In this type of referral it will also be crucial that the student has an opportunity to reflect on their own personal experience of family life and how it has moulded perceptions of (a) 'family', (b) labels such as 'normal', 'unusual', 'deviant', etc. attached to families, (c) the roles of men and women, and (d) child-parent relationships. Such openness and self-reflectivity is crucial, as taken-for-granted ideas about family life may mask stereotypes and assumptions which can lead to discriminatory attitudes and practices. It is also important because many of the paradoxes and contradictions of family life are often painfully exposed by relationship breakdown:

> The family is supposed to be a place of intimacy and support and yet it is also the place where violence against women is most tolerated... The family is supposed to be a sanctuary for children and yet being a 'child' in the family can mean being subject to discipline and control which is near absolute. If family life becomes hell, there may be no escape from it. (Muncie and Sapsford 1995, p.30)

Muncie and Sapsford suggest that core issues of power and authority are at the heart of these paradoxes and contradictions in family life. As the student moves into this contested arena, self-knowledge and identification with a set of professional values will help them grapple with the dilemmas they are likely to confront regarding post-separation relationships between men, women and children.

Values

As with the Central Council for Education and Training in Social Work (CCETSW) revised Paper 30, the new National Occupational Standards make it clear that students' practice must be 'founded on, informed by and capable of being judged against a clear value base' (Department of Health, Social Services and Public Safety 2003). Marion Roberts identifies four core principles underpinning practice:

1. The impartiality of the mediator.

2. The voluntariness of the process (because the mediator has no power to impose a settlement).

3. The confidentiality of the relationship between the mediator and the parties.

4. The procedural flexibility of the mediator – in contrast to the court system where communication with and between the parties is dictated by legal norms. (1997, p.7)

She also describes the mediator's main ethical responsibilities – to be clear about the nature of their authority, to protect the rights of the parties to be architects of their own agreement, to ensure the process is fair and equal, and that the parties consider the impact of their agreement on others. These responsibilities will present a number of challenges where mediation is undertaken in a social work setting. Social workers normally build alliances as part of the process of engaging and contracting with individuals. In mediation, they must avoid such alliances and be extremely even-handed with both parties from the start. It will also be important for the social worker/mediator to use every opportunity to recognise and affirm parental competence without unwittingly taking on the role of 'child development expert' or 'advocate'. All of this implies that the social worker will have thought carefully about the nature of their power and authority – something we will demonstrate in the case study which follows.

Skills

The mediator is often described as the orchestrator of a structured and staged negotiation process. Their primary task is to 'help disputants move through a natural process, from telling their story and view of events to eventual building of an agreement between them' (Liebmann 1998, p.46). They have no stake in the dispute and they have no power to impose a settlement. Important skills will include observation, attending and listening skills, questioning and summarising, but the delicate business of how and when these skills are used is linked to the particular stage in the negotiation process and the different strategies (power/balancing, mutualising, partialising) needed to orchestrate the exchanges between the couple. The illustration of 'The mediator' in Figure 2.1 (Evans 2006) captures the essence of what it means to be a mediator – a combination of skills, principles, pragmatism and personal warmth and humanity. Competent practice will involve providing information about mediation, contracting, focusing on the issues, maintaining control of the pace, balancing power, managing conflict and ensuring the parties feel responsible for, and happy with, the outcome. In the next section we focus on illustrating these skills and interventions in the early phases of the work, when considerable patience and

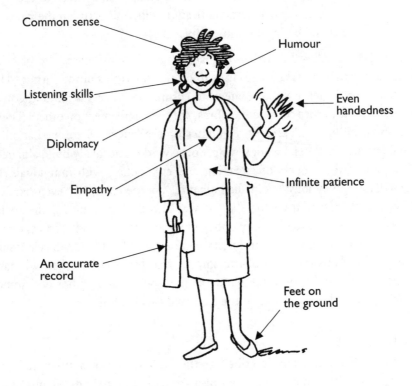

Figure 2.1: The mediator (Source: Evans 2006)

even-handedness is required, as the student and her co-worker face the challenge of setting up the process and engaging with Mr and Mrs Brady.

Developing and achieving competence

Setting up the process

PREPARATION

Unit 1 of Key Role 1 requires the worker to *prepare for social work contact and involvement*. And, right from the start, the student needs to be alert and self-aware regarding factors which could compromise careful preparation. In particular, the student's anxiety about taking on her first case could lead to an ill-informed rush into action with serious consequences. She could fail to clarify and negotiate her role with other professionals. She could become prematurely involved before adequately assessing the suitability of the referral, or she could be unwittingly drawn into taking sides in what are often complex and bitter marital disputes. A competent response to this referral will start with preparatory reading, reviewing information, reflecting on her organisational role and liaison with other professionals.

As a first step, the student is asked to set up a referral meeting involving Merál to clarify roles and plan the necessary steps to initiate contact with the Brady family. The practice teacher also asks the student to prepare an *ecomap* of the systems involved with the case and to note any initial questions she might have. Based on systems thinking, an ecomap is a drawing of the networks surrounding an individual or family. It provides 'an at a glance perspective on who is involved with whom and in what way' (Parker and Bradley 2003, p.46). It is a flexible tool which can start out as a thumbnail sketch in the worker's notepad, and it can be expanded and developed as the referral progresses (Figure 2.2).

Questions

1. Has this family consented to mediation or been referred under duress?

2. Have they been given any information on how mediation works?

3. Is there a timescale in which the work has to be completed before court proceeding would start?

4. The referral alludes to a 'bust up' between the couple. Has there been any violence involved?

5. What is the couple's attitude to social work involvement?

6. Would they regard the Family Centre as a 'neutral' venue?

7. Will the presence of two female mediators create an imbalance in the mediation process?

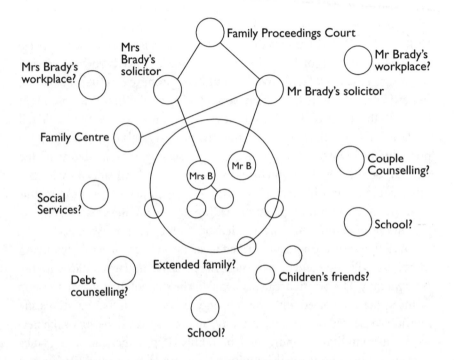

Figure 2.2: The Brady family ecomap

The student discusses the ecomap with her practice teacher and demonstrates knowledge and a critical understanding of the relevant systems. The map identifies the different kinds of resources, formal and informal, which may be important in circumstances of marital breakdown. The student is aware of different referral pathways and of the need to be able to respond to a range of scenarios. Her list of questions demonstrates her awareness of the potential for discrimination in the dynamics of court systems, which can sometimes alienate families and undermine the principles and values which mediation seeks to foster (Butler *et al.* 2003). Additionally, she has highlighted significant gaps in information, particularly in relation to the question of domestic violence. Mediation is intended to be a fair process, one in which participants are able to construct and shape the dialogue, express their interests and needs, and participate in reaching outcomes. If disputants cannot have an effective presence – either because of mental health issues, ongoing alcohol or drug dependency, domestic violence or other external factors, then mediation should not take place. The practice teacher suggests that all of these questions will need further consideration in both supervision and case planning starting with the meeting with Merál.

Liaison with other professionals

Unit 17 of Key Role 5 requires the social worker to *work in and across multi-disciplinary and multi-organisational team, network, systems and agencies*. This can seem a daunting prospect to the student. Her inexperience and sense of 'not knowing' can cause her to feel deskilled and lacking in confidence when starting to network with experienced professionals. She may find herself doubting the value of spending time on preliminaries. It would be all too easy to skip these preliminaries or to allow the agenda and pace to be to set by others. Planning, negotiating and exchanging information are all essential activities at this stage. They require the student to be well prepared and assertive, yet able to take direction and guidance when needed.

In this referral the process starts with the student setting up a planning meeting with Merál, who will be the lead worker responsible for the overall conduct of the case. It is suggested that the student takes responsibility for (a) drafting a letter to the parties and (b) contracting in the first session. The possibility of a direct consultation with the Brady children is also mentioned as a task to be agreed at a later stage. The student welcomes this responsibility. Already she is contemplating questions about the process, not least about the allocation of two female mediators. Co-working has obvious resource implications and each agency will vary in its capacity to allocate male/female pairs or to match disputants' backgrounds. The student is alert to the importance of striving to uphold the integrity of the mediation process whatever the context, and she takes the opportunity to raise her concerns about agency practices. Might the allocation of two female mediators be seen as biased and uncomfortable for the man? Her question prompts an acknowledgement from Merál that this is a valid concern. A range of options are considered:

1. Raising the issue directly with Mr Brady at the start of mediation.

2. Indirectly giving each of the parties time to air any concerns they
    have about mediation as part of the contracting process.

3. Requesting a re-allocation of the case to a male worker.

After some discussion Option 2 is agreed upon as the one which would
gives both parties the right to air their concerns without attempting to
pre-judge or pre-empt what these might be. It would still allow Option 3 to
be considered if serious objections were raised.

The student is encouraged by the consideration that has been given to
her question. What is being modelled for her is the negotiation and resolution of ethical questions as they arise within the mediation process. The
discussion moves on to the practicalities of initiating contact. The student
shows her ecomap (see Figure 2.2) of the systems involved in this case and
outlines her other questions about the referral process and gaps in information. After listening carefully, Merál advises the student to phone each
solicitor, starting with Mrs Brady's, to check if there have been any court
orders or indications of domestic violence, and to confirm the understanding that each party is willing to commit to joint mediation. If there are no
contraindications, the solicitors can be asked to confirm a suggested date
and time with their clients to attend the centre. Only then can follow-up let-
ters be sent inviting the parties to attend. In this way initial contact can be
made safely, without bias, and without getting caught up in an inappropriate referral. For the student this is a valuable lesson on the importance of
step-by-step negotiations in setting up the process. Practical advice such as
this is seldom found in any textbook. It forms part of the informal knowledge which will be a rich source of learning for this student as she works
alongside her more experienced colleague. Thompson cautions that informal knowledge or practice wisdom tends to be 'covert, implicit, and less
open to critical challenge' (1995, p.27). What this student has demonstrated, however, is her capacity to begin to question some of the assumptions and received knowledge of day-to-day practice in the agency (Key
Role 6 Unit 20 Element 2).

As the meeting draws to a close the student now has two provisional
dates pencilled in for when the work might commence. She has a clearer
understanding of her role. She also has a strategy for addressing some of the
gaps in information, and, as she actions the agreed steps, the student's initial
checks reveal no evidence of domestic violence. The outcome is confirma-
tion with the parties and their solicitors of a date and time for Mr and Mrs
Brady to attend the Family Centre for joint mediation.

Setting the scene and exploring the issues

Preparation

Most mediators will undertake further planning and preparation before each session. The next section introduces two important preparatory rituals – tuning-in and pre-session briefing – in which the student grapples with issues of risk management before moving on to her account of the first session. Under the requirements of Key Role 4 social workers must demonstrate competence in managing risk. In mediation practice the worker has important responsibilities regarding pre-mediation screening and the management of conflict during the process. While they do not have an investigative role they need to be knowledgeable and aware of protocols if new information emerges regarding spousal abuse or children's safety – an aspect of practice which the student demonstrates in the notes below.

Tuning-in

The student is tasked to prepare a written tuning-in for supervision. Given the themes and issues raised, the practice teacher asks the student to pay particular attention to how information gathered from her contact with solicitors might fit with agency procedures regarding the assessment of risk regarding domestic violence. Each agency will have its own particular risk assessment protocols and in the extract from the tuning-in notes (Box 2.1) the student outlines her understanding of the agency's Domestic Violence Risk Assessment Framework (Healey and Bell 2004) and its application to this case.

From these notes it is clear that the student has understood the essentials – the risk factors pertinent to the referral, the inter-agency protocols and the strategies to assess and manage risk in the next phase of the work. She has evidenced her thinking from current research literature and demonstrated a balanced approach to the topic with her references to protecting women, safeguarding the best interests of children, acknowledging the possibility of violence and noting gaps in research regarding cultural minority groups. As she actions these strategies, the student is demonstrating some of the key competencies in managing risk – identifying and assessing the nature and level of risk (Key Role 4 Unit 12 Element 1), working within the risk assessment procedures of her own and other relevant organisations (Key Role 4 Unit 13 Element 2), and planning and implementing action to reduce risk (Key Role 4 Unit 12 Element 3).

Box 2.1: Extract from tuning-in notes

Policy and procedures

What agency policy and procedures on domestic violence (DV) are relevant in this case?

The Domestic Violence Risk Assessment Framework deals specifically with male to female violence in families where children are present. Provides a structure for social workers to gather information in a consistent way about any evidence of domestic violence, risk factors and protective factors. Assessment of overall level of risk to mothers and children then rated from Moderate (Scale 1) to Severe (Scale 4). Framework also links these Scales to different types of intervention from family support services (Scales 1 and 2) to child protection (Scales 3 and 4). Framework currently in use in the Family Centre and the local trust. Also being piloted in other parts of UK to test its applicability with a range of ethnic minority group.

How does the Domestic Violence Risk Assessment policy impact on, or direct, this case?

It impacts on this case indirectly. Background knowledge of these risk factors helps us as mediators to distinguish between 'marital conflict' and 'domestic violence'. Feedback from solicitors indicates no evidence of DV. This would suggest that a family support type intervention is appropriate. Mediation aims to reduce conflict and get parents talking to one another.

However, because DV is often hidden and not reported, Merál and I need to ensure safe practice. It is important to minimise risk at intake stage – couple in separate waiting rooms, seating, rules agreed for the conduct of the session.

The referral indicates that since separating, Mr and Mrs Brady's relationship has become 'more acrimonious'. In the light of research evidence which suggests that women are at an increased risk when they leave a relationship (Lees 2000) we will also need to be aware of any significant changes in the pattern of conflict since the separation.

If new information emerges or fresh allegations are made about DV during mediation the policy and procedure guidelines indicate that different protocols may be required – seeing the couple/children separately to establish the overall level of risk – referring to social services for a full Domestic Violence Risk Assessment – reviewing if mediation is an appropriate intervention as contact may not always be in the best interests of the children in these circumstances.

Pre-session briefing

For the mediators, the first session begins 15 minutes before the couple arrives. They spend most of the time working out the details of the session plan – arrival, introductions, session outline, contracting and agenda setting (Fawcett and Lewis 1996, p.33). They agree how they will co-work the gathering of information about the pattern of conflict and they confirm with reception that Mr and Mrs Brady will wait in separate areas. Last minute tasks include re-organising the seating in the family interview room and checking that flipchart paper and pens are available. Because the student is now more aware of the potential risks involved in the work she finds herself admitting to Merál that the prospect of engaging an estranged couple suddenly seems really daunting. *What happens if a row breaks out and things get out of control? What if she makes a mistake or does not know what to do?* This is an ever present professional challenge – how to manage risk situations without becoming defensive or preoccupied with the fear of getting it wrong (Kelly 1996). Merál responds helpfully, stating that such fears are normal for even the most experienced worker. She reminds the student that this is a couple who have indicated their willingness for conciliation, and who have been able to agree and sustain contact arrangements in the recent past – all positive indicators for good outcomes.

By the end of the briefing the student, far more positive, feels prepared for the first contact with the disputants. The following section records the student's commentary on it. We will then analyse and reflect on her practice with reference to the three core elements underpinning social work – professional competence, accountability and ethical practice.

STUDENT NOTES – FIRST SESSION

Mr and Mrs Brady seem such an ordinary couple. They are both tense and nervous. Apart from a first glance they haven't looked at each other since they came into the room. Mr Brady is sitting in that seat as though it is a hot plate! He's fidgeting a lot with his tie and shifting from side to side. Mrs Brady is staring fixedly at Merál. She hasn't taken her coat off and her hands are clamped on her handbag as though she's ready to leave at any moment. You could cut the atmosphere between them with a knife. They're making me more nervous that I am already. Thank goodness Merál is looking and sounding confident.

MERÁL: You're both really welcome… We appreciate how
             difficult it is for a couple to come together at a time
             when their own relationship has broken down…
             Conciliation is about enabling separated parents to plan
             and sort out the practical arrangements for their
             children… For all sorts of reasons parenting across two
             households is more complicated… It is our hope that
             here will be a place where the two of you can have a
             constructive conversation about the issues which need
             sorted out… First, I need to check the basic information
             we have been given and then Clare [the student] will help
             you agree some ground rules for how you both want to
             work together when you are here…

I find myself relaxing a little. Mr and Mrs Brady are answering some of
Merál's factual questions and in my mind I drift on to the next task. It is my
turn now and as I get up from my seat to go to the flipchart the couple's eyes
follow me. Then I notice that Mr Brady has taken a notebook and pen from
his jacket. Oh No! He's going to take notes. I haven't planned for this. The
session has hardly started and I haven't a clue what to do next. I glance
quickly at Merál…a wordless 'Help'. She notices my glance and quickly
steps in.

MERÁL: Mr Brady, can I just check? Was it your intention to try
             and take notes?

MR B: Well, I want to make sure I remember everything for my
             solicitor.

MRS B: If he's up to that nonsense I'm out of here.

MERÁL: Mr Brady, we, too, think it important (*now glancing at Mrs
             Brady*) that each of your solicitors gets feedback. What we
             do here is encourage you both to agree a summary note
             at the end of the work which records any agreement that
             is made. A copy is sent to each solicitor. In our
             experience it seems the fairest way of doing things and it
             takes the pressure off any one person feeling either that
             they have to keep notes or that what they say is going to
             be written down immediately. Does that seem OK to you
             both?

Mr and Mrs Brady nod and the notebook remains unopened on the coffee table. Merál glances at me and, taking my cue from her, I move on.

ME: That's why the next bit is so important, agreeing ground rules for how the two of you are going to work together when you are here. For some couples it may be important to have rules about how and when information gets shared. For others it may be very difficult to have a conversation without arguing, so rules about talking are really important. I wonder what you both might think are important.

Given that Mrs Brady had just hinted that she was ready to leave (coat and handbag still at the ready!) I invited her to speak first and then invited Mr Brady to take his turn. Over the next ten minutes they agree to listen, not interrupt, and not to name-call.

Even though the atmosphere is still really tense I feel a sense of relief that they have each engaged with the task. Hoping desperately that I've got the timing right I probe a little bit further about how to manage the session. This time I make sure to start with Mr Brady.

ME: How would I know if things were to become difficult for you in this session?

MR B: Oh, well, I'd just get really impatient and frustrated because she's not seeing sense and then to top it all she usually starts to turn on the waterworks (*glancing at his wife as she says this*).

ME: And what usually happens next?

MR B: Oh, I just start to shout and then I just have to go off somewhere to cool down.

ME: And Mrs Brady?

MRS B: (*She turns to her husband*) Well you start to steamroller me and want things all your way…

ME: (*I interrupt*) Mrs Brady, I suspect you will both have very different ways of managing the stress of trying to talk with each other. At this point I'm really interested in knowing how I would know if it was becoming difficult for you here?

MRS B: Well I just go quiet, like I've given up on getting him to listen.

ME: *(Addressing them both)* So it sounds like when communication is difficult, Mrs Brady, you go quiet and withdraw a bit while, Mr Brady, you find yourself becoming frustrated and maybe starting to shout.

Both of them nod.

ME: So what could we agree, so that the communication here is different?

The tension eases a little and they agree two further rules:

- fairness (*taking turns to speak*)
- time out (*taking a break if things become difficult*).

I'm not sure about the mutual 'put downs', i.e. 'turning on the waterworks' and 'steamrollers'. I know I should challenge this but I'm not sure how. Things are going quite well and I don't want to rock the boat! I have asked some questions about their pattern of conflict. I feel reassured by what I have heard so far. I know Merál will gather more details later. I then take a lead and suggest that another important ground rule for most couples is about confidentiality of information. I write it on the flipchart.

I have done lots of preparation for this item. I give information and they each ask me questions. We cover really important areas about the limits of confidentiality and how feedback will be given to solicitors, the court and the children. It seems to take ages and I know I need to move things on.

ME: We have given a lot of time to these rules but it is really important that both of you are clear about how mediation works, and how information discussed here will be shared. Before we move on, have either of you any questions or concerns?

MRS B: It seems okay to me. The place is nicer than I thought. Mind you I don't fancy the look of those cameras on the wall. Are they on?

ME: No. I should have mentioned that earlier. The cameras are switched off and they are never used without a family's prior consent.

MRS B: That's a relief. As long as I know there is no Big Brother watching us! (*At this point she and her husband exchange a mutual glance.*)

ME: What about you, Mr Brady? Have you any concerns or questions we haven't dealt with so far?

MR B: Well, what happens if her and I can't come to an agreement?

ME: If couples are unable to reach an agreement in mediation we simply confirm this outcome with each party's solicitor. We normally provide no further details. If the case is returned to court and a welfare report is requested another social worker from the Family Centre would be allocated to the case. Merál and I would have no further involvement.

MR B: All of that seems fair to me. I just don't want any more delay. I just want to get on and see the kids.

ME: I guess the issues around contact are one of the reasons for you both being here, so maybe it's time to move on to explore the concerns and issues you each bring.

By the end of this phase, Mr Brady's notebook was still on the coffee table. Mrs Brady's handbag was now at her side. Handing back to Merál I felt I could relax a little. It was an opportunity for me to observe Merál using the skills I had read so much about.

Summary and conclusion

The primary task of the mediator is to facilitate the mediation process. The student has demonstrated her competence in the early stage of engaging and contracting with the couple.

- There was an even-handed approach to the structuring of the information exchanges.

- Policies and procedures were carefully explained.

- Respect was demonstrated for each of the parties' concerns.

- There was evidence of a good use of core skills.

- A range of strategies were used including normalising, mutualising and powerbalancing.

- The student kept to the session plan – even when temporarily unsure what to do next.

- She used her co-worker appropriately and combined structure with a responsive approach to client concerns.

The student has facilitated the beginnings of a process whereby Mr and Mrs Brady will be able to move on to the next stage of telling their story. Given the opportunity to hear that story, it is likely it would have uncovered a dispute with numerous strands of tensions – the issues resulting in the couple's estrangement, practical issues about fitting children's school timetables alongside parents' working arrangements, the weekly hassles of organising life between two households and the impact of introducing a parent's new partner. Successful mediation would facilitate the hearing of this 'human' story in a way that allows each party to learn about how to negotiate – to act rationally, communicate effectively, and how to be open to persuasion rather than bullying, shouting or withdrawing. This would require the same core skills but very different strategies as the couple grow in confidence in their capacity to negotiate.

In conclusion, this case study has illustrated the opportunities for learning and development of competence across a number of Key Roles. The material generated from this first phase of the mediation process (ecomaps, process records, tuning-in notes, supervision records) would readily count as verifiable evidence in any practice portfolio. While any claims to competence in mediation are ultimately tempered by the knowledge that it is the participants who retain ultimate control of settlement making (Roberts 1992), the student's proven abilities in preparing for social work involvement, working co-operatively with others and contracting with clients would be as applicable and effective in other areas of social work practice as it was instrumental in allowing the disputants in this case to engage effectively with the process of mediation.

References

Amato, P.R. and Keith, B. (1991) 'Parental Divorce and the Well-being of Children: A Meta-analysis.' *Journal of Marriage and the Family 61,* 3, 557–573.

Butler, I., Scanlan, L., Robinson, M., Douglas, G. and Murch, M. (2003) *Divorcing Children: Children's Experiences of their Parents' Divorce.* London: Jessica Kingsley Publishers.

Children Order Advisory Committee (2005) *6th Report.* Belfast: Department of Health, Social Services and Public Safety.

Coulshed, V. and Orme, J. (1998) *Social Work Practice: An Introduction,* 3rd edn. Basingstoke: Palgrave.

Crockett, M. and Tripp, J. (1994) *The Exeter Family Study: Family Breakdown and its Impact on Children.* Exeter: University of Exeter Press.

Davey, C., Dwyer, C., McAlister, S., Kilkelly, U., Kilpatrick, R., Lundy, L., Moore, L. and Scraton, P. (2004) *Children's Rights in Northern Ireland.* Belfast: Northern Ireland Commissioner for Children and Young People.

Department of Health, Social Services and Public Safety and the Northern Ireland Social Care Council (2003) *Northern Ireland Framework Specification for the Degree in Social Work.* Belfast: Department of Health, Social Services and Public Safety.

Evans, P. (2006) 'The Mediator'. In A. Murfin and V. Reid (eds) *What is Mediation? A Guide.* Advicenow's Family Mediation Campaign. Available at: www.advicenow.org.uk/family mediation.

Fawcett, M. (1999) *What Hurts? What Helps? A Study of Needs and Services for Young People whose Parents Separate and Divorce.* Belfast: Relate (Northern Ireland).

Fawcett, M. and Lewis, K. (1996) 'Competence in Conciliation Work.' In K. O'Hagan (ed.) *Competence in Social Work Practice.* London: Jessica Kingsley Publishers.

Geldorf, B. (2003) 'The Real Love that Dare Not Speak its Name.' In A. Bainham, B. Londley, M. Richards and L. Trinder (eds) *Children and their Families: Contact, Rights and Welfare.* Oxford: Hart Publishing.

Healey, J. and Bell, M. (2004) *Assessing the Risk to Children from Domestic Violence.* Northern Ireland: Banardo's.

Hester, M. and Radford, L. (1996) *Domestic Violence and Child Contact in England and Denmark.* Bristol: Policy Press.

Holland, Sir Antony (2006) 'Foreword.' In M. Fawcett *Getting it Right for Children When Parents Separate.* Belfast: Conference Report funded by the Legal Services Commission.

Kelly, G. (1996) 'Competence in Risk Analysis.' In K. O'Hagan (ed.) *Competence in Social Work Practice.* London: Jessica Kingsley Publishers.

Lees, S. (2000) Marital Rape and Marital Murder.' in J. Hanmer and C. Itzin (eds) *Home Truths about Domestic Violence: Feminist Influences on Policy and Practice: A Reader.* London: Routledge.

Liebmann, M. (1998) 'Mediation.' In Y. Craig (ed.) *Advocacy, Counselling and Mediation in Casework.* London: Jessica Kingsley Publishers.

Lord Chancellor's Department (2002) *The Government's Response to the Children Act Sub-Committee report 'Making Contact Work'.* London: Lord Chancellor's Department.

Mantle, G. and Critchley, A. (2004) 'Social Work and Child Centred Family Court Mediation.' *British Journal of Social Work 34,* 1161–1172.

Muncie, J. and Sapsford, R. (1995) 'Issues in the Study of the Family.' In J. Muncie, M. Wetherell, D. Dallos and A. Cochrane (eds) *Understanding the Family.* London: Sage.

Montgomery, A. (2005) *Scoping Paper on the Provision of Family Mediation Services in Northern Ireland.* Belfast: Office of Law Reform.

Parker, J. and Bradley, G. (2003) *Social Work Practice: Assessment, Planning, Intervention and Review.* Exeter: Learning Matters.

Roberts, M. (1992) 'Who is in Charge? Reflections on Recent Research on the Role of Mediator.' *Journal of Social Welfare and Family Law 5,* 372–387.

Roberts, M. (1997) *Mediation in Family Disputes.* Aldershot: Arena.

Robinson, M. (1991) *Family Transformation Through Divorce and Remarriage. A Systemic Approach.* London: Routledge.

Rodgers, B. and Pryor, J. (1998) *Divorce and Separation: The Outcomes for Children.* York: Joseph Rowntree Foundation.

Thompson, N. (1995) *Theory and Practice in Health and Social Welfare.* Buckingham: Open University Press.

UK College of Family Mediators (1995) Code of Practice for Family Mediators.' Available at: www.ukcfm.co.uk

Acknowledgements

I wish to thank Tony Macklin (Independent social worker/guardian ad litem/practice teacher) and Ursula McKeown (social worker/family therapist) for their advice and guidance in the writing of this chapter.

I am grateful to Advice Services Alliance Publishers for permission to use Phil Evans's cartoon 'The Mediator' taken from *Family Mediation: What is Mediation?* edited by Antonia Murfin and Val Reid.

CHAPTER 3

Competence in Residential Child Care

John Gibson and Raymond Taylor

Introduction

Residential child care in Britain provides temporary placement for some young people who experience severe emotional and behavioural problems (Milligan and Kendrick 2004). Many children, however, spend exceedingly long periods in residential care, which is required to meet a broad range of needs. This presents challenges in a sector that is also, at times, characterised by instances of abuse of young people (Kent 1997; Utting 1991; Waterhouse 2000). Caring for children in residential care has a long and at times inauspicious history. The current provision is not the outcome of a smooth and continuous progression to an ever improving quality of experience. Residential child care has a distant past which casts long shadows, and a recent past that has done little to dispel those shadows. The abuse of power by adults over young people and the 'blind eye' of managers (Levy and Kahan 1991) show marked similarity with other abuses in the history of institutional care (Robins 1987).

Parker writes about the consequences of this historical legacy, a 'persistent image of residential child care as nothing more than a repugnant type of institutional life' (1988, p.8). This is no mere academic observation. It is tangible enough to be felt, seen and heard. For children and young people the image becomes manifest in the resulting stigma of telling friends in school that they live in a 'home'. For staff members, and students undertaking practice learning, the image becomes manifest in the attitude of colleagues in other parts of the child care system who view admission to residential care as failure or at best as a last resort. Perhaps the most regrettable manifestation occurs when social work leadership expresses similar views: the Warner Report quoted one director of social services saying that residential child care was a 'necessary evil' (1992, p.7). Warner suggested that debate and opinion about residential child care was 'still dominated by historical attitudes towards looking after children as women's work in which skills are inherent or intuitive and the commitment of the work-force is exploitable' (p.2). Three major reports (Skinner 1992; Utting 1991; Warner 1992) have stressed the need for strategic leadership at government level as a prerequisite for the necessary conditions and resources that will lead to more positive outcomes for children and young people.

Over the last decade the UK government has sought to provide this leadership and direction, through the development of National Care Standards and the creation of national bodies responsible for the inspection of services and regulation of the workforce. Increased regulation of care services has required the creation of new legislation, in each of the four jurisdictions of the UK, which has led to the formation of four Care Councils (see Chapter 1). Standards for Social Workers and the Codes of Practice for Social Care Workers and Employers are very similar and provide a unifying framework, although since devolution differences are increasingly emerging in how care services are regulated across the United Kingdom.

In the context of caring for the whole child, the desire to raise standards and the idea of competence, meaning effectiveness, has great appeal. Winnicott wrote that children and young people in residential care need 'good experiences of care, comfort and control' (1971, p.30). Many interactions in residential child care require that workers provide care, comfort and control simultaneously. In the case study that follows (p.56), we illustrate this integration in relation to Key Roles from the National Occupational Standards. In Part 1 of the case study, we illustrate competence in making an entry to the group living context of residential child care (Key Role 2 Unit 5.1: *Develop and maintain relationship with individuals, families, carers, groups, communities and others*), and in responding to an individual in crisis (Key Role 4: *Manage risk to individuals, families, carers, groups, communities, self and colleagues*) in Part 2. In demonstrating their competence in these areas, students must also adhere to the new Code of Practice. They must:

1. protect the rights and promote the interests of service users

2. establish and maintain the trust and confidence of service users and carers

3. promote independence of service users while protecting them as a far as possible from danger or harm

4. respect the rights of service users while seeking to ensure that their behaviour does not harm themselves or other people

5. uphold the trust and confidence in social services

6. be accountable for the quality of their work and take responsibility for improving their knowledge and skills.

Group living: The general context

Brown and Clough comment that, 'life in day and residential centres is multi-layered and complex' (1989, p.6). Douglas says that although a residential unit can be referred to as a group 'it is most often an organisation containing many groups' (1986, p.1). Students are expected to evidence competence in this multi-layered, complex organisation of small groups where a primary goal is to 'place the individual at the heart of the system' (Ward 1993, p.158). The range and depth of activities encountered can be a very intimidating environment for a student beginning placement. Unlike fieldwork settings where one may be afforded time to acclimatise, adjust and respond to the demands of the setting before meeting clients, no such moratorium can be given in residential child care. From the first day, the student can expect to meet clients who are eager to find out about this new adult. Young people have a need to make sense of any new adult entering their living space, because, entering their world – their living space – is precisely what the new adult is doing. Their unspoken questions will be:

- Do I have anything to fear from this person?
- Will I like them?
- Will they like me?
- Will they respect me?
- Will they be fair in their dealings with me?
- Will they be afraid of me?

- Will they be trustworthy?
- Will they trust me?

These tuning-in questions are essentially about discovering the value base of adults who are charged with their care. We return shortly in more detail to the subject of values.

Structuring

Most residential units are busy places. Staff often work a 24-hour shift; Figure 3.1 provides a typical day in a residential unit. On the left-hand side are tasks and activities arising during specific phases; on the right-hand side are designated core themes in residential care and core roles.

Table 3.1 is adapted from Clough and Brown's 'mosaic of groups and groupings' (1989, p.21), commonly found in residential care settings. It shows the potential complexity of the situation the student will encounter.

Figure 3.1 and Table 3.1 demonstrate that the worker often operates in a public arena. The practice of social work in most other settings can be a private transaction between worker and clients. In a group living setting, work is often 'public', carried out in full view of colleagues, other clients, family members and sometimes other visiting professionals. This public arena can be intimidating, but it can also be supportive, as when colleagues share work with each other and, as a consequence, learn together.

In the next two sections of this chapter we present a two-part case example. In Part 1, the student records how she enters the living space of the group-as-a-whole. She begins the important transition from being 'the student' to being 'a student', who, like the residents, has a name, a past, a public and private life, a sense of humour, a personality; characteristics that will make her different from other staff colleagues, but through which she will have to give expression to the values embraced by the agency and the staff team. The student also encounters one of the core dilemmas of residential child care: 'enabling people to live private lives in public places' (Ward 1993, p.vii). In Part 2 the student is required to demonstrate competence in responding to a crisis which takes place in the context of group living.

Case study: Part 1

Entering the group space

The group living setting described here is a residential adolescent unit. Ten places are provided for the use of social service departments. The young people admitted to the unit are of mixed gender, they are aged between 12

Tasks and activities	Themes and Key Role					
	Care and control	Teamwork / communication / consistency	Develop and maintain relationships with individuals, families, carers and groups	Inter-agency communication / Provide for physical need	Plan, carry out, review and evaluate social work practice, with individual, families and groups	Demonstrate professional competence in social work practice
2pm–3pm shift change and handover meeting planning response to issues from previous shift						
3pm–4pm attend to afternoon administrative task including meeting social workers, afternoon telephone calls, anticipation of issues on forthcoming shift						
4pm–6pm evening meal time – engage with individuals as group-as-a-whole regarding evening activities • home visits • recreation • individual talk time						
6pm–10pm direct contact / work with wide range of situations / events • contact with families • respond to opportunity led work • respond to major / minor crisis						
10pm–12pm transition time from group time to individual time, i.e. bed time and settle for night						
7am–9am transition from individual time to various role demands, e.g. school pupil, worker, student, member of residential group						
9am–3pm deal with a wide range of professional tasks, recording, participate in supervision, preparation for handover of shift to colleagues, communicate with other agencies						

Figure 3.1: The 24-hour shift in residential child care

Table 3.1: Groups and groupings in residential settings

Groups and groupings	Signs and symbols of identity / belonging
The residential unit as a whole community	Totality of residents and staff
Living together groups	Groups determined by the programme of the unit – mealtime groups, bedroom groups
Informal friendship groups	Common interests / spontaneous friendships – individual choice regarding whether or not to 'join' – process of acceptance and rejection
Groups to discuss group living issues	Meetings to discuss shared concerns – frequently symbolises interface between staff and residents
Staff group and groupings	1. Staff meetings 2. Grouping of staff with shared responsibilities, i.e. art and craft 3. Informal affinity groupings – shared personal interests outside the work situation
Groups and grouping whose membership crosses the physical boundary of the unit	Membership composed of 'insiders' and 'outsiders', e.g. case conferences, family groupings, teams of residential and field social workers

and 18, and there is no selection on grounds of religious belief or ethnic origin. Competence in making effective entry into a group living situation depends on the integration of knowledge, values and skills. Before describing the work we need to explore the knowledge, values and skills underpinning social work in residential child care.

Knowledge

The knowledge base which informs social work practice in residential child care is extensive in its range and can be categorised as:

1. utilising theory
2. essential information
3. self-knowledge.

UTILISING THEORY

The theory base which informs residential social work practice can be daunting for student and practitioner alike. Figure 3.2 includes many of the theories and frameworks used.

ESSENTIAL INFORMATION

This is most easily understood in diagrammatic form. Table 3.2 presents our view of what constitutes essential information. The list is not exhaustive, neither is it presented in order of priority.

In the first few days and weeks of placement the student can expect to spend a considerable amount of time and energy in 'making sense' of how all this essential information fits together to inform the work of the particular unit.

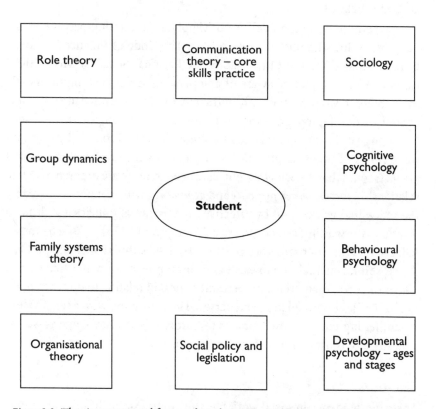

Figure 3.2: Theories, concepts and frameworks underpinning residential work

Table 3.2: Essential information

• Nature of managing agency	• Location of policy and procedure documents
• Purpose of the unit	• Daily routine
• Aims and objectives	• Key working system
• Names of staff	• Pattern of meetings
• Pen picture of young people	• Physical layout of building
• Social climate	• Recording system
• Theory base	• Values

SELF-KNOWLEDGE

'To try and understand oneself is not simply an interesting pastime, it is a necessity of life' (Bannister 1990, p.111). The Code of Practice for Social Care Workers (Training Organisation for Personal Social Services 2004) states that they should be aware of any personal issues that might impede their ability to work competently and safely (6.3, 6.4). Knowledge of self is central to developing professional competence. The importance of self-knowledge or insight is explained by Winnicott (1971, p.72): 'Insight into the feelings of others implies insight into our own similar feelings'. Ward (1993) argues that workers in group care need to be aware of three dynamic relationship forces, *power, prejudice* and *dependency*, which, if not managed by the individual worker and by effective organisational policies, can lead to discriminatory attitudes and practice. Thompson (1993) links self-knowledge with anti-discriminatory practice. He issues this challenge: 'perhaps the most fundamental step towards anti-discriminatory practice that we can take is to become, and remain open and critical in relation to our own practice' (p.153). The articulation and personal identification with a set of values is another ingredient in the worker's inventory of self-knowledge as well as a means of ensuring anti-discriminatory practice.

Values

There is a 'tendency in social work literature to list routinely and indiscriminately a series of so-called social work values as if nothing more need to be said for all to understand' (Levy and Kahan 1991, p.2). Values are integral to rather than separate from competent practice. It is the clear, consistent integration and application of values that students must demonstrate, drawing principally on the Codes of Practice. The student therefore also needs to be aware of her own values, as these will influence the quality and effectiveness of her relationships in the group living context.

Residential child care now has a well-developed value base. The impetus for its development comes from at least two sources. First, as a reaction to the abuse and exploitation by adults of young people and second, from the more positive dynamic of the United Nations Convention on the Rights of the Child. The Convention is a 'public avowal by all signatory countries that children are especially vulnerable'. Its ethos is 'to listen to and respect the voice of and needs of the child. For the first time all currently defined rights of children – from protection to self-expression – have been brought together in a single and internationally agreed document' (Kahan 1994, p.28). Kahan uses the Convention and the Children Act 1989 to delineate the rights of children in residential child care: the rights to be heard, to see health, education and social work files, to complain, to have contact with others, to health and education.

Discourse on children's rights cannot exclude responsibilities. Whilst it is true that 'some rights do not impose responsibilities on children and young people ('the right to protection from abuse is an absolute right')' (Kahan 1994, p.56), other rights do exact responsibilities. For example, the right to privacy requires respect of others' rights to privacy in return. This value base has provided a powerful mechanism for influencing policy and practice, and workers need to make sure that there is no clash between their personal values and children's fundamental rights.

Skills

The use of verbal and non-verbal communication, listening, questioning, pausing, pacing, timing, observing, summarising, planning skills, giving and receiving feedback apply equally in one-to-one social work encounters as in the group living setting. However, in the group living setting there are two important differences, the first of which, the public arena of practice, we have already discussed. The second refers to intensity and pacing. Often residential workers operate on the basis of a 24-hour period (including a sleep-over). Ward refers to the total shift as the 'unit of work' (1993, p.88) and suggests it is a process, having a beginning, middle and end. At the beginning the worker uses skills to engage with what will become a 'unit of work'. Information-gathering skills are crucial at this stage; information about what happened during the previous shift and about work to be done during the forthcoming shift. Anticipation and rehearsal skills will also predominate at this beginning stage. Based on information from colleagues who worked the previous shift, the student will need to ask: what is the anticipated mood of individuals and of the group as a whole? In the middle part of the shift, the student will need to engage directly with young clients in carrying out identified work as well as responding to events that require a response. As the shift progresses the worker will need to use planning skills to think ahead to the end of the shift so that she can hand over to other colleagues. What we have described here can be defined as the macro process of the shift. There is also the micro process. By this we mean the myriad encounters that take place between workers and young people during the shift. Each of these has its own beginning, middle and end; the quality of each such encounter will contribute to a residential unit that communicates a climate of warmth, acceptance and safety or one of suspicion and detachment, a place in which there is no emotional investment.

The following section of the chapter is the student's account of entering the group living space of an adolescent residential unit. Successful entry necessitates competence in the ability to plan, carry out, review and evaluate social work practice, with individuals, families, carers, groups and other professionals (Key Role 2) and in particular to develop and maintain relationships with individuals, families, carers, groups, communities and others. (Key Role 2 Unit 5.1)

STUDENTS' NOTES DAILY DIARY: 3 SEPTEMBER 2006

When I entered the living room there were five young people present watching TV and chatting. I had already been introduced to each of them very briefly during my induction period. I said hello, smiled and sat down on the nearest available seat. I was pleased that my voice sounded confident but no one said anything to me, some of them didn't even glance at me. The sense of isolation, of not having a relationship with any of them was quite unnerving – for a moment or two I felt like an intruder. Like the young people I too have a 'right' to be here but I am aware that I have to earn that right by showing respect. I decided that it was up to me to initiate the contact. I asked one of the young people whom I'd met before, 'Did you enjoy your home visit?' To my relief he said, 'Yeah, it was good. I stayed overnight and my dad is going to decorate my room.' I was then able to continue the conversation along the lines of what his preferences were regarding décor, sport and leisure facilities. One of the other young people then asked me, 'Are you the student?' I said, 'Yes I am,' and went on to say that I would be here for four months. I also said that my purpose in being here was to learn about what it was like to live in residential care.

They did not seem terribly interested. One of the boys asked did I ever play sport. I replied, 'I'm not good at sport but I really enjoy swimming, do any of you ever go to the leisure centre?' One replied that he went weight training; I said I wouldn't mind trying that. Some laughed and I laughed as well; some turned to look at me directly for the first time. I soon began to feel that I was beginning to be included. There were lots of questions but I was not asked anything that I felt awkward about answering. A member of staff then came in to inform us that some others were going out to town. As I left the room one of the girls, whose name is Mary, asked another worker, in what I felt was a hostile tone, if 'the student was going on the outing'. The worker asked me, I said 'Yes I am.' Mary looked away and did not seem too happy. I felt uneasy about this and knew I would need to consult with colleagues and practice teacher about what had happened. The group broke up to organise and I took a few moments in the office to think over my reactions.

Commentary

The student has begun to demonstrate that she has the knowledge, skills and values to interact with the group and contribute to improving young people's life opportunities (Key Role 2 Unit 5). This is the beginning stage of relationship building, a crucial phase in entering group care. All other work with individuals, sub-groups and the group-as-a-whole stand on the success of this stage. This process of relationship building has been described by means of the following process model (Dickson, Saunders and Stringer 1993, p.161–172):

> *Acquaintance*: 'literally the act of meeting other people either in voluntary or non-voluntary association'; 'developing meaningful fellowship' 'this can be accomplished simply by being physically present' (p.164).

> *Build-up*: The core process can be described as mutual discovery of the 'attitudes and beliefs' (p.166) of the various partners in the relationship. Judicious self-disclosure is an important skill at this stage.

Consolidation: during this phase participants typically look for ways of maintaining 'variety and interest in being together' (p.167).

Ending: Either through break-up or planned ending of association.

Conceptualising the experience

In the recording of her entry to the group living space the student's actions can be analysed against the first two stages of this framework as she begins to 'get acquainted' and we witness 'build-up' as she becomes involved in a process of mutual and appropriate self-disclosure. The student shows a mature sense of self-knowledge. She is aware of potential sources of stress, feeling isolated and vulnerable and feeling a sense of discomfort at Mary's hostility. She is aware of territory: it is their living room, she is the outsider 'joining' the group, she is aware of her own feeling and the sources of these. She has an understanding of the children's rights value base and is aware of the need to show respect. She displays good use of knowledge and uses this to engage directly with one of the boys by talking to him about his own visit. She also uses knowledge to inform her thinking about being part of the team, i.e. not wanting to earn the disapproval of colleagues. The student has made good use of relationship-building skills through her physical presence, through giving information, through initiating conversation, through humour, through tone of voice and physical control of her anxiety – 'I was glad that my voice sounded confident.' She shows skill in active listening as she correctly 'hears' the hostility in Mary's communication.

The student recognises that other Key Roles have relevance:

Key Role 1: *Prepare for work with individuals, families, carers, groups and communities to assess their needs and circumstances.* Assessment is a constant, and sometimes immediate element in the thinking processes of residential workers. The student has gathered information valuable to assessment of immediate, short and long term goals.

Key Role 6. 21.3: *Work with colleagues to contribute to team development.* The growth in her understanding of the importance of team work will help the student to gain confidence in her own contribution to the team.

Key Role 5.14.3: *Use professional and managerial supervision and support to improve your practice.* The student recognises the importance of bringing her feelings about Mary's hostility to her practice teacher during supervision.

Case study: Part 2

Competence in responding to crisis in a group living context

Many situations will require an immediate response from a student in residential placement. She may not have time to consult with other workers. These situations can be seen as crises that intrude into and disrupt the routine, or as opportunities that can offer a deeper understanding of the person being cared for, and opportunities for that person to learn mature and healthy ways of coping with problems.

CRISIS

We will assume that the student is now in week four of her placement. The hostility which she initially encountered has lessened but she has not really engaged yet with Mary. The pace has been slow and she has encountered Mary's mistrust of adults. Another young person, Jill, comes to the student and informs her that Mary is cutting herself in her bedroom. An immediate response is required.

Knowledge

We use the same three categories as for competence in entering the group-living space:

1. essential information

2. self-knowledge

3. utilisation of theory.

ESSENTIAL INFORMATION

What we provide here is a check list that a student will need to be aware of in responding to a situation of reported self-injury. This essential information can be subdivided into the three categories:

1. information about the specific context

2. worker self-check list

3. post-incident procedural requirements.

1. Information about the specific context

- What is the name of the young person reported as injured?

- What is the exact location of the young person?
- Where is the first aid equipment kept and where is that in relation to the location of the young person?
- Has another member of staff been informed?
- Where is the nearest phone in case an ambulance is required?
- What is the young person's legal status in care?
- Is this a characteristic response for this particular young person? What are the significant events or concerns in this young person's life? Are other young people involved?
- Has the young person taken any substances?
- Where are the other young people at the moment?
- If the situation requires the immediate intervention of more than one adult, are other staff free to attend?
- Will the remainder of the group require supervision or can they be left alone; if they require supervision who will do this?

2. Worker self check list

- What am I feeling right now – am I in control of myself?
- Can I cope with the sight of blood and physical injury?
- Am I competent in first aid?
- What will I say on first point of contact with the young person?
- What is my relationship with the young person?
- Have I made sure that another adult has been informed?

3. Post-incident procedural requirements

- Has the incident been written up?
- Has the young person's social worker been informed?
- Have arrangements been made to relay the information about the episode to parents, and other residential workers including the young person's key worker?
- Has a risk assessment been undertaken?

- Has someone talked through the episode with the young person? Is there need for psychiatric or psychological consultation?

SELF-KNOWLEDGE

A student finding a teenager who is involved in self-injury will need to be aware that this can provoke personal reactions including shock, denial, anger, disgust and pity, or a reluctance to see the episode as nothing more than attention-seeking behaviour. An understandable initial reaction can be that of fear, because of the amount of blood or the number of cuts or because the cuts are facial. Young people do not contrive self-injurious behaviour simply as a means of getting attention. Fundamentally, the student must be prepared to ask 'What do I feel about what has happened?' There is a good reason for doing so. If the student's answer is that they are annoyed, or disgusted, or repulsed and that they believe that the behaviour is designed as an attention-seeking strategy, then that response will inevitably act as a block on the student's ability to see self-injury for what it is: a communication of distress. A young person who self-injures is in crisis. We turn now to crisis theory as the final element in the knowledge base relevant to this particular episode.

UTILISATION OF THEORY

Crisis theory is particularly relevant to residential work. Crisis can be defined as an 'upset in a steady state'. In response to some hazardous or traumatic event the individual experiences a sense of helplessness, of not being able to cope or solve problems in their usual adaptive way. As Coulshed observes, 'If a human being is overpowered by external, interpersonal or intra-psychic forces…then harmony is lost for a time' (1991, p.68). With children and young people it may be that they have never learned healthy and adaptive ways of coping. Adult response to young people in crisis is vitally important, 'the outcome of a crisis is greatly influenced by the actions of the adult who handles it and it is the adult's attitudes and techniques that influence how a youngster responds' (Holden, Mooney and Budlong 2001). Drawing on the work of Coulshed we have assembled the following summary of crisis theory and how workers can respond:

- Crisis is generally self-limiting with a beginning, middle and end. A rise in tension in relation to some stressor is the main characteristic of the beginning phase; habitual ways of problem-solving are called on and found to be deficient; tension increases.

- The final phase is reached when the problem is solved or discharged in some way, perhaps by mobilising additional resources or perhaps, as we will see in the case of Mary, by turning the problem inward and acting aggressively against the self.

- On initial contact the worker needs to focus on the present circumstances. It is important to establish what happened and what were the circumstances that led up to the crisis.

- The next phase of intervention by the worker is to try and enable the client to state what is the most pressing issue and then to decide steps that can be taken to resolve this.

- During this early phase the worker seeks to communicate hope and optimism.

- Once the client's thinking has been concentrated on the immediate issues it may then be helpful to broaden out the exploration of circumstances. Has this ever happened before? What solutions have worked in the past?

- Reviewing progress and working toward ending the crisis intervention constitute the final phase.

STUDENT NOTES: RESPONDING TO CRISIS

Jill told me that Mary had a piece of blade from a safety razor and was in her room cutting her arm. I asked Jill to tell another member of staff that I would be in Mary's room and to check in with me as soon as possible. I was confident in my tone of voice and instruction to Jill, that she would do as I asked. For a moment I wondered if I was being 'set-up' by Jill as she knew that Mary had been hostile to me. I went to Mary's room and knocked on the door. There was no answer. I was aware of Mary's right to privacy and that this was an important part of the culture of the unit. I felt quite anxious – not knowing whether to go in or wait. I knocked again. This time there was an answer. I was anxious for Mary's safety and anxious for myself as I did not know what I would find inside the room. Another factor in my anxiety was that Mary had remained very distant from me; I had no sense of a relationship with Mary at all. Not only had she remained distant but had been openly hostile toward me. I could not make out what Mary said after my second knock on the door. It did not sound like 'come in'. I opened the door anyway. Here is some of the dialogue with my thoughts and observations.

MARY: What do you want?

Mary just gave a quick glance and looked away. I was relieved to see her sitting up on the bed. Her tone of voice was angry and hostile. There was quite a lot of blood and I could see she still had the blade in her hand.

ME: Can I come in?

I had decided I needed to stay but also felt I needed permission from Mary. If she had told me to get out I would have told her that I would send one of the staff to her.

MARY: If you want – but there's no point.

Mary seemed less hostile. I asked if I could sit down on the bed beside her. I still kept a bit of distance from her. I was very relieved that she stopped cutting herself and had actually set the blade down.

ME: Mary, I'm here because Jill told me that you were hurting
              yourself. I know she told you that she was going to get
              someone. What you're doing looks sore. Do you want to
              talk to me about it. What's wrong? I've got plenty of
              time to listen – and I won't lecture you.

One of the other staff arrived and asked if we needed help. I said I would call if I needed to. Mary gave me another quick glance. She looked at the staff member as if to say 'okay' and we were left alone again. There was a long silence. I broke it with the following comment.

ME: Mary, I don't know you all that well but I want to tell
              you that talking about things really can help. Seeing you
              like this makes me feel that you are being really hard on
              yourself.

I was beginning to feel that the distance put up by Mary had suddenly gone. I was worried that this might frighten her.

MARY: I do this more than you think. The staff just don't know
              about it.

Mary rolled up her sweatshirt and showed me previous scars. They looked quite old.

MARY: I used to do it at home but my Ma never knew. She was always out with her friends.

ME: Perhaps you would have liked her to notice?

Mary looked at me intently but said nothing. I was aware that Mary had had a home visit yesterday. I also knew from discussions at handover that the last time Mary cut herself was following a home visit. Other questions were coming quickly to my mind, but I did not want to push, yet on the other hand I felt that Mary was ready to talk.

ME: Mary there are other things I would like to ask you, but I'm not sure that I should just at the moment.

She shuffled a bit on the bed and started to pick at the blood on her arm. There was quite a long pause which was broken by Mary.

MARY: Go ahead – I don't mind.

ME: I knew that the last time you cut your arm was after a home visit. (*I paused here before going any further – I was looking for some sign that I should go on. I got a glance from Mary and a slight nod.*) I also knew that your dad was home at the same time. (*Mary was watching me intently.*)

MARY: Did you know that I told Karen (key-worker) that I hate my dad?

ME: No. I didn't know that. Is that why you are cutting yourself?

MARY: It's because of what he done to my sister. He called at the house yesterday when my ma was out. There was just me and him in the house. I want to say things but I can't.

At this point two other girls arrive at the bedroom door. They were not too sympathetic toward Mary. I had to firmly ask them to leave. I was glad of the momentary distraction to give me a little thinking time.

I was struck by the determined note in Mary's voice when she had said 'I can't,' indicating to me that Mary has things that she wants to share but feels that she cannot do so safely at this time.

ME: Mary, you say there are things you want to say but can't.
            Do you think you might be able to write them down?

MARY: I really hate my dad. If I wrote things down who would
            have to see it.

ME: Who do you think you could allow to see it first?

MARY: My key-worker, Karen.

ME: Karen is on duty tomorrow.

MARY: I can ask her then. Will you get me something to write
            on – and an envelope?

I agreed to this and then asked Mary if she would let me clean up her arm. I
also told her that I would like her to give me the piece of blade. I really was
very unsure about doing this. I knew she could easily get another piece. I felt
it was an important sign of caring for her that I removed the dangerous
object. She handed it to me and we went downstairs.

Commentary

In her response to Mary in crisis, the student illustrates many aspects of residential child care which we have described and discussed above:

- The necessity of having a personalised value base that
  convincingly communicates respect for individuals.

- The ability to respond to the opportunity-led orientation of this
  work setting.

- The tension between the public and private aspects of the setting.

- The need for workers to have well developed self-knowledge.

- The ability to draw from a wide range of theories.

- The ability to put individual clients at the 'heart of the system'.

- The ability to quickly identify with the philosophy and working
  practices of the unit.

- The ability to use core social work skills in a wide variety of
  formal and informal settings.

The student demonstrated integration of values, knowledge and skills. She convincingly communicated values of respect and acceptance in all her actions with Mary, including knocking on the bedroom door and the tone of her intervention. The student utilises knowledge in various ways. She knows and acts on the importance of informing a colleague about what is happening; she draws on the information obtained at the handover meeting about Mary's home visits; she is acutely aware of and listens to her own internal dialogue of anxiety about herself as well as anxiety about Mary; she draws on her knowledge of crisis intervention theory and responds to the immediacy of what is happening with Mary; she works toward helping Mary identify adaptive coping mechanisms. The student's recording conveys that she is demonstrating professional competence in social work practice (Key Role 6). Throughout the recording she provides evidence of her ability to manage complex ethical issues, dilemmas and conflicts (Key Role 6 Unit 20).

It should also be noted at this point that producing evidence of competence creates strong temptation for students and practice teachers to compartmentalise their practice learning experience, i.e. seeing competences as discrete and separate, thereby running the risk of students not developing an holistic view of practice. Students must be assessed for their understanding of knowledge, theory, values and capacity to work within the Care Council's Codes of Practice.

Summary and conclusion

As a result of her experience on this placement the student is able to provide written evidence that she has met a number of the Key Roles within the National Occupational Standards for Social Workers. This has included Key Role 2 Unit 5.1: *Develop and maintain relationships with individuals, families, carers, groups and others.* By communicating her role and engaging with the young people in the residential unit, the student has begun to demonstrate her ability to form relationships to enable her to plan, carry out, review and evaluate social work practice.

The student can also draw on evidence contained in her diary to highlight the fact that she recognises the need to consult with colleagues in her team, thereby contributing to team development as required by Key Role 6 Unit 21.3: *Work with colleagues to contribute to team development.*

Similarly the diary can be drawn upon to illustrate a developing awareness of self. For example, she recognised that her feelings of hostility towards Mary were something that requires to be discussed with her practice teacher during supervision, i.e. *using professional and managerial supervision to improve her practice* (Key Role 5 Unit 14.4).

In responding to Mary's self-harm with a razor blade, the student effectively demonstrated the management of risk which Mary's action posed to herself and others. Mary is in desperate need; those around her are in danger, including and possibly, primarily, the student herself. The student essentially fulfils Key Role 4 Unit 13: *Assess, minimise and manage risk to self and colleagues* and demonstrate a mature understanding of complex ethical issues and conflicts (Key Role 6 Unit 20)

As in all social work settings, good practice in residential care is informed by an ever expanding corpus of knowledge. The transition of that knowledge into social work tasks and activities is dependent on the use of skills soundly based on professional values. Debate about the value of residential child care appears to have been a constant theme over the past 20 years (Gibson 1995). There are, however, signs that positive change is taking place. Many organisations are investing heavily in new facilities to meet National Care Standards, and levels of qualification among the workforce are undoubtedly increasing throughout the UK. Recent studies demonstrate that residential child care workers have a clear sense of purpose, feel valued and that morale is high (Milligan and Kendrick 2004). Such developments have much to offer future generations of residential social work students, in their continuous striving to achieve competence.

References

Bannister, D. (1990) 'Knowledge of self.' In M. Herbert (ed.) *Psychology for Social Workers*. London: British Psychology Society and Macmillan Publishers.

Brown, A. and Clough, R. (eds) (1989) *Groups and Groupings: Life and Work in Day and Residential Settings*. London and New York: Tavistock/Routledge.

Coulshed, V. (1991) *Social Work Practice: An Introduction*. London: Macmillan.

Dickson, D., Saunders, C. and Stringer, M. (1993) *Rewarding People*. London and New York: Routledge.

Douglas, T. (1986) *Group living: The Application of Group Dynamics in Residential Settings*. New York and London: Tavistock Publications.

Gibson, J. (1995) 'Residential Child Care in Northern Ireland: Confronting Old Images and Preparing for Partnership with Parents and Families.' *Northern Ireland Journal of Multi-Disciplinary Child Care Practice 1*, 4, 26–39.

Holden, M., Mooney, A. and Budlong, M. (2001) *National Residential Childcare Project – Therapeutic Crisis intervention – Version Five*. Ithaca, NY: Cornell University.

Kahan, B. (1994) *Growing Up in Groups*. London: National Institute for Social Work, HMSO.

Kent, R. (1997) *Children's Safeguard Review*. Edinburgh: Scottish Office.

Levy, A. and Kahan, B. (1991) *The Pindown Experience and the Protection of Children. The Report of the Staffordshire Child Care Inquiry 1990.* Staffordshire County Council.

Milligan, I. and Kendrick, A. (2004) '"Nae too bad": A Survey of Job Satisfaction, Staff Morale and Qualifications in Residential Child Care in Scotland.' Glasgow: Scottish Institute of Residential Child Care, University of Strathclyde.

Parker, R.A. (1988) 'Residential Care for Children.' In I. Sinclair (ed.) *Residential Care: The Research Reviewed.* London: HMSO.

Robins, J. (1987) *The Lost Children of Ireland: A Study of Charity Children in Ireland 1700–1990.* Dublin: Institute of Public Health.

Skinner, A. (1992) *Another Kind of Home: A Review of Residential Care.* Edinburgh: HMSO.

Thompson, N. (1993) *Anti-Discriminatory Practice.* London: Macmillan.

Training Organisation for Personal Social Services (2004) *National Occupational Standards.* London: TOPSS.

Utting, W. (1991) *Children in the Public Care – A Review of Residential Child Care.* London: HMSO.

Ward, A. (1993) *Working in Group Care – Social Work in Residential and Day Care Settings.* Birmingham: Venture Press.

Warner, N. (1992) *Choosing with Care. Report of the Committee of Inquiry into the Selection, Development and Management of Staff in Children's Homes.* London: HMSO.

Waterhouse, R. (2000) *Lost in Care. Report of the Tribunal of Inquiry into the Abuse of Children in the former County Councils of Gwynedd and Clwyd since 1974.* London: Stationery Office.

Winnicott, C. (1971) *Child Care and Social Work.* London: Bookstall Publications.

CHAPTER 4

Competence in Social Work Ethics

Derek Clifford and Beverley Burke

Introduction

Ethics is commonly understood as referring to moral philosophy – the study of morality, and the norms and standards of behaviour that are used by people in order to do what is right (Banks 2006, pp.4–5). Social work students need to demonstrate knowledge of standards expected within their profession, but they also need to have a basic understanding of wider moral concepts. The latter should be able to enlarge their understanding of expected norms in a critical way – making it clear that statements about ethical behaviour and the values underpinning it have a certain variability and can be interpreted and applied in different ways. Values are usually defined in broad terms as beliefs about what is good (Banks 2006). Social work values have historically been regarded as central, and are currently recognised as such in the National Occupational Standards (NOS). Parallel developments in the UK include Codes of Practice, to which students need to adhere, and the registration of social workers. Both developments are designed to support and uphold expected norms and standards.

There is however, some tension between trying to suggest minimum standards of ethical behaviour that employers and users might expect, and the view that since ethics and values are contested and related to specific cultural, geographical and historical variables, the demand for a common minimum standard becomes an ethically and intellectually dubious proposal. The NOS refer unequivocally to the importance of professionals working within *agreed standards of social work practice* (Unit 19), and further defines the relevant values and principles as *those specified by the profession, government and employing organisation* (Unit 21, paragraph 21.4a). One may perceive the NOS therefore as enforcing supposed consensual values espoused by a particular government or agency to which an individual may well have justifiable ethical objections. Ethical competence requires responsible, reflective and reflexive actors, aware of their multiple accountabilities, and of their socially and historically differentiated locations.

Another objection to the concept of competency in ethics arises from contemporary writers interested in postmodernism and virtue ethics, where the importance of professional character and judgement is emphasised, rather than ethical principles. These ideas originate in ancient Greek philosophy, but are revived in recent times as a conscientious way of working through the complexities of (post)modern life (Clark 2006). The onus here is on the individual to develop qualities of moral excellence, such as integrity, courage, empathy, honesty and truthfulness. The Codes of Practice currently endorse the need for social workers to demonstrate moral qualities of character: 'Being honest and trustworthy' (Code of Practice, 2.1), and 'reliable and dependable' (Code of Practice, 2.4). Virtue ethics highlight the inadequacy of an approach based on the technical application of rules – or 'competency training' in its uncritical sense – without the personal *commitment* of the professional (Banks 2006, p.70). One problem with this is the variability of what differing cultures regard as excellence of character, and raises again the difficulty of identifying the minimum to be counted as necessary for competency in practice. Our approach requires social workers to be sensitive to various concepts in traditional and contemporary ethics including virtue theory.

Competent social work ethics thus needs to be pluralist, aware of different traditions in ethics, and critically informed by an awareness of power and inequality between social groups and individuals. We follow this introduction with a framework for ethical practice, a summary of which is provided in Table 4.1.

The reflexive ethical practitioner

The ability of a professional to recognise ethical issues is paramount. Lack of awareness of them leads to unquestioning application of whatever current norms and standards are in operation, and/or an egoistic approach to conduct which offers a poor basis for social work with vulnerable service users.

Box 4.1: Framework for ethical competence in social work

The reflexive ethical practitioner:

1. *recognises key aspects of social life that engender ethical issues:*
   - social location of the self in relation to others
   - the range of interdependent social systems that influence behaviours
   - the multiple directions and effects of different kinds of power
   - personal, family and social histories that shape present behaviours
   - social differences, especially those involving significant and enduring inequalities.

2. *critically evaluates relevant evidence:*
   - referral and case details, including case histories
   - research evidence
   - service user and carer evidence and their perspectives on the evidence
   - multi-professional evidence and perspectives.

3. *critically applies and interprets law, codes of practice and policy:*
   - relevant aspects of Codes of Practice
   - general laws relevant to ethical issues
   - particular laws relevant to cases
   - policies relevant to implementation.

4. *critically understands key ethical concepts:*
   - autonomy and respect for persons
   - maximising good outcomes, minimising harm
   - fairness and social justice
   - good character and intentions
   - ethical responsibility
   - care, interdependency and social support.

5. *takes responsible action on the basis of the above considerations*
   - What am I willing to be responsible for in the light of the relevant ethical, legal and anti-oppressive issues?
   - What therefore should be done?

The existence of ethical issues is sometimes regarded as a matter to which workers are alerted by the presence in discourse of words such as 'ought', 'right' or 'wrong', or of issues known to be contentious (Thomson 1999, pp.10–11). These are indeed key indicators but, in social work, the professional needs to have broad awareness of potential differences where there is no direct evidence or textual indicators. This is especially the case in relation to values which are different from the worker's own, and may not be easily 'known' to be contentious. In particular, social workers need to recognise that 'gender, race, class hegemony and subjectivity are not optional aspects of moral theory but necessary elements of any account of morality' (Hekman 1995, p.48).

The ethical practitioner, therefore, will be aware not only of the range of values and differences between social groups and cultures, but will be concerned to think through the implications in any situation of their own membership of the social divisions. The notion of 'reflexive' thinking, popularised by Schon (1983) and applied in social work by Taylor and White (2000), is inadequate if it does not focus on actors' recognition of their own social location and relative powers in relation to others: 'all significant differentials in power are critical hot spots in social-moral order' (Walker 1998, p.218). We introduce the reader at this point to a practice situation, which we will use to illustrate the above points.

Case study

Sue is a white English student social worker co-working on a child care case. The child, A, a ten-year-old girl, was of Bangladeshi ethnic background and neglected by the parents, who had a history of domestic violence, in which the child had suffered emotionally, and her development had been impaired. The child had been taken to a place of safety following an episode of violence in which the mother had been injured and the child hurt. Following a court welfare report which had favoured returning the child to the parents with a view to rehabilitation, Sue's co-worker, an experienced childcare specialist advised that it was important to plan for long-term stability for this child. She was expected to prepare for the likely failure of rehabilitation by recruiting potential adoptive parents ready to take over the child when the present situation deteriorated. The agency and related professionals were clear that the situation was untenable and that future stability for A lay away from home. However, both the court welfare report and a local Bangladeshi community advocate had strongly advocated support for the family who wished to keep the child at home, in her own community.

Sue had made a good relationship with A, and with A's mother, but her co-worker began to investigate the possibility of an adoptive placement with a couple of mixed Asian and English background. Sue had been asked to work in partnership with the parents and support the rehabilitation decision, yet she also had to be honest about her agency and its plans for the future. How could she be honest without alienating the parents and jeopardising both rehabilitation and future co-operation over adoption? How could she genuinely assist the family if she believed the agency view that support for the family would only prolong an unacceptable situation, putting the child's welfare at risk?

This case study will illustrate the way a student needs to consider ethics in relation to the National Occupational Standards. This documentation has four distinct areas focused on ethics and values (in addition to the opening international definition of social work):

1.   the GSCC Codes of Practice

2.   the Statement of Expectations of Service Users and Carers (section 6)

3.   the statement of 'Values and Ethics' that forms a part of the repeated 'Indicative Knowledge Base'

4.   Units 19, 20 and 21 of Key Role 6 setting out requirements for professional standards and values.

These statements are not entirely consistent. They vary in emphasis and need to be interpreted. Unit 21 refers to the *values and principles specified by the profession, government and employing organisations* (21.4a) as though they were exactly the same. They are not, but they overlap. Consequently, the student needs to reference as broadly and as consistently as possible, using their judgement as to what is particularly relevant, but using the framework as a guide to ensure that all the main areas are covered. In the case analysis below quotations from the NOS are in italics.

The competent reflexive ethical practitioner

1. Recognising key aspects of social life that engender ethical issues

Awareness of ethical issues needs to extend not only to the assessment of the immediate 'facts' of the situation facing the worker, but also to the range of factors relevant to ethics. The following concepts need to be systematically explored. They represent key aspects of social life where ethical analysis is required, and are drawn from anti-oppressive practice and the perspectives of subordinate social groups on the 'social world' (Clifford 1998).

REFLEXIVE SOCIAL LOCATION OF THE SELF

This requires Sue to consider how her own social location will impinge on the process. As a white, female social worker, she will need to think about the impact of her own particular experiences and values, how others will see her, and the limits of her own cultural awareness. She needs to consider her own ethnicity and how she might be able to understand the needs of a Bangladeshi child. She is faced with different accountabilities to service users, carers and employers, and the law. She may need to judge how other aspects of her social location, including her professional and social status, will also impact, and how she will be able to understand both child and parents, given her own particular experiences of child and adulthood. (NOS, Unit 19.3d): *Evaluate your own values and principles, and identify any conflicts and tensions*; Unit 19.4: *Critically reflect upon your own practice*; Unit 1.3a: *Reflect on your own background, experiences and practice that may have an impact on the relationship*; Indicative knowledge 3a: have an *Awareness of your own values, prejudices, ethical dilemmas and conflicts of interest and their implications*.)

SOCIAL DIFFERENCES

In this case study there are both obvious and hidden social differences. Some of the obvious differences concern a specific Bangladeshi ethnicity, but different ages and religions, social class and gender issues also intervene. Sue would need to contemplate *all* the possibilities (in accordance with Key Role 1 Unit 3) and consider appropriate levels of intrusiveness about personal information in order to understand family dynamics and personal values. She should also consider how social differences arise in relation to colleagues and managers, and how these might reflect differences of values, interests and status. How far can she assess the values of both colleagues and service users and their ethical implications? In addition to *The ability to view situations from multiple perspectives* (Unit 19.4 keyword: 'reflective practice'), Unit 3 indicates that the scope of assessment activity needs to consider *issues of gender, ethnicity, culture, impairment and diversity.*

THE RANGE OF INTERDEPENDENT SOCIAL SYSTEMS

The informal social systems in this case include a family and local community in which there are close ties and specific histories. Sue needs to guard against facile assumptions about the functioning of social systems, and must be ethically and 'politically' aware of how various formal and informal local systems, including the social services and community organisations, impact on this situation. She should think *Holistically...taking account of the social, economic and ecological context in which the individuals, families, carers, groups and communities are living* (Unit 2.3a). In this case she has to consider the importance of working with the local Bangladeshi community as a positive strategy to help reduce discrimination (*Ensure that the professional principles, codes and values are used...especially in relation to anti-discriminatory and inclusive practice*, NOS 19.3g) but also as a potential problem in their opposition to the plans of the agency for which she works (*Identify and work with disagreements, conflicts and tensions between stated values and principles*, NOS 19.3b).

POWERS

Different kinds of powers and the different directions in which these powers flow need to be considered by Sue, including influences upon herself (such as agency managers) and those which she herself wields (including her status in a powerful agency, and her membership of dominant as well as subordinate social divisions). These inequalities give rise to ethical issues – they make A and her mother vulnerable. Sue needs to have an awareness of the varying aspects of power – political, social, psychological, sexual and economic, and the possibilities for abuse, but also for positive change. On the one hand she needs to *Use power constructively and appropriately* (NOS 19.2b) but she also needs to *identify ways in which your own service may stigmatise and increase the exclusion of individuals...and communities* (NOS 20.2b).

PERSONAL AND FAMILY HISTORIES

By listening carefully Sue will gain insight into the unique values which mould current identity and behaviour: the history of the family and its settlement in this area, as well as individual social and psychological histories, and the impact of factors such as racism and religion. A and her parents have a lot to tell Sue, but there may well be problems both about telling and about 'listening', including different languages and cultural experiences and views: listening to a very different child, as well as a potentially violent male. These considerations equally apply where the ethnicity of the family is similar to that of the worker: awareness of difference in personal and family stories is related to *all* the significant social differences that divide the experiences of workers from others. Social workers should 'have respect' *for the expertise and knowledge users and carers have about their own situation* (Statement of Expectations 6a). Units 2.2, 2.3 and 2.4 are also highly pertinent, requiring the student to work with individuals and families to identify their needs, and this task is spelled out more clearly in the indicative areas of knowledge accompanying the NOS: she must *value, recognise and respect the diversity, expertise and experience of individuals, families, carers, groups and communities* (Indicative Areas of Knowledge 3d)

2. Critically evaluating relevant evidence

The range of evidence must at least be considered in principle even if sometimes it is not always possible or ethical to investigate fully.

REFERRAL AND CASE DETAILS

At the referral stage, ethical values are already embedded in different people's interpretation of the case evidence. Sue will need to consider critically the values expressed, and further study and interviews will be necessary. She has also to be careful about how much investigation can be ethically justified, especially when that can be seen as intrusive and unnecessary. She needs to satisfy herself that she understands the differing perspectives, and weigh up differing hypotheses. Some of the relevant standards for this overlap with the previous section on personal and family stories. However, Sue needs to demonstrate *The ability…to search for alternative explanations* (Unit 19, keyword: 'reflective practice') and, in doing so, she will have to consider the alternative explanations of users and carers, and information from inter-professional colleagues. This is a service user expectation (Statement of Expectations 4b) and also of Unit 17: *Work within multi-disciplinary and multi-organisational teams, networks and systems.*

RESEARCH EVIDENCE

Sue needs to know and understand evidential research:

1.   on the experiences of, and services to, minority ethnic families

2.   relating to adoption as a stabilising factor in children's lives

3.   about long-term fostering and the different ways that family and community ties can be maintained

4.   on domestic violence, its implication in child abuse

5.   on resilience in child development and how the child might develop, wherever placed.

However, all this research has to be interpreted and applied to the case. Unit 19.1 requires Sue to consider the evidence and use *best knowledge-based practice* in her work, but in a critical, ethical way.

SERVICE USER AND CARER EVIDENCE AND THEIR PERSPECTIVES

The Code of Practice urges Sue to work in partnership with the service users and carers, but there is an obvious difficulty. The family is divided on some things, but united on others. On religious matters they may share common values. A's mother *may* not see the violence as significant in the same way as Sue, nor easily work in partnership with someone different from her own culture. This raises ethical issues relative to the welfare and rights of mother and child, justice for the family, and cultural sensitivity. The whole Statement of Expectations is an indication of the importance of this issue, yet its advice to *put users and carers first* (6e), does not help Sue when the users' and carers' interests are not necessarily the same, and may be in conflict, and both may be in conflict with her own and her agency's values.

MULTI-PROFESSIONAL EVIDENCE AND PERSPECTIVES

The evidence of numerous 'scandals', as Sue knows, suggests that the failure of communication between professionals is a major issue. She needs a critical approach to assess conflicting evidence from differing sources. In A's case the court has not upheld her agency's view on the matter. She needs to pay attention to views which *differ* from her agency brief, taking account of both high and low status professions, the evidence base for their views, and the social locations through which they are filtered. This practice is ethical both in respecting colleagues having (possibly) disconfirming 'expert' evidence, but also in following a policy of rigorous assessment and dialogue, likely to get nearer to a more valid constructive account. The whole of Unit 17 is relevant, and is particularly apt in requiring Sue to *Deal constructively with disagreements and conflict within relationships* (17.4).

3. Critically interpreting and applying law, policy and codes of practice

Our ethical values will influence how we interpret the law (Banks 2001). It should be used as a tool to work with people to enable them to assert their right to resources, to challenge rules which diminish individual and collective rights, and to promote individual and social change. Deciding when and how to use the law is not a neutral act: it is one that has a value and ethical dimension to it. A legalistic approach to human problems fails to address questions of inequality, and such an approach can compound the oppression felt. Sue has to be knowledgeable about the law, as well as 'possess independent critical judgement, practical wisdom and the capacity to act responsibly' (Pattinson 2001, p.7).

GENERAL LAWS RELEVANT TO ETHICAL ISSUES

In recent years there has been a steadily developing range of laws relevant to ethics. Human rights represents a powerful global discourse which has significant implications (Ife 2001; Williams 2001). The United Nations Declaration of Human Rights is referenced by international social work organisations, and along with the United Nations Convention on the Rights of the Child 1989, is incorporated into national UK legislation. Particularly important are laws such as the Disability Discrimination Act 1995 (amended and extended by the Disability Discrimination Act 2005), and the Race Relations (Amendment) Act 2000. The Equality Act 2006 will establish the Commission for Equality and Human Rights (CEHR), and other recent legislation in relation to discrimination will ensure that equal opportunities and rights for members of different social groups are recognised. There are numerous laws promoting individual and collective rights and social justice, which underpin ethical practice, and Sue needs to have a good understanding of such laws in relation to the particular service users and carers she works with. No legislation stands above ethics, and interpreting and using the law requires awareness of ethical, anti-oppressive dimensions. In some cases (for example in the area of immigration and asylum) it may be regarded as ethical to resist the law (Hayes and Humphries 2004; Humphries 2004).

PARTICULAR LAWS RELEVANT TO SOCIAL WORK

Legislation has to be actively and critically interpreted and applied, so the needs of service users and subordinate social groups are robustly protected, and where appropriate their autonomy expanded – but balanced against the claims of others affected by their actions. This clearly requires thoughtful consideration of the rights and obligations of different people, including social workers themselves. Sue will also need to be aware of the Children Acts 1989 and 2004, and, if adoption is being planned, the Adoption Act

2002, and the associated policies and procedures developed by agencies in response to the legislation.

SOCIAL WORK CODES OF PRACTICE

Codes of practice are often used to articulate the ethical responsibilities of professionals. Such codes regulate their conduct and distinguish their role from others (Banks 2003, pp.106–124). They usually incorporate a range of values which have been found to be: 'useful in structuring moral life. These may include seeking justice, equality and liberty for all, and respect for persons and their autonomy' (Pattinson 2001, p.7). The British Association of Social Workers Code of Ethics and the General Social Care Council Codes of Practice for Social Care Workers and Employers are examples of such documents. Some codes have begun to emphasise the importance of the character of the social worker, rather than simply list the principles under which they should operate (Clark 2006). There is thus a personal challenge for Sue, as well as accountability to her employer, to the law and to the profession, for the interpretation of and compliance with the ethical standards in such codes.

4. Critically understanding ethical concepts

The following ethical concepts are drawn from classical and contemporary ethics. There is no absolute basis for the following selection, but they do cover most of the ethical ideas that recent commentators have thought to be relevant to social work (Banks 2006; Beckett and Maynard 2005; Hugman 2005). They need to be interpreted in the light of the above anti-oppressive concepts.

AUTONOMY AND RESPECT FOR PERSONS

The classic obligation to have respect for others includes the rights of both A's parents and also their child, and these are each in potential conflict with the other. The differing ethnicity of A's family means that Sue needs to have respect for their different culture, as well as for each as individuals of different age and gender. A particular problem here is how far she can justify taking a parentalist view of A's needs against the wishes of her parents, and possibly even A herself. How can she support their right to determine their own lives? How can she respect their right to honest information? Being honest is desirable, yet is regarded as secondary to safety (Loewenberg and

Dolgoff 1996). However, Sue will need to pay attention to the Codes of Practice which lay emphasis upon respect for the service user's rights (3.1), and also *Being honest and trustworthy* (2.1). There is thus an obligation here for Sue to be aware of the *complex ethical issues,* and *devise strategies* to deal with them (Unit 20). She has to balance the rights of the child (and of the legal and social obligations) to its protection and care, against the rights of the parents to honesty and justice. She will need to seek advice from colleagues, supervisors and others to act in a way she can herself respect.

MAXIMISING GOOD OUTCOMES AND MINIMISING HARM

Sue will need to take 'utilitarian' ethics seriously – she needs to assess what outcome will ensure the 'greatest happiness' for all. To achieve this she will need to pay close attention to the case history, the wishes of A and her parents, the evidence of past events, of strengths and needs, and the evidence of research into comparable situations. This is a strong ethical argument for 'evidence-based' practice, but how are complex and conflicting interests and values to be reconciled? How easily can they be 'measured' or outcomes predicted? These difficulties should not be used as an excuse for avoiding careful assessment of best strategies. The Codes of Practice require social workers *where appropriate* to promote the *individual views and wishes* of service users (1.2) and *minimise the risks of harm to themselves or other people* (4.3).

FAIRNESS AND SOCIAL JUSTICE

Sue needs to think about the justice of the situation in relation to the different individuals, and in relation to them as a family group. Are they being targeted unfairly because of their membership of a minority ethnic group, or because of their lack of material resources? How can Sue balance justice for the parents and for the child, including justice for A's mother who has tried to bring up her child whilst under attack at home and in the community? The Codes of Practice have a relatively mute tone on this issue, yet they are clear that social work includes *promoting equal opportunities for service users and carers* (1.5), and a social worker must not *discriminate unlawfully* (5.5). However, there is a clear call to social justice at the head of the National Occupational Standards, in its use of the international definition of social work, and its call for the *empowerment and liberation of people,* based on *Principles of human rights and social justice* (Training Organisation for Personal Social Services 2004, NOS p.2).

GOOD CHARACTER AND INTENTIONS

Sue wants to practise with integrity, and would like to display genuine warmth and empathy to A and her parents. She is well aware that A's mother expects her to be trustworthy and reliable. However, Sue feels uncomfortable about the plans that she is making which go against the parents' wishes. She will have to find ways of carrying out what she feels is best for the child and the family whilst making it clear to A's mother especially that there are difficult balances that she is required to hold. She will want to be as truthful and trustworthy as she can. The Codes of Practice agree with the service users' Statement of Expectations, that social workers should be of good character – *honest and trustworthy* (2.1), and *reliable and dependable* (2.4).

ETHICAL RESPONSIBILITY

Sue owes both the family and its different members some accountability for her actions, but also the employing agency and society at large. However, the endpoint in uncertain situations is that she is responsible herself for her own actions. It is not *just her* decision, but it *is* her decision too: how far can she allow her own personal values – religious or secular – to influence a professional decision, and how far is it possible to avoid that? The NOS say that the social worker has a professional responsibility for dealing with ethical dilemmas and problems: they are not something to be left for someone else to resolve. Social values and principles should be *Integrated…into your own practice* (19.3a), *especially in relation to anti-discriminatory and inclusive practice* (19.3g), and conflicts and disagreements should be worked with (19.3b). The Code of Practice has a whole section (6) on being 'accountable'.

CARE, NURTURE AND SOCIAL SUPPORT

Sue knows that a care perspective in ethics emphasises the importance of the network of interdependent relationships, and especially the process of dialogue. Sue needs to demonstrate that she has shown appropriate care and empathy for service users. She also needs to maintain a professional distance that will enable her to make difficult decisions. The Codes of Practice are not very explicit about the importance of care – surprisingly for a caring profession – yet they insist that service users need 'respect' for their dignity and culture (1.4; 1.6) 'support' (1.3), 'help' (3.7), as well as information and advice. Throughout the service users' Statement of Expectations there is the assumption that the social worker is there to 'work with', 'help', 'involve', 'empower', and *link users and carers to support groups and networks and support them* (Statement of Expectations 2.l).

5. Taking responsibility for acting on the basis of the above considerations

Sue needs to consider the ethical issues arising from analysis of the evidence, and the interpretation of relevant laws, codes of practice and policies. She will have questioned the actions and interpretations of all involved (including her own) from the perspective of the complex inequalities that drive individuals from subordinate groups into the care system. It will be a decision which has been checked out against the key concepts in this ethical framework, demonstrating that the issue has been thoroughly thought through. However, there is no absolutely 'correct' outcome. Sue has to take responsibility for her views after rigorous, thoughtful consideration.

Sue needs to prioritise values, if for example, she feels the safety of the child would be at risk if she was too honest. She might need to abandon some aspects of confidentiality if they conflicted with the future welfare of the child. Loewenberg and Dolgoff (1996) suggest that there is a hierarchy of values with safety and the meeting of basic needs at the top of the priority list. This is helpful up to a point, but the ethical concepts discussed above are not always easily commensurable, and the choices to be made between them have to be the subject of personal judgement in changing circumstances. How can Sue balance the rights of differing carers and service users?

She will need to:

1. be reflexively aware of her own values, her social position, and of her feelings, including fear of consequences for herself

2. maintain a balance between commitment and professional distance

3. be aware of her own attitudes to religion in general, and in this case specifically

4. respect their freedom of worship, their culture and hopes for their child

5. draw a line between respecting religious – or secular – values and ensuring the safety or welfare of the child.

But where exactly should this line be drawn, and how far is Sue reflecting her own values in making this judgement?

EVIDENCE OF ETHICAL COMPETENCE

Sue needs to demonstrate that she has engaged with the five steps in the above summary, with reference to the NOS, Statement of Expectations and Codes of Practice. Since ethics is central to the whole social work process, it follows that the evidence provided for *previous* Units and Key Roles will be relevant to Key Role 6 – the over-arching requirement to *Demonstrate professional competence in social work practice,* and especially Units 19 and 20 which specifically refer to standards and ethics. This means that some of the evidence does not need to be repeated, but simply referred to at this point.

For example, Sue should already have demonstrated that she has critically referred to relevant laws, policy, case and research evidence. Taking account of differing inter-professional values and of service user and carer views and working ethically with others should have been demonstrated. However, sections 1, 4 and 5 in the above Framework need to be separately evidenced by the student, and Units 19 and 20 are especially relevant. There are various ways in which these competences could be evidenced. The following might be a hypothetical statement of evidence (NOS quotations in italics).

SUE'S WRITTEN REPORT:

Evidence for Key Role 6 Unit 19

Element 1 of Unit 19 requires me to exercise *professional judgement,* made difficult in this case by conflicting views emanating from different sources. I had to work sensitively with conflicting opinions and *issues of diversity.* This required me to make judgements about relative risks and opportunities, demonstrating understanding of ethical considerations and seeking good outcomes for as many as possible, but especially (as decreed by the Children Act 1989) the most vulnerable, child A. My role was to support the family and monitor the care of child A whilst considering alternative courses of action, twin-tracking the possibility of either rehabilitation, or removal and eventual adoption.

It was a difficult situation, but the evidence from both family and advocates is that they maintained contact with me even when they did not agree. In both cases my strategy was to contact them, offering to visit the community centre and speak to them on their territory, respecting their customs and views, and thus integrating into my practice basic ethical requirements of the Codes, and Expectations of service users and carer. I therefore had more than ample opportunity to demonstrate my competence in relation to element 2 of Unit 19, when I had to justify decisions and outcomes, and challenge others' views where I thought there might be significant harm to child A, and do so in a sensitive way that would not undermine my relationship with the family. Written evidence of some of these exchanges can be seen in contemporaneously recorded notes, and minutes of discussions with my practice assessor. I also depended heavily on these discussions concerning my values in relation to understanding the cultural and economic circumstances of the family, thus providing evidence for Unit 19.5 – using supervision to meet developmental needs, especially in relation to respecting other cultures.

Another strategy here was to study the community background, using community centre resources to access information with support and approval from workers there. The evidence of that relationship and the knowledge gained also exists in some of the materials that I was able to bring back, providing information and posters that have been widely shared, thus contributing to agency policy and practice as required in Unit 21.1. This included an implicit challenge to current agency practice where the culture of this particular community was not well represented.

I have tried to *work within the principles and values underpinning social work practice* (Unit 19.3), and believe that the above narrative and the associated evidence bears this out. I argued in professional meetings that the long-term interests of the child required a dialogue, with continued involvement of the different parties. There was a danger that I would identify too strongly with the mother, having a child of my own, and not balance this with the known risks. But there was also a danger that I would be too judgemental about culturally different forms of child care. This discussion took place in supervision, and in team meetings, as recorded in supervision minutes, and evidences my commitment to meeting the requirements of 19.4: *to critically reflect on…own practice*, in respect of ethical issues.

Evidence for Key Role 6 Unit 20

Much of the evidence for Unit 20 – that I should *manage complex ethical issues, dilemmas and conflicts* – is implicit in my discussion of evidence for Unit 19. There were clearly conflicts between agencies, and between service users, carers and agencies. I was faced with personal dilemmas about how I could maintain an honest – and effective – relationship between the different members of the family, myself and my agency, in view of the serious differences of perspective, culture, powers and social positions. I found myself as a mother very sympathetic to A's mother and her struggle against racism from the majority community, and against violence from her husband. I had to explore with my supervisor whether my attitude to A's father was Eurocentric or justifiably feminist. I considered that there was a serious danger of discrimination on my part if I either underprotected or overprotected child A. In order to get an appropriate balance I sought advice from my supervisor, and discussed the general issue of child abuse with community members.

Evidence for Key Role 6 Unit 21

I referred above to evidence of contact with the community centre, and contribution to informing and changing ideas about the family and their community. Additionally, I used my contact to initiate discussion of *policy review and development* within the agency about continuing and enhancing relationships with community workers. I have suggested that proactive measures need to be considered unless there is not to be a suspicion of institutionalised poor practice, and have written notes for consideration by my practice teacher and senior staff. I have thus evidenced my attempt to meet the performance criteria in relation to 21.2: *to inform a course of action where practice falls below a required standard.*

Evidence relating to the Codes of Practice, the Service Users' and Carers' Statement of Expectations, and anti-oppressive social work values

The evidence for these ethical requirements should by now have been produced in the context of discussing the competences relating to the above Key Roles and Units. Sue should conclude her statement of evidence by referring to the Codes and Expectations, identifying and explaining any apparent gaps, and highlighting the ethical issues that were of most importance, and emphasising how the anti-oppressive social work values listed above have been integrated throughout her practice.

She needs to make it clear that although her personal values may inform her understanding of the social work task, she has been careful to follow the *broader* framework provided by social work ethics. This means that whatever kind of religious or secular view she has, she has refrained from imposing her judgements on service users. The framework provided here allows for social workers themselves to have differing personal values, yet it challenges the worker to place them within the wider framework where accountabilities to others require them to refrain from imposing their views, and question their own values. This kind of 'bilateral view' is necessary for competence in social work ethics (Hugman 2005), but the connection between 'local' and 'universal' values is complex, and cannot rest on assumptions about uncontestable universal human values.

Conclusion

Competency in ethics in social work requires judgement and responsibility for decisions, practices and understanding, in which a person is involved, directly or indirectly. It requires a reflexive attitude of deliberation and review of personal and social processes in which unequal needs, strengths and powers are assessed and the implications considered. It also needs a pluralist appreciation of the varied ethical concepts and norms that are relevant to personal and social life. It needs an ability to understand and tolerate the variety of local values to be found in communities and families, but also a commitment to critical questioning of local values (including the worker's own) in the light of wider norms. This notion of competency not only implies a positive attitude towards the development of character, but also critical assessment of the collective social systems in which the person is situated, including the organisations in which they work. It thus requires a commitment to a professional approach to ethics that overlaps with but may be in some tension with personal ethics. The commitment to be (and to stay as) a post holder in a profession that is governed by codes of practice and laws relating to human welfare, and in an organisation driven by various stakeholder interests and powers, is a demand for competency in ethics made upon oneself. The minimal requirement is that the issues have been systematically considered in the light of contemporary best practice, and the above framework provides the basis for this. Excellence in ethical social work practice would be demonstrated by the thoroughness and level of commitment shown.

References

Banks, S. (2001) Ethics and Values in Social Work, 2nd edn. Basingstoke: Palgrave Macmillan.
Banks, S. (2003) Ethics, Accountability and the Social Professions. Basingstoke: Palgrave Macmillan.
Banks, S. (2006) Ethics and Values in Social Work, 3rd edn. Basingstoke: Palgrave Macmillan.
Beckett, C. and Maynard, A. (2005) Values and Ethics in Social Work: An Introduction. London: Sage.
Clark, C. (2006) 'Moral Character in Social Work.' British Journal of Social Work 36, 1, 75–89.

Clifford, D.J. (1998) *Social Assessment Theory and Practice, a Multi-Disciplinary Framework*. Aldershot: Ashgate.

Hayes, D. and Humphries, B. (eds) (2004) *Social Work Immigration and Asylum: Debates, Dilemmas and Ethical Issues for Social Work and Social Care Practice*. London: Jessica Kingsley Publishers.

Hekman, S. (1995) *Moral Voices, Moral Selves, Carole Gilligan and Feminist Moral Theory*. London: Polity Press.

Humphries, B. (2004) 'An Unacceptable Role for Social Work: Implementing Immigration Policy.' *British Journal of Social Work 34*, 1, 93–107.

Hugman, R. (2005) *New Approaches in Ethics for the Caring Professions*. Basingstoke: Palgrave Macmillan.

Ife, J. (2001) *Human Rights and Social Work: Towards Rights-Based Practice*. Cambridge: Cambridge University Press.

Loewenberg, F.M. and Dolgoff, R. (1996) *Ethical Decisions For Social Work Practice*. Illinois: F.E. Peacock.

Pattinson, S. (2001) 'Are Nursing Codes of Practice Ethical?' *Nursing Ethics 8*, 1, 5–17.

Schon, D. (1983) *The Reflective Practitioner in Action: How Professionals Think in Action*. New York: Basic Books.

Taylor, C. and White, S. (2000) *Practising Reflexivity in Health and Welfare: Making Knowledge*. Buckingham: Open University Press.

Thomson, A. (1999) *Critical Reasoning in Ethics: A Practical Introduction*. London: Routledge.

Training Organization for Personal Social Services (2004) *National Occupational Standards*. London: TOPSS.

Walker, M.U. (1998) *Moral Understandings: A Feminist Study in Ethics*. London: Routledge.

Williams, J. (2001) 'The 1998 Human Rights Act: Social Work's New Benchmark.' *British Journal of Social Work 31*, 6, 831–844.

CHAPTER 5

Competence in Child Abuse Referral-taking: Coping with Discriminatory or Malicious Referrals

Kieran O'Hagan

Introduction

Much of the impetus for change in child care legislation and policy has been generated by the government's, the media's and the public's response to a seemingly relentless stream of child abuse inquiry reports criticising many of the professionals involved (Parton 2004). An inevitable though often temporary consequence to inquiries is that agencies adopt an over zealous response to referrals of any kind, investigating every referral immediately, irrespective of the quality or quantity of information obtained, and in the process subjecting families and children to exceedingly intrusive and some-times damaging bureaucratic procedures. This chapter tells the story of a student dealing with a particularly difficult type of referral, an anonymous referral. She attempts to adhere to National Occupational Standards, the agency's procedures and guidelines, child care law, comprehensive assess-ment and referral frameworks, and to the values and ethics espoused in the code of practice governing her work. The case explores the challenges and complexities of anonymous referrals. It suggests that the context and condi-tions of many single mothers, particularly those from minority groups, are vulnerable to discriminatory or malicious referrals. The student demonstrates knowledge, skills, values, rigour and discipline that not only help expose such referrals, but remain the principal attributes underpinning competent practice in response to all genuine referrals, the foundation stone upon which equally competent investigation and assessment is made.

Child protection: giving student opportunities

How much responsibility should be given to students on placement? In some child protection placements responsibility is minimal and students may be deprived of real opportunity. This is despite the fact that the new degree courses are committed to ensuring students carry out statutory tasks. The nature and extent of criticism levelled against child protection agencies over many years has been such as to induce extreme caution in those supervising students. In the author's recent random telephone poll of child protection agencies, the question: 'How do you provide meaningful experiences in child abuse referral taking for students on placement?' invariably provoked awkward silences, followed by commitments to enquire and to get back to me, which none of them did. Although I am sure they exist, I was unable to find an authority that permitted students to take child abuse referrals, or had a specific policy on the matter.

It is a dilemma not only about students, nor is it a uniquely British dilemma. McPherson and Barnett (2006) provide a detailed description of a comprehensive (and otherwise commendable) induction course for *qualified* social workers embarking upon child protection work in the Australian state of Victoria. The nearest these newly qualified workers get to taking a child abuse referral is, apparently, 'sitting in on the reception of a report of child abuse' (p.195).

This regrettable state of affairs may stem from a number of root causes:

- ultra caution (*we wouldn't dare allow a student to take a child abuse referral*)

- the perennial crisis in recruiting and retaining practice placement supervisors (Torry, Furness and Wilkinson 2005), particularly in child protection agencies

- reorganisation and specialisation, with the merest whiff of a child abuse referral case instantly re-referred to specialist individuals or teams.

Such structural safeguards and/or caution on the part of agencies are understandable in the light of incompetent referral-taking forensically exposed in
child abuse enquiry reports (e.g. Blom-Cooper 1995; Lambeth 1987; Laming 2003). But the sometimes disastrous consequences, which are the direct
result of such incompetence, are the surest evidence we have of the importance of referral-taking in child abuse work. The Department of Health's
Framework document (DoH 2000) stresses the 'critical importance' of
referral-taking, and its fundamental role...'At that point the foundation is
laid for future work with the child or family' (p.42, 3.3).

Competence during the *referral* phase of child protection

In the following case, a social work student responds to an anonymous telephone child abuse referral. She is shadowed by her experienced practice
teacher. She is in the second year of a degree course, and is placed in an
authority that has integrated child protection services. In her first year she
completed a two-week observation placement in a centre providing refuge
for asylum seekers.

Case example

The duty officer (hereinafter referred to as the 'student') takes a telephone
call from a man who refuses to give his name. He is agitated, and is obviously anxious about the consequences of his actions. He says that he
believes there is a child being abused in his neighbourhood. It is a baby; he
doesn't know what gender; he thinks it's about four months old. The baby
lives with his/her mother quite near him, in a home owned by the Catholic
church. He thinks the mother and baby are African. He thinks the mother
can't speak 'the language'. He and his neighbours have seen this mother and
baby leave the home late nearly every night. He thinks she's 'on the game'.
Occasionally she has come back to the home with men and women. He
believes most of them are of the same nationality. He hears the baby crying
often when they come back, and he thinks he/she is distressed. He stresses
that he is not racist, that he has nothing against this mother, that he and his
neighbours have tried to reach out to her, have offered to help, but she can't
even communicate with them. He and his neighbours are concerned about
what's happening to this baby.

The knowledge base

Competence requires knowledge, values and skills. The knowledge base underpinning effective referral-taking is outlined in the National Occupational Standards but only in the form of generalities applicable to virtually all social work practice itself. Students need a more sharpened focus. Referral taking requires (a) basic information, (b) understanding (possibly assisted by theories, concept or frameworks), (c) self-knowledge and self awareness (O'Hagan 1986; Trevithick 2005).

The most basic, important information required is:

1. the *legal context*, i.e. the law pertaining to Child Protection (e.g. Children Act 2004; Children Act 1989, Ss.42–52) and in particular, the statutory obligation to investigate all referrals alleging child abuse of any kind (Children Act 1989, S.47, 1(b)). Morris (2005) analyses the shift in emphasis between 'children in need' in the 1989 Children Act, to 'children at risk' in the 2004 Children Act

2. *Framework for Assessment of Children in Need and their Families* (DoH 2000)

3. the agency's policy and procedures on child abuse referrals (as contained in child protection handbooks, made available on placement)

4. knowledge of the areas to be explored in referral-taking generally (see below)

5. child abuse enquiry reports which have identified poor referral-taking as a contributory factor in the chain of events leading to the deaths of children, or to the unjustified removal of children (see above)

6. relevant child protection research and literature

7. statement of principle regarding values and ethics in NOS.

1, 2, 3, 5 and 7 are quite straightforward: in addition to being available in the agency's literature, such knowledge will be demonstrated daily by other more experienced workers. In respect of 6, students should be aware of the prevalence of and of the particular challenges posed by anonymous referrals. Besharov (1990) and Thorpe (1994) provide evidence of their prevalence, and O'Hagan (1989, 1993) has analysed anonymous referrals in practice, and provided guidelines for coping with them. O'Hagan and Dillenburger (1995) are particularly concerned about anonymous referrals alleging abuse or neglect by single parent mothers. They contend that such referrals, and how agencies often respond to them, are an intrinsic feature of abusive child care and child protection systems. In respect of 4 (knowledge of the areas to be explored), the student will need to establish in so far as is possible:

- person making the referral
- age and gender of child
- nationality/group identity of family of child
- position of child in family
- whether or not child is disabled in any way
- identity of alleged abuser
- type of alleged abuse
- location of child at time of referral
- location of child at time of alleged abuse (see Table 5.1).

In addition to these factors, five specific lines of enquiry should be made about:

1. the nature and extent of the alleged abuse
2. the circumstances surrounding the abuse
3. the family, extended family and significant others
4. the welfare of the child: their emotional, social, psychological, educational and physical wellbeing
5. the involvement (and reasons for it) of other child care agencies.

The importance of each of these information factors in enhancing understanding of the referral is self-evident; they also help determine the appropriateness and urgency of an investigation. Unit 4.1 of Key Role 2 requires the worker to *Assess the urgency of requests for action*. The above referral is very urgent for one obvious reason: the age of the alleged victim. Generally, the younger the child, and the closer the relationship between child and alleged abuser, then the greater the risk (O'Hagan 1989, 2006a).

Table 5.1: Facts to be established in referral-taking

Person making referral	Age of child and gender	Place of child in family	Nationality, group identity, status etc. of family	Disability	Alleged perpetrator	Type of abuse	Location of child at time of referral	Location of child at time of alleged abuse
Relative	0–1 year M/F	Youngest	British	Physical	Mother	Physical	Home	Home
Neighbour	1–2 years M/F	Oldest	Afro-Caribbean	Sensory	Father	Emotional	School	Home of neighbour
Friend	3–4 years M/F	Middle	African	Mental disability	Stepmother	Social (deprivation)	Surgery	Home of relative
GP	5–10 years M/F	Other	Asian	Emotional	Stepfather	Psychological	Care home	School
Teacher	11–12 years M/F		East European		Grandparent	Sexual (or grooming for)	Clinic	Nursery
HV	13–17 years M/F		Economic migrants		Aunt/Uncle	Failure to thrive	Neighbour-hood	Foster home
Community nurse			Asylum seekers		Neighbour	Ritual	Nursery	Care home

Continued on next page

Table 5.1 continued

Person making referral	Age of child and gender	Place of child in family	Nationality, group identity, status etc. of family	Disability	Alleged perpetrator	Type of abuse	Location of child at time of referral	Location of child at time of alleged abuse
Police			Travellers		Professional	Satanic	Hospital	Other
Psychiatrist			Other		Putative father	Bullying	Unknown	
Abused child					Cohabitee	Neglect	Other	
Anonymous					Babysitter			
Other								

The referrer believes the alleged victim is only a few months old, and that the mother's behaviour is a cause of the alleged abuse.

Values and ethics

The value base for child protection work in general and for response to this anonymous referral in particular consists of much more than the para-mountcy principle, i.e. 'the welfare of the child is paramount'. The welfare and rights of the mother and the welfare and rights of the person making the referral have both got to be considered. The mother has the right not to be prejudged on the basis of an anonymous referral. An agency which responds immediately to the referral as it stands, by rushing out to investigate, will generate an enormous crisis for the mother, thus risking incapacitating her caring adequately for the children she is allegedly neglecting. The referrer too has rights: the right to be listened to and taken seriously; the right to be helped and comforted (if needed) during the probable ordeal in making the referral; the right not to be forgotten if the referral leads to an investigation and intervention, and he holds himself responsible for some future drastic resolution (e.g. court proceedings, children permanently removed, etc.). NOS spell out the ethical imperatives; here are some of the most pertinent to this particular case:

Awareness of your own values, prejudices, ethical dilemmas and conflicts of interest, and their implications for your practice
The student needs to be rigorous in exploring his/her attitude to single parent mothers, fragmented families and mother–cohabitee relationships (O'Hagan and Dillenburger 1995). The referrer believes that the mother may be of African origin; therefore (particularly in the light of the current intensifying animosity towards economic migrants and/or asylum seekers and the draconian measures taken by most governments to block them) the student must be fully aware of their own views and feelings on these broader issues of immigration and asylum seeking, and of the level of their cultural competence generally (O'Hagan 2001). Concomitant with these obligations are two statements from the new Code of Practice for social care workers: they must not 1. *discriminate unlawfully or unjustifiably against service users carers or colleagues* (5.5), nor 2. *condone any unlawful or unjustifiable discrimination by service users, carers or colleagues* (5.6) (Training Organisation for Personal Social Services 2004).

Respect for and the promotion of (a) each person as an individual; (b) dignity and privacy of individuals; (c) Recognise and facilitate each person's language and form of communication of their choice

These requirements under Values and Ethics reaffirm the necessity of careful assessment in a case of potentially competing rights. The Framework document emphasises that 'initial assessment is deemed to have commenced at the point of referral' (DoH 2000, 3.9).

Skills

The skills required for referral-taking include:

- listening skills

- accurate interpretation (of words, voice, tone, emotion, attitude)

- empathy (important to convey to the referrer that you understand and 'feel' the likely predicament they are in)

- patience (avoid putting referrer under pressure)

- pacing and sensitivity (uttering words or sounds of encouragement at the appropriate time

- written recording (contemporaneous)

- report writing (necessary for future consultations, case conferences, submission to court etc.)

- computer literacy (eliciting, adding to, correcting, updating existing files on computer; creating new files).

The exercise of all these skills requires self-control and discipline, and a continuous awareness of, and being able to respond within, the bounds of legal obligation and departmental procedure.

A student encountering an anonymous referral for the first time will soon realise the necessity of these skills, and gain a deeper understanding of the nature of such referrals. Much of this understanding will come on hearing the referrer's words, tone, mood, warnings, threats, apprehension and/or fear. At the outset, the student should keep an open mind as to whether or not this is a genuine referral. It may be a malicious referral, which is not uncommon, but on the other hand it may be genuine. Either of these possibilities will become more apparent if the student succeeds in communicating and engaging with the referrer. Assuming for the moment that it is genuine, the student should understand that:

- the referrer's tension, apprehension, and fear, are reasonable; he may be taking considerable risks in expressing his concern about the child (Key Role 4 in the NOS requires workers to *manage risk*)

- the referrer may find it difficult to phone an agency like social services to allege child abuse. Most anonymous referrers need help and support, to say what they need and want to say

- following on from that point, the referrer may give the very strong impression that they want to get the referral over with as quickly as possible and put the phone down; but in fact, they will most often welcome a well-timed, suitably toned interjection.

Self-knowledge and self-awareness

In Chapter 1, reference was made to the substantial literature that contributes to the knowledge base of social work practice. But referral-taking is not just about reading and accumulating knowledge from books; it is also about how the worker deals with entirely new knowledge (true or false) from an unknown source, alleging abuse or expressing concern. The worker is not only meant to receive the information, but possibly to influence and shape the knowledge. As Osmond writes: 'The individual (i.e. the worker) is seen as an active sense maker and will craft the knowledge according to the specific situation, circumstance, place and time in which they act... Knowledge then can be personalised and idiosyncratic' (2005, p.887).

Self-knowledge and self-awareness enlighten you about how certain features of the referral-taking task impacts upon you, and how that impact may affect the quality of your response (O'Hagan 1986). Students should carefully explore this impact in practice and in reflection, with the help of Table 5.1. Which referrer for example, is likely to pose the greatest challenge to them: an anonymous neighbour, a timid inarticulate family friend, a confident, assertive overpowering GP? In attempting to respond to the information provided by the referrer, which category of child poses the greatest difficulty – a referral about a newborn, or about an adolescent boy (or any other age category)? Which alleged perpetrator will be the most problematic – mother, father, cohabitee, grandfather, etc? What type of abuse does the worker instinctively regard as difficult – sexual abuse, neglect, emotional abuse, etc.? Asking any of these questions is important, the answers more so. Such answers may include the following: 'I am apprehensive about taking a referral from a GP because GPs always seem to be confident and demanding and I find it difficult to cope' or 'I find it emotionally difficult, and even more difficult to concentrate in listening to a referrer telling about some infant being sexually abused'. It is this kind of self-exploration and the sharing of findings with the practice supervisor that will contribute towards the attainment of competence in referral-taking.

Self-knowledge and self-awareness are even more crucial in coping with anonymous telephone referrals. Students should contemplate how a voice (anxiety laden, hesitant or in haste), without a face, without a name, alleging or hinting at something bad happening to a small child, impacts upon them. The referrer may also warn the student, that if nothing's done 'you (*or your agency*) are in trouble!' Whatever the impact, the student should learn precisely how that impact affects the quality of their response to the referrer; for example, does the referrer's anxiety and fear make the student anxious and fearful (thereby seriously limiting the student's capacity for logical and objective responses) or does the referrer's hint of something terrible happening to a child preoccupy the student to the exclusion of all other necessary enquiries?

The process of referral-taking

Let us now explore how the student progresses in her attempt to achieve and maintain competence in responding to this referral. We will assume that the student, through college training, placement supervision, the studying of texts (including some of those mentioned above), and previous attempts at supervised referral-taking during the placement, has had the opportunity to acquire essential knowledge, values and skills.

Managing the referrer's crisis

In the hurried, anxious referral-giving, there are two utterances of particular interest to the student: 'I'm not a racist' and 'I don't want to give my name'. The student realises that, despite the difficulty created by anonymity, she must respect it. She also knows that she must take the first opportunity to reassure the referrer. At the outset, she says 'Okay…it's all right', and listens carefully to the remainder of the referral. She notes the increasing anxiety and fear in the referrer's voice, and the lack of detail and context of the message; she knows she first has to deal with the anxiety and fear. She occasionally and gently interjects with 'okay…right…I see…'. She then says slowly, genuinely, reassuringly: 'Look that was really helpful…You've done the right thing and we appreciate it…I'm sure it wasn't easy…we *will* look into it…could I ask you…could you give me a little more information…I mean about this baby…that would be appreciated…could you do that?'

The student has reduced some of the tension and burden carried by the referrer: she has acknowledged and praised his effort; she is not going to press the referrer about his identity, nor adopt a morally censorious tone about anonymous referrals. In effect, she has begun creating a relationship and atmosphere conducive to meaningful communication, which may yield information important enough to establish the seriousness and/or the genuineness of the referral.

Consolidating engagement: practical considerations

She checks that the referrer is able to talk to her a little longer, that he is not under pressure using someone else's (his employer's?) phone. She does not offer to ring him, knowing that he might feel that was an attempt to identify him. The referrer tells her that he is able to talk for a while longer. The student continues to encourage the referrer at numerous points as she begins attempting to explore the five specific areas and necessary factual data (see Table 5.1). It is not yet time to embark upon a straight question and answer session; she encourages the referrer to give additional information in his own way, at his own pace.

Impact of certain referral information

The referrer gives the precise address of mother and baby, confirming that it is one of a number of temporary shelters provided by the local Catholic church, particularly for asylum seekers. This information has a major impact upon the student. She cannot stop instant and opposing thoughts coming to mind. Perhaps the referrer is right: this mother is engaged in prostitution, taking advantage of an unsupervised domestic facility granted her; on the other hand, this mother may be doing no such thing, and may in fact be subject to pressures which compel her to leave her home each night. She recalls some of the experiences relayed to her in the asylum seekers centre in which she was an observer.

Clarifying information given

The student realises that she must proceed with caution in order to 'ensure that referral processes discriminate effectively' (DoH 2000, p.12) There are questions that may enlighten her on the two opposing possibilities that have come into her mind, but she senses that she may at this stage only proceed in exploring the first. Before doing that however, she must express gratitude to the referrer; she knows that she must always be attempting to reassure him, encourage him, maintain contact with him.

> 'That's very helpful...We really appreciate that information...it makes it that bit easier when we start looking into it. You say you don't know the name...does anybody in the neighbourhood know their names?'
> 'No...it's a foreign name...African...'
> 'And you don't know the nationality?'
> The student senses a hesitation in the referrer's response. She knows that the country from which asylum seekers come is usually the greatest source of curiosity (and sometimes hostility) amongst the community in which they are temporarily settled. She suspects that the referrer is withholding this information and that that is linked to his protestation that he is not a racist.
> 'I don't know' he says hesitantly... 'Somebody said they're from Somalia.'
> What about the other people you see her with...do you think they're from Somalia too?'
> 'Probably.'
> 'And they all speak Somali, and you and the neighbours can't communicate with them?' the student asks, understandingly. 'Do you know what their religion is?'

The referrer says he thinks they're Muslim.

The student pauses; she instantly wonders has she unintentionally mentioned a factor that today, has all kinds of connotations, good or bad, for different people; she also wonders whether or not she was permitted to ask that question.

Breach of departmental procedure?

The student then realises (as does her practice teacher sitting opposite her) that departmental policy does not actually permit her to enquire about religion or religious convictions, during referral-taking. Yet she also knows, from her experiences with asylum seekers, that these matters are of crucial significance in some people's lives. The research of Gilligan and Furness (2006) highlights the neglect of religion and spirituality in social work training in Britain. They say that despite the statutory requirement (1989 Children Act), questions about religion 'are not asked during assessments, in review or case conferences, in supervision or in training' (p.634). Consequently, social workers are in danger of 'imposing culturally incompetent "secular" and "rationalist" interventions on service users who may have very different actual needs and wishes' (p.634).

There is the briefest mention of religion in the NOS, a requirement to *gather information that addresses cultural, religious needs* (Unit 2.2). But there is a much more robust statement in the Framework document (DoH 2000). It is a quote from Dutt and Phillips (2000) in the Practice Guidelines accompanying the Framework: 'Issues of race and culture cannot be added to a list for separate consideration during an assessment. *From referral through to core assessment, intervention and planning*, race and culture have to be taken account of' (my italics) (DoH 2000, p.39, 2.27).

The student automatically thinks that if the family are Somali, they are likely to be Muslim, and that will have a bearing on the strategy of approach in investigating the referral. She also knows that Islam is not merely a religion; it is an all-embracing culture, a way of life. Islam 'makes no division between secular and religious matters "Daily life, food, dress, manners, education politics and law are all religious issues"' (Henly 1982, p.17). The student therefore believes that the question was warranted, but she is acutely conscious of the fact that she attempted to learn of the mother's religion through someone else. Her practice teacher's expression remains inscrutable.

The Somali community

The identification of nationality also impacts upon the student. Somalis constitute the largest immigrant group, with long-standing historical links with the city. Their numbers have increased more rapidly in the previous five years as a result of the government's policy of dispersion. Local authorities with an established minority group were persuaded, pressurised and bribed to accept more of that same group. The sharp increase in the number of Somali people has generated disquiet in the city as a whole, and they have frequently been the subject of racist abuse.

Exploring the five core areas in child protection referrals

Already, the student has learnt (although, as with every referral, all this information needs verification in subsequent enquiry) that the referrer is a neighbour, the approximate age and nationality/culture of child being referred and that the mother is either the alleged abuser, or aware of the alleged abuse. The abuse being alleged is not specified, though the daily routine described hints at emotional and psychological abuse (O'Hagan 1993, 2006a, 2006b). The student now feels she must focus on the detail of the referrer's observations. She proceeds, sensitively, patiently, to explore the five core areas (see above), the most crucial of which is what precisely is happening to the child.

'Have you or your neighbours ever seen the baby being abused?'
'No.'
'Have you or neighbours ever seen any marks of injury on the baby?'
'No.'
'How often do you and your neighbours see the baby?'
'Every day.'
'Wherabouts?'
'In the pram…going to the shop, getting in and out of the car.'
'Have you or the neighbours ever had the chance to hold the baby?'
'No.'
'Okay…so…am I right in saying you're not suggesting the baby's being physically abused?'
'We don't know…we just hear it crying, inside and outside the house.'
'Every day?'
'Yea…well…nearly every day.'
'You still did right to report it, and we appreciate that. Now… can I just make sure again…you said this woman doesn't have any contacts in the neighbourhood?'
'That's right.'

> 'And that you and the neighbours have tried to reach out to her…?'
> 'Yes.'
> 'Can I ask you how often you've tried to reach out to her?'
> 'Lots of times.'
> 'When was the last time?'
> 'About a week ago.'
> 'Can you tell me about that?'

The referrer says nothing for a few seconds. Then he speaks with a slight agitation.

> 'It wasn't me…it was one of the neighbours.'
> 'Tried to reach out to her?'
> 'Yes.'
> 'Did she meet her in the street…or something?'
> 'No…she went to her door.'
> 'Was that during the day…or evening?'

The student thinks this neighbour may have seen something untoward that she has conveyed to the referrer. The student is contemplating, anticipating and curious, yet senses the slightest hurriedness in the referrer's voice, as though he had anticipated these particular questions, and was reluctant to answer, yet keen to get such questions out of the way. Perhaps he was irritated too, she thought, maybe feeling that these questions were irrelevant to the reason he was phoning in the first instance. The student however, feels that she must enquire further along this particular path, despite sensing that it may irritate him more.

> 'In the morning', the referrer replies.
> The student asks: 'Was there a particular reason why the neighbour went to the door last week?'
> There is a long pause; then the referrer without notice terminates the call.

Aftermath of a terminated referral

The student wonders what she may have done wrong. She is acutely conscious of the fact that not only does she not have the name of the referrer but, more importantly, she hasn't got the name of the child or his/her family. In the few referral-taking tasks she's already done, under the same close scrutiny of her supervisor, she felt she was doing something really useful in checking computer records and files, and considerably expanding knowl-edge about the families in question, but she cannot do that without a name. Her supervisor assures her that anonymous referrers often hang up, and that the address (owned by the local Catholic church) will enable them to estab-lish the family's names and circumstances.

This raises the question of confidentiality in the student's mind. How can one enquire of the church without disclosing the nature of the referral? Can an 'allegation' that has not been investigated, and that has been made by an anonymous referrer, be construed as confidential information? Does it constitute the 1989 Children Act stipulation that enquiry should be made *Where a local authority has reasonable cause to suspect...harm* (S47 (1) (a) (b))? And would such inquiry breach in any way the Data Protection Act? The student recalls and rereads the department's child protection manual. It does not unambiguously answer those questions, but it clearly states that in some circumstances the safety and welfare of a child necessitate the sharing of information without seeking consent (from the family involved).

The student is disappointed because of another aspect of the case; she so much wanted to establish what was happening to the child, and to explore the situation of the mother insofar as the referrer was able to provide infor-mation. Her experiences as an observer in a refuge centre for asylum seekers enlightened her in two main respects: 1. the formidable difficulties of pov-erty, homelessness, racism, and harassment often faced by many of the families, and 2. the lack of training and preparation in her course for work-ing with and helping asylum seekers. Warwick, Neville and Smith (2006) acknowledge this deficit in training, and provide a detailed account of their successful attempts to counter it in the new BA degree course in Huddersfield.

The supervisor advises the student that in the light of the allegations and the age of the child the authority is entitled to seek out the identity of the family and establish whether or not there is a risk to the child. The supervisor will make contact with the church; church and social services often mutually help in respect of asylum seekers. To all intents and purposes the task of taking an anonymous referral is now over for the student.

Written evidence of competence in referral taking

Much of the knowledge, values and skills underpinning competence in child abuse referral-taking (anonymous referrals in particular) are provided above. In writing evidence of competence students will be guided by the

National Occupational Standards or by whichever practice specifications their college and/or Care Council has derived from them.

Key Roles 1, 2, 4 and 6 of the NOS have been much in evidence in this brief but challenging piece of work. The first *statement of expectations* prefacing and summarising the NOS is highly applicable: *Communication skills and information sharing*, one of which, (g), is *Listen actively to what individuals... have to say*. Whatever the overall rating of the student's competence, it is clearly evident that she has listened actively to the referrer.

Key Role 1 *Prepare for and work with individuals, families, groups and communities to assess their needs and circumstances*

The three Units of this first Key Role are:

1. *Prepare for social work contact and involvement.*

2. *Work with individuals, families, groups and communities to help them make informed decisions.*

3. *Assess needs and options to recommend a course of actions.*

THE STUDENT WRITES:

I *prepared* myself for the task of referral-taking and initial contact with referrers through consultation and exercises with my supervisor. This included study of relevant law (1989 Children Act (S47 (1) (a) (b)), departmental procedures, the child protection manual, the Framework for Assessment (DoH 2000), and drawing up comprehensive lists of questions to ask. In college I had opportunity to practice referral-taking through role play. This included working with anonymous referrals, though I have to admit that I was not fully prepared for an anonymous referrer who could not even give me a name, was hesitant and anxious, made a very serious allegation, then terminated the call without notice.

Performance criteria under Key Role 1 in evidence (NOS quotes in italics)

Given that this was an anonymous referral, I strove to *identify the source and nature of the referral,* and to *establish areas of consistency* in the information being given to me (Unit1.1b). The referrer was exceedingly guarded and hesitant, giving the least possible information, and in some respects no information at all. My *underlying strategy* therefore was to consolidate the contact between us, regularly reassuring him that he was doing the right thing and that the department very much appreciated his efforts and, parallel with this strategy, continually attempt to clarify and to expand on the information he was providing (i.e. *dealing with information gaps* Unit 1.1d).

During the referral-taking process, I was conscious of the experience I gained in an observation placement in a centre for asylum seekers, and on how my own *anti-discriminatory values* were impacting on my interpretation of the information being supplied (Unit 1.2b). I remained aware of this impact, and open to the contrasting possibilities which interpretation offered. These possibilities were 1. that the mother was abusing the child, and 2. that it could be a malicious (or racist) referral and that no such abuse was taking place. There were of course many possibilities between these particular two. I later fully discussed these contrasting interpretations with my supervisor.

Having recognised the anxiety of the referrer at the outset, I was particularly careful about the timing of any information I gave him about the department's response to child abuse referrals, or about any questions I was asking him about the referral he was making (Unit 2.1b).

In carrying out this task of referral-taking, I believe I identified a lack of clarification in procedural guidelines (Unit 3.1d). I enquired about the religion of the family, because I thought such knowledge would be helpful if they were going to be contacted and investigated. But I realised as soon as I had asked this question that the department does not permit such direct enquiry. In retrospect, whilst I recognise that asking people about the religion of others can be construed as an infringement of privacy, nevertheless I believe that knowing the users' culture, nationality and religion can and should enhance the sensitivity with which one approaches the users in the particular task of referral-taking. The DoH (2000) Framework document would appear to support this view. I don't think the department's child protection manual and, in particular, its section on referrals has explored this issue sufficiently.

Key Role 2 *Plan, carry out, review and evaluate social work practice*

Unit 4 of the NOS, under Key Role 2, is entitled: *Respond to crisis situations.* The task was a crisis for me and, I believe, for the referrer. Not to be able to see a person who is anxious and agitated, and who is alleging harm being done to an infant, is a situation that has many features of crises: the unknown, fear, initial lack of control, unpredictability and risk (O'Hagan 1986, 1991).

Throughout the referral-taking process, I was attempting to do precisely what Unit 4.1 spells out: *Assess the urgency of the request for action.* At the same time, I was attempting to establish a relationship with the referrer, in which I listened carefully to what he had to say, and tried to elicit additional information for the completion of the referral (Unit 4.1a,c). I also attempted to gain a wider perspective on what the referrer was telling me by inviting him to recall what others in the neighbourhood had seen and heard in relation to the infant at the heart of the referral (Unit 4.2b).

The *urgency of the department's response* (Unit 4.1b) could not be determined on the basis of the incomplete information provided and the termination of the call by the referrer. At the end of the referral, all my efforts to cope with the pervasive crisis of anonymity were fully discussed with my supervisor (Unit 4.1e)

In attempting to manage the crisis situation, I tried to exercise discipline and control and avoid being overwhelmed by the nature of the referral. I did not allow the referrer to project his anxiety and fear onto me. I realised on initial contact that I had to allay his anxiety and fear (or at least minimise it) in order to establish a meaningful relationship, which would allow me to explore with him the information he was providing.

Social work skills demonstrated

I believe I minimised the referrer's initial anxiety by:

- communicating and listening effectively; not interrupting anything he wanted to say

- accepting and respecting his wish for anonymity

- encouraging, reassuring and thanking the referrer for that initial information

- emphasising that in making this referral out of concern, he was doing right

- empathising with and being sensitive to the referrer

- being patient, encouraging him to respond to my queries in his own way, at his own pace.

All of these efforts I believe, fulfilled the criteria of Unit 5.2, i.e. *work with individuals... to avoid crisis situations and address problems and conflict.* My efforts avoided escalating the crisis to an extent whereby (I'm sure) the referrer would have terminated the call earlier. The reason I was able to do this is because I had a reasonable grasp and understanding of the relationship between myself and the referrer (5.2a).

Key Role 4 *Manage risk to individuals, families, carers, groups, communities, self and others*

I recognise that most anonymous referrals are perceived and felt by the referrer to be risk-laden (Unit 3.2b). The referrer feels at risk if their identity is disclosed. The worker often feels at risk of not being in control of an anonymous referrer and not getting all relevant information about the child alleged to be at risk (Unit 12.1). I believe that I responded to the referrer in such a way as to minimise his sense of risk, yet also to ensure that he stayed with me long enough to question him. He provided me with key information about the family, but his replies also raised many more questions. The skills listed above were instrumental in minimising the sense of risk experienced by both the referrer and myself.

At the heart of the challenge facing me was the need to elicit sufficient information enabling my supervisor to make a decision on whether or not to investigate. The alleged abuser has the right not to be investigated unnecessarily, whilst the referrer has the right to be taken seriously on the basis of the information he was providing. The more qualitative and quantitative information he provided, the easier it would be to invoke legal and organisational procedures to determine the most appropriate course of action (12.2a,b,c.).

Key Role 6 *Demonstrate professional competence in practice*

I believe I demonstrated professional competence in the skills listed above and by the values underpinning them. I have repeatedly 1. re-examined my experiences and actions during this referral-taking, 2. read relevant *legislation, policy and procedural requirements, and recording processes* (Unit 6.18.1a), 3. read recommended standard social work texts for the course, particularly 'skills' oriented texts (e.g. Trevithick 2005). I have also repeatedly referred to the Framework for Assessment (DoH 2000) and the National Occupational Standards.

I valued my supervisor's support and encouragement in re-analysing the experience (Unit 18.2), and being directed to particular areas of study (Unit 18.2a,b,c,d) that would prepare me more adequately the next time I take an anonymous referral (e.g. Langan and Day 1991; O'Hagan 1986, 1991; Trevithick 2005).

Unit 18.2a and b are of particular relevance: *Identify sources of knowledge that can inform best practice*, and *Identify areas of practice that require broader more in-depth and up to date knowledge*. It seems to me in the light of this experience that the most useful source of knowledge to underpin effective, competent responses to anonymous child abuse referrals is *research* on anonymous referrals. I was particularly struck by my supervisor's comment that many anonymous referrers 'hang up' before the referral is completed. I believe all child protection agencies should research anonymous referrals, and that this research be collated on a national basis. I am inquisitive about the relevance of the nationality and the circumstances of the family at the heart of this referral. I am aware of the fact that single mothers are often the subject of anonymous, malicious referrals (Besharov 1990; O'Hagan 1997; O'Hagan and Dillenburger 1995), but this experience raises the question as to whether or not single mothers from minority communities (asylum seekers) may be even more vulnerable to such maliciousness, infused with racism.

Elements 19.2 and 19.3 (Key Role 6) both focus on social work values. This experience of referral-taking posed a significant question: who is/are the user(s) of services? I concluded that the referrer of alleged child abuse *is* a user, and that the family being referred may become users. I believe that my thoughts and actions recorded above reveal that I adhered to the values and ethics expounded in the new code of practice for social care workers, in respect of both the referrer and the referred, that I *upheld professional social work practice values and ethics* (19.2) and that I *worked within the principles of social work practice* (19.3). The principal ethical and professional challenge for me was in not prejudging, or rushing into a judgement, that the referrer was racist or discriminatory towards Somali people or towards single mothers, to remain open and active in listening to what he had to say, and always to attempt to enable him to clarify and expand on the information he was providing.

Element 21.1 of Unit 21 requires a *contribution to policy review and development*. The performance criteria (a) states: *Identify contexts and procedures where you can contribute to national and local policy*. This very much ties in with Unit 18.2a and 2b above: *Identify sources of knowledge that can inform best prac-*

tice, and *Identify areas of practice that require broader more in-depth and up to date knowledge*. The research on anonymous referrals, which I suggested above, would be essential before amending, adding to and/or expanding existing departmental guidelines on child abuse referrals in general and anonymous referrals in particular.

Subsequent enquiry

The supervisor's subsequent enquiry confirmed that the mother was an asylum seeker from Somalia, awaiting a decision from the Home Office on the legitimacy of her status. She had been subject to various forms of racist abuse since residing in the accommodation provided by the church. Police and the local council had been informed about this abuse. It included offensive graffiti on the door and walls, youths screaming obscenities outside the home and, worst of all, a police visit following anonymous telephone calls alleging that they were illegal immigrants creating trouble in the neighbourhood. The mother was petrified about the safety of her four-month-old son and the possibility that all of these incidents would adversely affect the decision of the Home Office. She reasoned that her presence provoked the attacks, and that the less visible and more absent she was, the greater the possibility that the attacks would reduce. So she spent most of the day at the asylum centre, and literally fled from the house each night, shepherded out and returned by members of the Somali community, but also, as it turned out, by volunteers from the asylum centre. A number of volunteers provided her with alternative accommodation in their own homes.

The mother and infant were temporarily registered with a GP, one of the primary objectives of the asylum centre staff for all of their users (asylum applications must be accompanied by rigorous medical reports). The infant had already been examined by a GP and health visitor. Both assured social services that the child was not subject to abuse.

The referrer's information that a neighbour had 'tried to reach out' was true. She was one of a number of neighbours disgusted by the racist attacks, and simply wanted to 'reach out' to a mother with whom she could not communicate, on a morning after new graffiti was scrawled on the front door. Clearly this whole incident and the referral stemming from it reveal a family in need rather than a child being abused, although it could be argued that the anxiety induced in the mother by racist attacks could have adversely impacted upon the quality of care she was able to provide for her child.

Conclusion

One never really knows if these types of anonymous referrals are either racist or malicious, or what precisely the motivation of the referrer may be. A more important focus however is the preparation of the student for *all* types of referrals. In this case the student had a comprehensive framework which addressed every important area of enquiry, and despite the difficulty of anonymity, she doggedly persisted in pursuing these lines of enquiry insofar as the referrer permitted (see Table 5.1). Referral-taking in child protection, irrespective of the culture, religion, nationality or status of whoever is being referred, must have such a framework, must be rigorous and disciplined, professional and competent, and ethically based. That is the most effective way of protecting children, respecting their parents and exposing malicious intent or discriminatory motivation. As the Framework for Assessment (DoH 2000) reiterates, competent referral-taking is the foundation stone upon which equally competent investigation and assessment can be built.

References

Besharov, D. (1990) *Recognising Child Abuse: A Guide for the Concerned*. Washington: Free Press.

Blom-Cooper, L. (1995) *A Child in Trust: Jasmine Beckford*. London: Brent.

Department of Health (2000) *Framework for the Assessment of Children in Need and their Families*. London: Stationery House. Available at www.dh.gov.uk

Dutt, R. and Phillips, M. (2000) 'The Assessment of Black Children in Need and the Families.' In Department of Health *Assessing Children in Need and the Families: Practice Guidance*. London: Stationery Office.

Gilligan, P. and Furness, S. (2006) 'The Role of Religion and Spirituality in Social Work Practice: Views and Experiences of Social Workers and Students.' *British Journal of Social Work 36*, 4, 617–637.

Henly, A. (1982) *Caring for Muslims and their Families: Religious Aspects of Care*. London: DHSS.

Lambeth (1987) *Whose Child? The Report of the Public Enquiry into the Death of Tyra Henry*. London: London Borough of Lambeth.

Laming, H. (2003) *The Victoria Climbié Inquiry: Report of an Inquiry*. London: HMSO.

Langan, M. and Day, L. (eds) (1991) *Women, Oppression and Social Work: Issues in Anti Discriminatory Practice*. London: Routledge.

McPherson, L. and Barnett, M. (2006) 'Beginning Practice in Child Protection.' *Social Work Education 25*, 2, 182–198.

Morris, K. (2005) 'From "Children in Need" to "Children at Risk" – The Changing Policy Context for Prevention and Participation.' *Practice 17*, 2, 67–77.

O'Hagan, K.P. (1986) *Crisis Intervention in Social Services*. Basingstoke: Macmillan.

O'Hagan, K.P. (1989) *Working with Child Sexual Abuse*. Milton Keynes: Open University Press.

O'Hagan, K.P. (1991) 'Crisis Intervention in Social Work.' In J. Lishman (ed.) *Handbook of Theory for Practice Teachers in Social Work*. London: Jessica Kingsley Publishers.

O'Hagan, K.P. (1993) *Emotional and Psychological Abuse of Children*. Buckingham: Open University Press.

O'Hagan, K.P. (1997) 'The Problem of Engaging Men in Child Protection Work.' *British Journal of Social Work 27*, 1, 25–42.

O'Hagan, K.P. (2001) *Cultural Competence in the Caring Professions.* London: Jessica Kingsley Publishers.

O'Hagan, K.P. (2006a) *Identifying Emotional and Psychological Abuse.* Maidenhead: Open University Press.

O'Hagan, K.P. (2006b) 'Catch the Meaning'. *Community Care* (July 13–19).

O'Hagan, K.P. and Dillenburger, K. (1995) *The Abuse of Women within Childcare Work.* Buckingham: Open University Press.

Osmond, J. (2005) 'The Knowledge Spectrum: A Framework for Teaching Knowledge and its Use in Social Work Practice.' *British Journal of Social Work 35*, 6, 881–900.

Parton, N. (2004) 'From Maria Colwell to Victoria Climbié: Reflections on Public Inquiries into Child Abuse a Generation apart.' *Child Abuse Review 13*, 1, 80–94.

Thorpe, D. (1994) 'Facing Reality.' *Community Care* (31 August), 32–3.

Trevithick, P. (2005) *Social Work Skills: A Practice Handbook.* Maidenhead: Open University Press.

Training Organisation for Personal Social Services (2004) *National Occupational Standards.* London: TOPSS.

Torry, B., Furness, S. and Wilkinson, P. (2005) 'The Importance of Agency Culture and Support in Recruiting and Retaining Social Workers to Supervise Students on Placement.' *Practice 17*, 1, 29–38.

Warwick, I., Neville, R. and Smith, K. (2006) 'My Life in Huddersfield: Supporting Young Asylum Seekers and Refugees to Record their Experiences of Living in Huddersfield.' *Social Work Education 25*, 2, 129–139.

CHAPTER 6

Competence in Protecting Adults with Learning Disabilities

Paul Cambridge

Introduction

The relationship between care management and social work is often ambiguous, because of the differences between a qualification and a role. This ambiguity is naturally part of what this chapter is about, although it is also a metaphor for some of the challenges currently facing social work and social work trainees, many of whom will enter their profession as 'care managers'. I decided to focus on adult protection process as a 'case study' of the skills and competences required of social workers and care managers because it represents a relatively newly emerging demand which has been little articulated and is a route by which the impact of a single policy area on practice can be assessed. Moreover, it provides an interface with recent statutory changes which affect practice and helps us sample the bureaucratic and procedural expectations increasingly being made of social work trainees. In relation to adult protection I consequently identify and discuss social work competence in some detail, referencing wider competence in care management through 'key' or 'core' competencies which underpin best practice.

I have taken the stance of an 'analyst' and 'commentator' for tackling the over-arching task of relating the National Occupational Standards required of social work (TOPSS 2004) to care management. I have also adopted a reflective as opposed to a directive stance. This is perhaps the most realistic way to approach the issue of social work competence and care management – first, because care management is not a standard intervention, varying widely in operation and organisation between client groups and local authorities and second, because to try to develop a comprehensive list of the competences required would distract attention from an interpretative understanding of the qualities required of effective care management.

Care management as a social policy instrument has been in operation for some 15 years since its promotion as part of a raft of changes in the organisation and management of social care and the social care market articulated in the 1990 community care reforms (Department of Health (DoH) 1989). It is consequently relatively new in social policy terms and, given the tendency for New Labour to introduce numerous policy initiatives and reorganisations in health and social care, it is surprising that care management has not been more systematically reviewed. The reviews that have been conducted (e.g. Cambridge *et al.* 2005; Challis 1994a; Sainsbury 1996) have been without a policy strategy.

Origins

Care management was introduced largely as an answer to the problems of organising social care services and resources around the needs of individuals in what was then a developing mixed economy of care and an emerging social care market. The rationale for introducing care management as a mainstream policy instrument was based on the success of a series of 'case' management experiments designed to support older people in their own homes who would have gone into residential care. The approach to care management developed in 1989 was also influenced by the Griffiths Report *Community Care: Agenda for Action* (DoH 1988). Although Griffiths introduced the term 'care' management, this was seen as a strategic management task focusing on local client group budgets and services.

The policy guidance was vague about the best approach to develop, promoting a variety of permissive models (DoH 1991). This tended to steer local authorities away from evidence based care management. In 'new wine into old bottles' approaches (Davies 1992), social workers were simply renamed care managers with a wide variety of arrangements developing (Cambridge 1999a; Cambridge *et al.* 2005), many overly influenced by administrative and resource management demands. Most current care management arrangements are as a consequence typified by large caseloads, dominated by the assessment task, with review even undertaken by letter.

There is rarely the capacity for care managers to get to know the people on their caseloads due to the sheer volume of cases. However, this also means that service users rarely have the opportunity to develop a close working relationship with their care manager. Care managers may work more intensively with an individual when undertaking a community care assessment but, longer term, any intensive contact is in response to a crisis, a placement breakdown or (as in the case study in this chapter) an adult protection concern.

Since the 1990s we have also witnessed a collection of additional social care reforms and service reorganisations which have affected the environment in which care management is expected to operate. These include the introduction of new purchasing and commissioning arrangements, best value, national standards and new inspection regimes and service frameworks and strategies for mental health, older people and people with learning disabilities. Care managers are expected to incorporate all such changes into their practice.

Specific policy initiatives such as *No Secrets* (DoH 2000) have also impacted on the knowledge and skills required by care managers and social workers. Adult protection is used as a case study in this chapter to explore some of the additional responsibilities and competences demanded by the implementation of such policy initiatives. Moreover, new initiatives in micro-organisation have impacted directly on some of the tasks and functions of care management, including direct payments (Commission for Social Care Inspection 2004; DoH 2001, 2005 and 2006) and person-centred planning (PCP) for people with learning disabilities (DoH 2001; Robertson *et al.* 2005). The focus throughout this chapter will be on learning disability, although generic lessons will also be drawn where appropriate.

Care management, social work and key competencies

Fundamental questions about what care management is and the nature of its relationship with social work have framed its design and implementation and influenced the direction in which it has developed. Care management and social work are not mutually exclusive professionally or operationally. In some instances it is evident that they have been perceived as interchangeable roles with observers referencing the relationship from a variety of perspectives (Cambridge 1999a; Cambridge *et al.* 2005; Onyett 1992). In many local authorities care managers are expected to have social work qualifications and historically a mix of qualifications has been deemed appropriate for care management.

In its original experimental approaches what was then termed case management comprised a series of core tasks: case finding and referral, assessment and selection, care planning and service packaging, monitoring and reassessment and case closure (Davies and Challis 1986). The key competences required directly related to the performance of these core tasks. The success of these experimental forms eventually led to care management being adopted in *Caring for People* (DoH 1989). Assessment received particular prominence due to the desire to match need to resources in helping manage the new financial community care landscape – e.g. Key Role 1 Unit 3 – but key tasks also centred on service planning and packaging and case review – e.g. Key Role 2 Unit 6.

The confusion over terminology stemmed from the Griffiths Report (DoH 1988) which had used the term care management to describe a new role and function, with client group managers holding local care budgets. In this formative phase, the organisation and targeting of care management was already diversifying through a wide range of emerging models (Brandon and Towe 1989; DoH 1991), with organisational and operational differences proliferating in the 1990s (Cambridge 1999a; Cambridge *et al.* 2005; Challis 1994b; Huxley 1993). Since its introduction as a mainstream policy instrument it has also been functionally redefined in response to the demands of working a social care market and characterised by increasing workloads (Ramcharan *et al.* 1999). Care management also varies in its relationship with team working – in addition to specialist care management teams, care managers may perform a role on a multi-disciplinary or joint agency team for a client group. In such situations skills at working with a range of professional perspectives (NOS Key Role 5 Unit 17) are required.

Assessment remains a core task for all care managers (NOS Key Role 1 Unit 3). It takes on particular significance in the context of British social and community care policy and practice due to the absence of nationally set eligibility criteria for services, which is in strong contrast to experience elsewhere in Europe (Cambridge and Ernst 2006). Assessment requires an array of knowledge and skills including familiarity with the needs of individuals, an understanding of the targeting criteria of the commissioning agencies, awareness of the range and scope of local services and familiarity with bureaucratic processes.

Care management and anti-oppressive practice

Little reference has been made in the literature on care management to anti-oppressive practice or notions of equity in caseload management. It is therefore important that care management is able to respond not just to the powerlessness that disability and dependency bring, through developing person centred and empowering approaches, but to issues of gender, race, culture, sexuality and age (Shah 2005). In short, it must be culturally appropriate if it is to have a positive impact on people's lives.

Care management systems require radical realignment if care managers are to be able to perform more effectively within a person-centred culture (Cambridge 2006). As a service intervention, it needs to return to evidence-based practice, incorporating some of the key devices of the earlier experimental models. These include smaller caseloads, creative budget-holding, possibly through the use of flexi-budgets to access informal community resources or affect service substitution (Key Role 5 Unit 15) and a greater level of specialisation across and within the client groups. For example, in learning disability, specialist experience in working with people with autistic spectrum disorders or people with challenging behaviours and their carers or support staff (Key Role 1 Unit 1; Key Role 2 Unit 9). Currently, people with profound and multiple learning disabilities are perhaps the most excluded group and care managers need to be able to work more intensively alongside carers, communication therapists, community nurses and GPs in co-ordinating high quality care (Bradshaw 2005; Carnaby and Cambridge 2002) (Key Role 2 Units 6 and 7). For example they will need to be able to engage users with non-traditional forms of communication using individual vocabularies within the context of total communication strategies (Jones 2000) (Key Role 1 Unit 2; Key Role 3, Unit 11). Achieving effective co-ordination and communicating with service users in supporting informed choices is part of the professional advocacy role of social work (Key Role 3 Unit 10).

Care management and adult protection

Care managers are sometimes the only people who are in a position to keep in contact with someone placed in residential care, such as an older woman with a learning disability or someone living at home with their parents. Inspectors from the Commission for Social Care Inspection have a responsibility for reviewing standards in residential services and may also lead on adult protection should neglect or other forms of abuse be evident. But for people isolated in community settings, such as with parents or relatives, the care manager may be the only form of scrutiny and protection. The situation is even bleaker for people placed out of area, where they may be no ongoing care management involvement (Pring 2004). Typically, the group most affected will be difficult-to-place people, such as men with learning disabilities who display seriously challenging behaviours.

I was involved in an abuse inquiry relating to a directly commissioned service in a London borough which supported two people with challenging behaviours and where physical abuse and neglect, staff intimidation and management failure had been characteristics of a culture of abuse for a number of years (Cambridge 1999b). Specialist behavioural support workers, care managers, social workers, psychiatrists and psychologists were all in contact with the staff and service users, yet the culture of abuse went unrecognised until one of the service users made a fragile non-verbal disclosure of physical abuse to her mother. Imagine the risks to people vulnerable to abuse by nature of their learning disability isolated in out of area placements. The misuse of control and restraint – euphemistically called physical interventions – within the closed worlds of institutionalised services is a prime example (Macintyre 1999), so much so that focused policy and practice attention has been invested in this area (Harris 1996). In such situations abuse can become normative practice and relatives or staff may be the only people who are in a position to blow the whistle.

It is therefore essential that care managers maintain regular contact with users placed both in and out of area and are able to detect and respond to crises in such placements (Key Role 2 Unit 4; Key Role 3 Unit 10) and that this is undertaken with awareness of the risks and signs associated with abuse and neglect, such as unexplained increases in challenging behaviours (Key Role 4 Units 12 and 13). Some independent service providers recognise that it is important, in the absence of professional advocacy from care managers, to access independent support and advice, as it is not just current abuse that may need to be addressed. Over a number of years I have undertaken individual psycho-educational work with six men with learning disabilities placed out of area in a local provider service in Kent. For one man the work centred on sexual abuse perpetrated by a family member, for another on his sexually abusive behaviour and, for two of the remaining four, sexual abuse was disclosed during work relating to difficulties the men were experiencing with sexuality or other behaviours. This snapshot provides an indication of the scale of adult protection issues that care managers and social workers have to deal with.

No Secrets (DoH 2000), provided a framework for local authorities to develop multi-agency adult protection policies and helped provide a common typology for abuse. For example, neglect or the misuse or withholding of medication was stipulated as a form of abuse. The way adult protection resources have been allocated and organised within and between social services departments varies, and this will have an impact on the adult protection responsibilities expected of care managers and others in the system. It is of course the local authority in which people are placed which holds responsibility for responding to adult protection issues. Kent has organised its adult protection resources to better respond to such demands. Kent and Medway share a multi-agency adult protection policy (Cambridge and Parkes 2004a) and training framework (ADSS 2005), which systematically addresses competence at various levels. Both authorities have also been recording adult protection alerts and their process and outcomes since 1998. Recent research on this data confirms that adult protection demands are disproportionately high for people placed in Kent by other authorities – the majority being men with learning disabilities (Cambridge *et al.* 2006). People placed out of area in Kent experience more multiple abuse and more neglect and discriminatory abuse than within area clients. However, they also appear to receive more robust and effective responses to adult protection alerts.

Care management competence in adult protection

Managing the adult protection alert/referral requires that practitioners are able to assess the relative urgency or potential seriousness of the alert and record the characteristics of the alleged abuse. For example, the immediate risk to the person or others, the type and seriousness of the alleged abuse, information about the potential perpetrator, where the alleged abuse took place and so on. This means that a capacity to ask basic questions whilst listening and keeping an open mind are important. It is critically important to manage disclosures of abuse effectively at this stage, for example, recording what was disclosed by the person, supporting them to disclose and reassuring them that they have done the right thing and also explaining your responsibility to report the abuse. It is also important not to attempt to 'interview' the person about the allegations, as this risks introducing leading questions and opening accusations of suggestibility and reliability, should there be a criminal prosecution. This is the task of those leading disclosure interviews at a later stage of the investigation. Basic information is needed, however, so that a priority can be given to the case and a place of safety can be sought if there is a risk that the abuse will be repeated, for example, abuse perpetrated by a staff member of a residential team or by a man with a learning disability who has access to other vulnerable adults.

Sexual abuse: ensuring police support

The actions taken or not taken at this stage will also be informed by the need to safeguard forensic or other evidence. For example, where sexual abuse is suspected the police should be informed so that they can undertake forensic examinations as soon as possible. There are also clear limits to the capacity of social services and care managers in criminal cases. For example, financial abuse, which is becoming more common in relation to older people living in community settings, requires particular forensic skills that only the police are likely to have. Ideally the alleged perpetrator should not be alerted to the fact that abuse has been reported, although the safety of the individual remains an imperative in high risk situations and the removal of the person, for example from an abusive family relationship, or the suspension of a member of staff may be necessary to achieve this. Moreover, no assurances relating to confidentiality can be given to the client or those disclosing abuse until a proper assessment of risks and issues such as capacity can be gauged.

Defining the student's role

In some situations trainee or newly qualified social workers might be supported in undertaking prescribed pieces of work or particular tasks associated with the alert stage. The work would be demanding and complex. It would require consultation and negotiation with the service provider organisations and/or family members in order to reach an agreement on the appropriate action (Key Role 1 Unit 2; Key Role 3 Unit 11; Key Role 5 Unit 17). Consequently, of course, the ultimate responsibility will remain with the supervisory practice teacher, i.e. an experienced senior worker, possibly an adult protection co-ordinator. They should be no less visible or available when the trainee social worker is allocated more mundane or less complex tasks, described below.

The information gathering and planning stage generally requires the selective opening up of information to other stakeholders. These will mainly be other professionals at this stage, for example the police, in cases where a criminal act is suspected, or health personnel where the case concerns an NHS trust. Skills required for this include negotiating skills, awareness of 'need to know' and confidentiality criteria as well as considerations of capacity to consent as defined in the Mental Capacity Act 2005 (implementation 2007). There will also be situations where the alleged victim has capacity to consent and does not wish the case to be continued. In such situations and where continuing risk to the person or others is evident, the care manager has responsibility for taking the case forward in a way which maintains confidentiality by not disclosing the identity of the person but protects them and others from further abuse. Should the person wish, for example, to return to an abusive sexual relationship, little can be done other than to monitor the situation and support the person unless an explicit sexual offence has been committed.

The Sexual Offences Act

The Sexual Offences Act 2003 has, for example, introduced new offences against people with a mental disorder – sex between a care worker and a person with a mental disorder whether or not it was consensual. Sexual acts have been redefined as including acts such as touching of a sexual nature, even through clothes, and exposing people with a mental disorder to sexual acts or images to encourage sex. In situations where the circumstances of the case involve other professionals or agencies, such as abuse reported by accident and emergency staff or a community nurse for a client of a care manager, a decision will need to be taken on who and which agency is best placed to lead the investigation, and it is often the care manager who will co-ordinate an investigation and advocate on behalf of the person. It may well be that a trainee care manager or social worker could be given the task of working closely with the client to keep them informed of progress and feedback the person's wishes to the investigating care manager, thus adopting an enhanced professional advocacy role (Key Role 3 Units 10 and 11).

The investigation stage requires a collection of quite specific skills relating to the collation, recording and management of evidence. The management of evidence includes issues of confidentiality and information sharing between professionals and agencies as well as with service users and, potentially, whistle-blowers. Up to this point, a whole series of questions will have been asked about the case, the people involved and the circumstances in which the alleged abuse took place. By collating and representing these, a framework for the investigation can be produced. This will include, for example, the different types of evidence to be sought or clarified – forensic, circumstantial, victim and witness disclosures etc.; and who might need to be interviewed and by whom – witnesses, victim(s) and alleged perpetrator(s); what records might need to be examined – care plans and PCPs, care guidelines, supervision policies etc. (Cambridge 2001). Most joint investigations will involve social services and health agencies and allocation of responsibilities (Cambridge and Parkes 2006b).

In some cases, such as sexual abuse or serious neglect, the police will usually lead the investigation, although a lead officer from social services will also be required and this might well be the care manager. For example, the police will have skills at organising disclosure interviews and have a suite for video interviewing. The lead role will, however, require specific liaison, co-ordination and communication skills, particularly with service users where non-traditional forms of communication are used or translators might need to be employed. Such methods have received greater prominence since the Youth Justice and Criminal Evidence Act 1999, which allows for special measures in court such as translators or intermediaries, screens, the removal of wigs and gowns, clearing the court, video links with witnesses and video evidence of disclosure interviews and cross-examinations.

It might well be appropriate for a trainee care manager to work between the communication therapist and the client in order to develop individualised communication in the form of symbols, pictures or signs that relate to the alleged abuse and the circumstances in which it took place (Key Role 1 Unit 2; Key Role 2 Unit 6; Key Role 3 Unit 11; Key Role 5 Unit 17).

Evaluating the evidence and the case conference requires key analytical and interpretative skills and the ability to summarise complex information. Most of these activities will be shared within the group, but the ability to retain an overview and act strategically remains important. That is why conference chairpersons should not be personally involved in the investigations, and should hold a position of rank (Adult Protection Co-ordinator or District Manager) commensurate with the gravity of the proceedings. Conflicts of interest and professional or agency level disagreements may emerge, necessitating authority and negotiating skills to resolve. In adult protection cases with a criminal element, the police are likely to provide significant input.

Feedback to stakeholders, particularly service users and whistle-blowers will remain important, as will space and time to reflect on the case and develop learning points. In particularly difficult cases, for example, where protection went badly wrong, the serious case review panel, part of the adult protection committee (Cambridge and Parkes 2004a) is likely to feedback and disseminate relevant learning.

Likely obstacles to resolution

In reality, of course, many adult protection cases do not run through such an idealised linear process, and there are often feedback loops between different stages, parallel investigations and, in many instances, the case will not proceed to an investigation. Even with investigations, outcomes may sometimes be inconclusive. Criminal investigations often never get off the ground because of lack of support from the Crown Prosecution Service, and if they do the evidence presented is often insufficient or the strategies adopted by the defence undermine the credibility of the victim, despite the potential availability of the special measures outlined above. Now, however, most constabularies will have specialist units and officers who are competent at supporting prosecutions and working with vulnerable witnesses and staff. For example, in Kent there are special investigation units across the county with dedicated officers allocated to work with vulnerable adults, making liaison at an early stage with such specialists essential to maximise effectiveness. Such specialist resources can provide guidance on legislation and access to facilities such as interview suites.

Those leading investigations also need to be aware that for many cases of institutionalised abuse, individual culpability will not be the primary concern, as systems failures at different levels will also be associated with the development and sustaining of abuse or abusive cultures (Cambridge 2004). It is often easier to blame individuals such as front line workers than to address failures in service management or staff supervision and training. Because of its co-ordinating and monitoring role, questions are likely to be asked of care management in such situations, similar to the profile given to social work in child protection (Reder and Duncan 2004).

Trainee social workers entering care management will therefore need basic competences which relate to adult protection per se as well as those relating to individual stages in the process of adult protection 'case management' (Cambridge and Parkes 2004a). Whilst most of these are intrinsic to good practice in social work (e.g. Key Roles 5 and 6) – they take on particular prominence in adult protection, for example, a familiarity with policies and procedures, an understanding of the potential of legislation and its application in the client's best interests, accurate and precise record keeping (Key Role 5 Unit 16), and an ability to work across a range of interests and perspectives, from family members to the police (Key Role 5 Unit 17). First and foremost, it will be maintaining professional advocacy and support for the person who was at the centre of the abuse or alleged abuse (Key Role 3 Units 10 and 11).

Promoting integrated micro-organisation

Currently, micro-organisation in services for people with learning disabilities is shockingly fragmented, risking interventions working towards different objectives. Put bluntly, it is important for example that the PCP (Person-Centred-Planning) facilitator and care manager communicate to ensure that service planning reflects the aspirations articulated through the PCP and that the financial assessments relating to direct payments build on the wider assessment and review information collated through care management. Moreover, evidence suggests PCP has been patchily and ineffectively implemented across user characteristics and living contexts (Robertson *et al.* 2005) and is more a paper exercise and tool for professionals than a device for user empowerment (Mansell and Beadle-Brown 2004, 2005). The take up of direct payments has been slow and disappointing (Commission for Social Care Inspection 2004; DoH 2005).

The possible models for a closer relationship between care management, PCP and direct payments and the rationale for greater integration have been articulated (Cambridge 2006). Given time and resources, care management should have the capacity to close such gaps by helping implement and maximise the effectiveness of PCP and where appropriate accessing direct payments. Care managers can also play an important role in bringing systems together and making them work effectively and efficiently, but this will require knowledge and understanding of systems and responsibilities held elsewhere (Key Role 1 Unit 1; Key Role 6 Unit 18). The irony is that care management will take on more of an advocacy and monitoring function as people are empowered to better plan their own futures and manage and access more of their own services. However, financial empowerment through individual budgets brings risks as well as opportunities and care management is well positioned to provide the monitoring and checks and balances essential for ensuring that someone is not abused or exploited financially.

Care management within learning disability necessitates broadening the perspective of approach to include all aspects of the needs of individual users. For some, basic budgetary and accounting skills will be required, although all care managers will need to access direct payments and person-centred plans when planning and reviewing services and undertaking individual work with clients. As such, they will also require knowledge of commissioning and funding arrangements more widely and the role played by learning disability partnership boards (Key Role 5 Unit 15). Increasingly care managers will need to be vigilant of the risk of financial abuse to those receiving direct payments.

Some concluding observations

Care management demands a collection of core competences relating to core tasks as defined by the original case management experiments (Challis and Davies 1986). Assessment, service planning and case review remain as important today as they were when these experiments were established in the 1980s. However, the rapidly changing policy landscape in social and community care has brought additional expectations, and the topography of care management is much more complex today than it has ever been. The 1990 community care reforms (DoH 1989) placed particular emphasis on the core task of assessment, and government guidance (DoH 1991) introduced a range of models which formed the basis for the diversification experienced since policy mainstreaming. Each approach, from micro-budgeting to social entrepreneurship demands particular skills. In reality, many current care management arrangements represent various combinations of such models, making broad competencies difficult to prescribe.

Market management and service co-ordination skills have generally come to the fore whilst those associated with an advocacy role have tended to retreat as caseloads have expanded and tighter targeting criteria have been imposed. Many of the skills currently required by care management relate more to accounting and administration than they do to social work. The policy reforms introduced by New Labour have also introduced additional requirements on care management, including an awareness of best value and cost effectiveness, a capacity to work with a wide range of interests in the social care economy from joint commissioners and partnership boards, to service providers and the Commission for Social Care

Inspectorate (CSCI). Particular policy initiatives have had a major impact on the care management role, for example, *No Secrets* (DoH 2000) as exampled in this chapter. Such is this impact that many social services departments have responded by reorganising adult protection resources within and outside care management (Cambridge and Parkes 2006a).

The future for care management is unclear. It has proven to be a relatively durable policy instrument for some 15 years, without being reorganised and, even more remarkable, without a review of its overall efficiency and effectiveness. Currently there is scope for it to better link into parallel micro-organisational activities such as PCP and direct payments, again as exampled in this chapter, but questions also remain unanswered about retaining the assessment role and the organisational location of care management itself (Cambridge 2006). We need to ask and answer such questions if the policy intent to promote social inclusion for people with learning disabilities and other disadvantaged groups is to be fulfilled, if services and resources are to be further de-institutionalised, and truly person-centred approaches to the organisation of care and support are to be planned and funded. Such an agenda will have an ongoing impact on the role of care management and the competencies required.

References

ADSS (2005) *Safeguarding Adults: A National Framework for Standards for Good Practice and Outcomes in Adult Protection Work.* London: Association of Directors of Social Services.

Bradshaw, J. (2005) 'The Role of Communication in PCP: Working with People with Complex Needs.' In P. Cambridge and S. Carnaby (eds), *Person Centred Planning and Care Management for People with Learning Disabilities.* London: Jessica Kingsley Publishers.

Brandon, D. and Towe, N. (1989) *Free to Choose: an Introduction to Service Brokerage.* Community Living Monograph. London: Good Impressions.

Cambridge, P. (1999a) 'Building Care Management Competence in Services for People with Learning Disabilities.' *British Journal of Social Work 29,* 393–415.

Cambridge, P. (1999b) 'The First Hit: A Case Study of the Physical Abuse of People with Learning Disabilities and Challenging Behaviours in a Residential Service.' *Disability and Society 14,* 3, 285–308.

Cambridge, P. (2001) 'A Framework for Managing Abuse Inquiries: Methodology, Organisation, Process and Politics.' *Journal of Adult Protection 3,* 3, 6–20.

Cambridge, P. (2004) 'Abuse Inquiries as Learning Tools for Social Care Organisations.' In N. Stanley and J. Manthorpe (eds) *The Age of the Inquiry: Learning and Blaming in Health and Social Care.* London, Routledge.

Cambridge, P. (2006) 'The Case for a New Case Management in Services for People with Learning Disabilities.' *British Journal of Social Work,* published online 31 October. Available at: www.bjsw.oxfordjournals.org/cgu/content/abstract/bcl359VI

Cambridge, P., Beadle-Brown, J., Mansell, J., Milne, A. and Whelton, B. (2006) *The Prevalence and Nature of Adult Protection Alerts in Kent and Medway* (report to the Nuffield Foundation). Canterbury: Tizard Centre, University of Kent.

Cambridge, P. and Ernst, A. (2006) 'Comparing Local and National Service Systems in Social Care in Europe: Framework and Findings from the STEPS Anti-Discrimination Learning Disability Project.' *European Journal of Social Work 9*, 3, 279–303.

Cambridge, P. and Parkes, T. (2004a) 'The Case for Case Management in Adult Protection.' *Journal of Adult Protection 6*, 2, 4–14.

Cambridge, P. and Parkes, T. (2004b) 'Good Enough Decision-making? Improving Decision-making in Adult Protection.' *Social Work Education 23*, 6, 711–729.

Cambridge, P. and Parkes, T. (2006a) 'The Tension Between Mainstream Competence and Specialization in Adult Protection: An Evaluation of the Role of the Adult Protection Co-ordinator.' *British Journal of Social Work 36*, 2, 299–321.

Cambridge, P. and Parkes, T. (2006b) 'The Management and Practice of Joint Adult Protection Investigations.' *Social Work Education 26*, 8, 824–837.

Cambridge, P., Carpenter, J., Forrester-Jones, R., Tate, A., Knapp, M., Beecham, J. and Hallam, A. (2005) 'The State of Care Management in Learning Disability and Mental Health Services Twelve Years into Community Care.' *British Journal of Social Work 37*, 7, 1039–1062.

Carnaby, S. and Cambridge, P. (2002) 'Getting Personal: An Exploratory Study of Intimate and Personal Care Provision for People with Profound and Multiple Intellectual Disabilities.' *Journal of Intellectual Disability Research 46*, 2, 120–132.

Challis, D. (1994a) 'Case Management: A Review of UK Developments and Issues.' In M. Titterton (ed.) *Caring for People in the Community: The New Welfare.* London: Jessica Kingsley Publishers.

Challis, D. (1994b) *Care Management: Factors Influencing its Development in the Implementation of Community Care.* London: Department of Health.

Challis, D. and Davies, B. (1986) *Case Management in Community Care.* Aldershot: Gower.

Commission for Social Care Inspection (2004) *Direct Payments. What are the Barriers?* London: Commission for Social Care Inspection.

Davies, B. (1992) *Care Management, Equity and Efficiency: the International Experience.* Canterbury: University of Kent, PSSRU.

Davies, B. and Challis, D. (1986) *Matching Resources to Needs in Community Care.* Aldershot: Gower.

Department of Health (1988) *Community Care: Agenda for Action.* London: HMSO.

Department of Health (1989) *Caring for People.* London: HMSO.

Department of Health (1991) *Care Management and Assessment: Managers' Guide.* London: HMSO.

Department of Health (1999) *Co-ordinating Care: the Care Programme Approach and Care Management.* London: Department of Health.

Department of Health (2000) *No Secrets: Guidance on Developing and Implementing Multi-agency Policies and Procedures to Protect Vulnerable Adults from Abuse.* London: Department of Health.

Department of Health (2001) *Valuing People: A New Strategy for Learning Disability for the 21st Century.* London: Department of Health.

Department of Health (2005) *Independence, Well-being and Choice: Our Vision for the Future of Social Care for Adults in England.* London: Department of Health.

Department of Health (2006) *Our Health, Our Care, Our Say: A New Direction for Community Services.* London: Department of Health.

Harris, J. (1996) 'Physical Restraint Procedures for Managing Challenging Behaviours Presented by Mentally Retarded Adults and Children.' *Research in Developmental Disabilities 17*, 99–134.

Huxley, P. (1993) 'Case Management and Care Management in Community Care.' *British Journal of Social Work 23*, 365–381.

Jones, J. (2000) 'A Total Communication Approach towards Meeting the Needs of People with Learning Disabilities.' *Tizard Learning Disability Review 5*, 1, 20–26.

Mansell, J. and Beadle-Brown, J. (2004) 'Person-centred Planning or Person-centred Action? Policy and Practice in Intellectual Disability Services.' *Journal of Applied Research in Intellectual Disabilities* *17*, 1–19.

Mansell, J. and Beadle-Brown, J. (2005) 'Person-centred Planning and Person-centred Action: A Critical Perspective.' In P. Cambridge and S. Carnaby (eds) *Person Centred Planning and Care Management for People with Learning Disabilities.* London: Jessica Kingsley Publishers.

Macintyre, D. (1999) 'Macintyre Undercover', broadcast on BBC 1, 16 November.

Onyett, S. (1992) *Case Management in Mental Health.* London: Chapman and Hall.

Pring, J. (2004) 'The Frequency and Potential Consequences of the Failure to Visit Learning Disabled Adults in Out-of-area Placements.' *Tizard Learning Disability Review 9*, 2, 35–42.

Ramcharan, P., Grant, G., Parry-Jones, B. and Robinson, C. (1999) 'The Roles and Tasks of Care Management Practitioners in Wales.' *Managing Community Care 7*, 3, 29–37.

Reder, P. and Duncan, S. (2004) 'From Colwell to Climbié: Inquiring into Fatal Child Abuse.' In N. Stanley and J. Manthorpe (eds) *The Age of the Inquiry: Learning and Blaming in Health and Social Care.* London: Routledge.

Robertson, J., Emerson, E., Hatton, C., Elliott, J., McIntosh, B., Swift, P., Krijnen-Kemp, E., Towers, C., Romero, R., Knapp, M., Sanderson, H., Routledge, M., Oakes, P. and Joyce, T. (2005) *The Impact of Person Centred Planning.* Lancaster: Lancaster University, Institute for Health Research.

Sainsbury (1996) 'Care Management: Is it Working?' London: Sainsbury Centre for Mental Health.

Shah, R. (2005) 'Addressing Ethnicity and the Multi-cultural Context.' In P. Cambridge and S. Carnaby (eds) *Person Centred Planning and Care Management for People with Learning Disabilities.* London: Jessica Kingsley Publishers.

Training Organisation for Personal Social Services (2004) *The National Occupational Standards for Social Work.* Leeds: TOPSS.

CHAPTER 7

Competence in Criminal Justice

Gerry Heery

Introduction

This chapter tells the story of a student beginning to work with a young person who has been involved in offending behaviour. The student forms a working relationship with the young person and assesses and plans a programme of intervention with him. The case explores the value tensions within the politicised world of criminal justice, and how the student deals with the perennial care and control balance and related issues of rights versus risks. The knowledge required for competence in this work is outlined, as is the student's efforts to integrate this knowledge into her practice. The skills required to bring the above values and knowledge to life are described and the need for the student to develop and improve in different areas is explored. Ultimately, the student demonstrates the necessary knowledge, skills and values to work positively with the young person and his mother while making some contribution towards helping him reduce the likelihood of offending. She is able to provide evidence of this through discussion in supervision; production of the case records; completion of various analytical and reflective exercises and from feedback taken from the young person and his mother. This body of evidence taken together shows the student's ability to fulfil requirements within the six key roles of the National Occupational Standards.

The criminal justice context and social work

In the first edition of this book, the example used was a social work student on placement within a probation team. At that time, the future of social work within the Probation Service was uncertain. There appeared to be an ongoing transition from a rehabilitative and caring approach in the direction of control and punishment. This trend has continued with a distinct politically driven push towards more overt toughness within probation with increasingly more emphasis on 'management, containment, punishment and control over social work and welfare approaches' (Whitehead and Statham 2006, p.144). Consequently, the Probation Service in England and Wales has undergone significant changes, including the ending of the social work qualification as a requirement for entry into the service. (Northern Ireland has retained the qualification and still offers some practice learning opportunities each year. Scotland continues to offer criminal justice work under the broader social work umbrella.) In order to make this chapter accessible to as many social work students as possible, it is now placed within the context of youth justice. This choice recognises the creation in 2003 of the Youth Justice Board and Youth Offending Teams in England and Wales and the Youth Justice Agency in Northern Ireland within which social workers (and other professionals) operate. (It also remains possible that some students may be asked to work with a similar case from within a probation, statutory social work or voluntary setting.)

Whatever the setting, there remains a range of ongoing ethical and practice dilemmas which continue to run through the politically volatile and polarised world of youth justice (Burnett and Appleton 2004). It is a contested and divisive area with competing ideologies on how best to deal with young people who offend. Not only in the UK, but throughout Europe, one will find some countries with welfare-based models focused on the needs of the juvenile and others with justice models emphasising retribution and public protection. 'Juvenile justice has no common vision or philosophy' (McCarney 2004, p.5). At the same time, a positive new factor to emerge within the world of youth justice has been the growing influence of the restorative justice model. This presents a positive and empowering vision of practice 'guided by values that honour the dignity of every human being and the importance of caring relationships' (Fox 2005). At the time of writing, it underpins the juvenile justice system in Northern Ireland, and is making significant inroads across the United Kingdom. It provides an additional strand alongside welfare and punishment, although questions remain as to the extent to which it can genuinely operate within existing justice and care tensions.

Case study

Joe is 15 years old. He and some friends vandalised a neighbour's car whilst stoning fire brigade personnel dealing with a fire. For the purposes of this chapter, it will be assumed that he has already been through a sentencing process and is required to undertake a period of community supervision. As stated above, this process will vary according to which jurisdiction within the United Kingdom that the young person lives. It is possible that the matter may have been dealt with in a more formal youth or family court, but we will assume it was dealt with using a restorative process involving the police and fire service. The neighbour, a 70-year-old man living alone, did not feel comfortable about participating. The student has not been involved in this process but she has been requested to take on the community supervision of the young person. The following additional information is given to the student in supervision approximately a week before meeting Joe.

Joe lives with his mother and 18-year-old brother. The family is dependent upon benefits. His mother has a part-time job in a local shop but sometimes finds it difficult to manage. His older brother has recently got a job and Joe would like one as well but isn't keen on attending training courses. The domestic situation is relatively stable at present, although there has been a difficult family history. Following a relationship marred by alcohol abuse and violence, Joe has had no contact with his father since he and his mother separated when he was two years of age. His mother became dependent upon alcohol and there were concerns about the parenting of her two sons. They were left unattended at times and had to fend for themselves from a young age. Social services were occasionally involved in seeking to support the family unit. As he moved into his teens concerns grew about aspects of Joe's behaviour, particularly at school and in the local community where he sometimes played truant and used solvents.

Joe's family lives in a difficult and disadvantaged community situation with a range of negative social indicators. These include high levels of unemployment, low income levels, significant health problems, above average truancy rates, limited recreational facilities for young people and high rates of anti-social behaviour, including drug taking and crime. On the positive side, Joe's mother has a large family network nearby from whom she receives support despite their disapproval of Joe's behaviour.

Joe's lifestyle is characterised by street loitering amongst friends, drinking alcohol, smoking cannabis and occasional law-breaking. He has received two previous cautions, for being in a stolen car and shop lifting offences, when he was 14. He dislikes school and wants to leave. He knows his offending is causing problems for his mother. The student has been told that his mother was distressed at the restorative meeting claiming that she was at the end of her tether with Joe and just didn't know what to do any more about him. Joe appeared moved by his mother's distress and tried to reassure her. From that meeting it is also clear that Joe is worried about the negative local reaction to his most recent offending. He was relieved that the neighbour did not participate, although research suggests that if Joe had faced his victim, it may have contributed a greater understanding of the effects of his actions and possibly impacted on his thinking, attitudes and behaviour (Campbell *et al.* 2006).

As part of his community supervision, Joe has been requested to make reparation, to complete a victim awareness programme, and to address his drug/alcohol abuse and offending behaviour.

Value issues

On receiving the information on Joe, the student's supervisor encourages her to be open and honest with herself in relation to her own values and feelings and to continue to reflect on these as the work develops. She needs to recognise and not underestimate the strength of her values in shaping her behaviour and responses (Thompson 2000). In particular, she needs to address one of the core value issues in this type of work. That is the degree to which Joe's offending is related to difficult care and protection issues in his life. Is he a victim of multiple adversities and is there a real danger of criminalising him rather than responding to his needs? On the other hand, is he responsible for his offending, for which he should be held accountable? Is he a victim or a villain?

In her preparation and tuning-in, the student recognises her strong feelings about anti-social behaviour. Simultaneously, she knows the estate that Joe comes from, that it is beset with many social problems and that, in her view, it would be hard for anyone to come out of it without getting into trouble, especially given the difficulties he has experienced as a young child.

The student also acknowledges that the people who live in the estate are of different religious and cultural backgrounds which causes her some anxiety about working there. She reflects on how these issues will impact on the relationship she forms with Joe. For example, will she tend to label or to stereotype him? She is also anxious about the power she has over Joe and how she will use it, particularly if he is resistant and does not want to engage with her. Much work with offenders is suffused with value dilemmas. They emanate from the difficulty of establishing a purportedly helping alliance within a wider context of restraint and coercion (Maguire 2002, p.168). The student is becoming more aware of, and anxious about, the challenges she will face in trying to integrate core social work values in her work with Joe. How is she going to demonstrate respect to him as an individual, encourage his self-determination, promote social justice, and also work for his interests in helping his situation within his family and community (Banks 2006)?

The knowledge base

There are two main areas of knowledge the student needs to acquire. First, there is the legal and policy context. (Space does not permit consideration of the legal context within all four jurisdictions. Suffice to say that students may be operating within different legal frameworks, e.g. the Criminal Justice (Children) (Northern Ireland) 1998 Order, the Children (Scotland) Act 1995 or the Youth Justice Criminal Evidence Act 1999 in England and Wales.) In her tuning-in, she is clear about the statutory basis of the supervision programme, and the responsibilities on her and the agency to deliver this to Joe as well as the requirements on him to adhere to what has been decided within the sentencing process. The student also recognises the relevance of the United Nations Convention on the Rights of the Child 1989. This is the most widely recognised, binding treaty in international law. It stresses children's rights to be involved in decisions that effect them and have their voices heard. It is applicable to children who come into conflict with the law.

The second area of knowledge consists of a range of theoretical material new to the student, who has little experience of the world of criminal justice.

Theoretical knowledge base for social work within criminal justice

- explanations of crime, particularly youth crime
- effects of crime on victims and communities
- effective responses to crime in terms of encouraging young people to desist, including: diversion, targeting and predicting risk, change and motivation theory, restorative justice, social learning,

systems and systemic family theory, cognitive behavioural theory, community development and safety issues

- anti-discriminatory practice

- adolescence and development

- attachment and family issues

- other social work methods such as group work, task centred, crisis intervention, solution focused and narrative therapies.

Initial thoughts and dilemmas

From the teaching and reading within the course, the student identifies various strands that appear most relevant. On a general level, she learns that a significant number of young people involve themselves in a range of anti-social, deviant behaviour. Delinquent or deviant behaviour forms part of the growing up process of Western adolescents – it is about testing boundaries, taking risks and challenging authority. It is a period of life that is mistake-prone by design: intellectual capacities and powers of reasoning are still developing, and young people learn from doing and making mistakes. In her tuning-in, this already raises a dilemma for the student. Is Joe's behaviour something that most young people grow through in the transition from adolescence to young adulthood, and in a way which will allow him to avoid ongoing persistent and serious delinquent behaviour? Much of the literature stresses that the overwhelming majority do grow out of it and that this is more likely to happen if society does not place a delinquent label on them and spoil their identities. However, how can she be sure that Joe is not in a more high risk group, and what will help her to make such a judgement? Is he a potential member of the 3 per cent or so of young people who become more serious and persistent offenders, responsible for over a quarter of all youth crime (Herbert 2000)?

Even at this early stage the student is addressing assessment and risk issues, recognising the complexity and challenge involved in assessing needs and circumstances and beginning to think about how she can, if at all, manage the risks that Joe presents in terms of his level of offending behaviour. This is not easy and in supervision and in her tuning in, she tentatively explores some of these issues. She accepts that it is critical that she is able to assess Joe's level of risk to help in deciding how best to respond, but she feels uncomfortable that it seems to be the risk factors around his offending rather than his needs that are already driving how the intervention should be shaped and how resources will be allocated (Kemshall 2002). She is experiencing the core value dilemma of care and control mentioned earlier.

Application of...which theory?

To further help her analysis, the student also considers some of the theories which seek to explain crime. She quickly rules out biological or genetic approaches, and is more drawn to psychological and social explanations arising from Joe's difficult early childhood experiences and the community he was brought up in. She reviews research which claims that low levels of affection and caring, coupled with erratic or harsh discipline as well as parental conflict and aggression are linked to subsequent involvement in offending (Farrington 1996). Is Joe going to be in this category? She is also intrigued by social strain theories which suggest links between crime and the desire to attain legitimate goals, which for some, because of how society is structured, can only be obtained through illegal means. This contrasts with social control theories which also assume that offending is a function of the social processes. However, they point out that the majority of people do not regularly commit crime in spite of economic pressures or the opportunity to do so. The focus is more on why so many do not become persistent offenders rather than why some do! The key concept is social bonding. Essentially, the more attached, committed and involved people are in positive relationships the more likely they are to observe the law. It is the disintegration of these bonds and the subsequent loss of social control which increases the risk of the onset of delinquency. 'Early developmental disadvantages begin in chaotic and abusive families and are perpetuated by chains of negative interactions, relationships and behaviours' (Halpern 2005, p.121). The loosening or 'neutralisation' of moral constraints lead to some drifting towards delinquent behaviour. The student feels that she is beginning to connect to Joe's situation and behaviour.

What works?

Although she finds the new area of criminology to be interesting, she is struck by the divergence of views and complexity of the material. These issues continue as she accesses what is known as the 'What Works' body of research. This material claims to have identified those factors which not only help explain why someone like Joe would offend but, more significantly, the factors that need to be addressed if he is to be helped to desist from offending. These include social circumstances and close personal relationships, individual temperament and personality characteristics, cognitive and reasoning skills, mental health and degree of addictions, and personal predispositions and attitudes to offending and potential victims (Roberts 2004). They are not static unchanging factors, rather they are dynamic and fluid and associated with persistence and desistence from offending. As such they need to become the focus for attention if it is going to be possible to help someone like Joe from going further into crime. They provide key assessment information in terms of how best to intervene. Even before meeting with Joe and based on the information she has, the student is able to begin to analyse these and begin to see how they may need to become part of her planned work with him. At a social level, he has problems within his family system, with his education and isolation from pro-social contacts. On an individual level the student tentatively identifies Joe's anti-social attitudes, feelings and associates, his poor decision-making and problem-solving skills, his lack of pro-social interpersonal skills, self-control, self-management skills, his dependence on alcohol/drugs, and maybe his lack of belief in legitimacy of the justice system.

The relationship perspective

The above material helps the student to begin to see that there is an evidence base to justify a targeted intervention in Joe's life, and that he has moved beyond diversion. However, there is still a large piece of the jigsaw missing and that is the type of relationship she will have with Joe. She is surprised, reassured and then daunted as she learns about how much emphasis the literature puts on the quality of the relationship. Successful outcomes are strongly influenced by effective workers who are warm, optimistic and enthusiastic, creative and imaginative and who use their personal influence through the quality of interaction directly with offenders (Trotter 1999). Change and motivational theory reinforce for the student the need to have a collaborative empathic relationship with Joe, trying to give him as much ownership as possible in terms of finding ways of sorting out his difficulties (Miller and Rollnick 2002). This also helps the student realise that the assessment she completes is not just about taking account of all relevant available information and the risk factors identified above but also about the need to address Joe's perceptions and perceived readiness for change. This can only be done in partnership with him, within a relationship that recognises and accepts his natural resistance or ambivalence about change and empathises with how difficult it is. The student begins to get a sense of the importance of her early work in trying to help Joe to face up to the 'why' question. From his perspective why does he want to do anything to change his lifestyle? Unless he has his own answers to this, then how likely is he to commit himself to different ways of behaving (Chapman 2000)? The restorative conference has already given some indications that Joe does not want to cause so much trouble to his mother and that he wants to be more accepted within his community. The student realises that she needs to try and build on this, and establish a relationship with him that is one in which Joe is encouraged and persuaded, no matter how adverse his circumstances, to buy into his own future with a different kind of enthusiasm, and to in some way become an agent for positive change in his own life. Research suggests that more is to be gained by trying to help Joe focus on, plan for and take control of his future rather than dwelling on past mistakes (Farrall 2002).

Critical appraisal of theory: limitation or overuse

The 'why' question will just be the beginning. Even if there is a sense that Joe is open to some change, then the 'how' also needs to be addressed. The student learns that much emphasis is placed in the literature on social learning and cognitive behavioural approaches. Social learning theory posits that children and young people learn behaviours, including undesirable ones, when positive outcomes are achieved without eliciting negative sanctions, through which behaviour is reinforced and repeated (Bandura 1986). The student recognises that Joe needs to experience 'negative' consequences as a result of his destructive behaviour within his community. She also hopes that she can help provide opportunities for him to receive positive feedback and outcomes through his making of reparation or participating in positive social experiences. The research-based literature also highlights the usefulness of cognitive behavioural approaches and the importance of challenging Joe's reasoning as much as his behaviour (Youth Justice Board 2005). The student is initially challenged by using this approach and focusing with Joe on his past or current behaviours and in particular in trying to challenge his 'faulty' thinking around his anti-social attitudes and feelings and his limited appreciation of the effects of his actions. In supervision, she refers to some of the literature which criticises the overuse of cognitive behavioural approaches. She reflects on the danger of focusing too much on

Joe and his responsibility to change, while ignoring the wider social problems within which he lives. The student asks herself if she is ignoring more challenging structural issues of inequality and discrimination, putting the onus on Joe to sort out his own problems whatever his circumstances? In supervision, she agrees that it is important that Joe is encouraged to understand the effects of his behaviours, on the car owner, his mother and his community. At the same time, she also recognises the links between crime and social exclusion and the need to be able to access services and resources for Joe that will assist his integration within the community (Scottish Office 1998).

Skills

The student has little experience of working with young people, nor has she worked within the justice system where issues of power and control are prominent. She is keen (though anxious) about using skills that bring to life the values and knowledge she has been reading and learning about. How do the interviewing, assessing and various communication skills she has learnt on the course fit within this setting? To begin, it is absolutely essential that she is able to form a warm positive working relationship with Joe and his mother. She needs to pay attention to how she presents, her body language, and tone of voice. Further core communications skills in explaining, listening, accurate interpretation, empathy and pacing are needed. More complex skills in integrating the motivational, change, social learning and cognitive-behavioural approaches, referred to above, will also be required, particularly as the work moves forward. To this end the student needs to improve her reflective listening and being able to encourage Joe to think and challenge himself. She needs to be able to develop her ability to recognise anti-social thinking and to be able to model and demonstrate real alternatives to this. She also needs to be able to reinforce and affirm the 'positive' when she sees it in Joe's words or actions. Other key practitioner skills within criminal justice work include modelling, positive reinforcement and effective disapproval, providing structured learning to develop problem-solving skills, and providing opportunities for restoration and making amends as part of examining offending. In addition, the student faces further challenges in seeking to demonstrate and develop her organisational skills around planning, time management and recording.

The supervisor reassures the student that although the tasks are demanding, they offer much opportunity for Joe's developmental progress.

The importance of establishing a positive relationship is emphasised, and from that her opportunity to develop more complex skills will develop. She needs to take it in stages and to recognise that

> people oriented skills are acquired over a considerable period of time through doing the job and gaining knowledge based upon experience; making mistakes and learning from them; training, coaching, and feedback from those who over many years, have themselves acquired these skills. (Whitehead and Statham, 2006 p.225)

The importance of her developing her ability to reflect on various aspects of her own practice and taking responsibility for her own learning is continually stressed.

The process of supervising the client

It will be assumed that the student, through college training, practice learning supervision (rehearsing many 'what if' scenarios with her supervisor), the studying of texts (including some of those already mentioned) has had the opportunity to acquire essential values, knowledge and skills. The process in demonstrating these will now be outlined. The student feels anxious, but reasonably well prepared for the first meeting with Joe and his mother, and looks forward to the challenge of working with him.

First contact

The student's supervisor attends this first contact meeting. The student welcomes Joe and his mother to the office, thanking them for attending as agreed, offering something to drink and trying to put them at ease by asking about their journey to the office and any difficulties in finding the place. The student introduces herself and explains that she is in training and indicates that whilst she is very happy to work with Joe and his mum, she can only do so with their permission as they have a right to a fully qualified member of staff. Confirming that she will be supported and supervised, both Joe and his mother indicate that they are satisfied with this arrangement.

The student then explains the purpose of the meeting. 'We are here today so that we can tell you what community supervision is about, what is expected of each of us, what each of us thinks about the situation and also to begin to get to know each other a bit.' She checks if Joe or his mum have issues that they need to raise or want explained. She then takes the opportunity to use an open question to Joe, 'Why have you decided to come here today and what do you want to happen?' From his answer she is able to get a sense that he accepts that there are consequences of his behaviour and is accepting of these (at least verbally). She reflects back his understanding of his situation, 'You know you had to come today, because of the damage you've done to your neighbour's car, but you would rather not have had to.' She keeps good eye contact and her tone is soft. She asks his mum if she has anything that she wants to deal with today. His mum replies that she just wants Joe to sort himself out before he puts her in an early grave!

'You're finding it tough going at the minute...' asks the student.

'Its not just at the minute, it's been desperate for the last couple of years with him,' replies Joe's mum loudly.

The student is unsure how to respond at this point. She is worried that Joe is about to react to his mum, particularly if her comments become more critical of him. Should she stay with the mother and reflect back her pain and hurt at how she is experiencing her son's behaviour or move things on? Before she can say anything, her supervisor gently indicates that this must be a difficult meeting for both mum and Joe, but hopefully the agency will be of help with some of the difficulties they have both been experiencing and to help Joe stay out of trouble.

The student then continues and explains to Joe and his mum that

> I am here to do what I can to help you stop getting into trouble and to try to help you to deal with some of the difficulties you have with your mum, your school and where you live. You have agreed from your meeting with the police that you would come here and also you would do some work in your area to make up for the damage caused. We need to meet every week, to get to know each other and to decide together what and when we will do things. How do you feel about that?

Reflections on first contact

When the student subsequently reflects on this initial session, she is able to analyse and evaluate her practice with Joe and his mum across value, knowledge and skill areas. With regard to values, she sees the care control tension playing out particularly in her use of power. She initially experiences some tension and feels that the power imbalance is oppressive. On reflection, and after discussion in supervision, she comes to see that she is confusing power, which in itself is not oppressive, with how it is used. Society is giving her the power to hold Joe accountable for his delinquent behaviour. She is not abusing power because she is asking Joe to engage even though he may rather do something else. She begins to see that it is about her learning to use her authority without being authoritarian. She recognises that she has been unambiguous and transparent in explaining procedures and the implications if he fails to co-operate with what he has agreed to do. She is being open and honest about what the deal is for Joe and what she will do to support him within the agreed boundaries. At the same time, she is pleased that she has been able to make a good start in forging a positive relationship with Joe.

Evidencing the NOS Key Roles

The student has now gathered several pieces of relevant evidence. These include her tuning-in piece plus related supervision minutes, her completed agency record of the first meeting with Joe and his mum, and her analysis and reflection on this. In addition, there is the direct observation report completed by her supervisor and feedback from Joe and his mum. Taken together, these provides evidence of her competence in several of the Units (known in Northern Ireland as the practice foci) across at least three of the NOS Key Roles. In relation to Key Role 1, her evidence shows that she has prepared thoroughly for contact and involvement with Joe and his mum, and has begun to help them make informed decisions (Units 1 and 2). In terms of Key Role 2, she has been able to make a start in developing a relationship with Joe to achieve change and improve his opportunities and also to address behaviour which presents risks (Units 4 and 5). Finally, and particularly in relation to her written tuning-in and analyses of her intervention so far, she has made inroads into Key Role 6 in being able to show her ability to analyse, evaluate and use up to date knowledge of best social work practice, work to agreed standards and contribute to promotion of best social work practice (Units 18, 19 and 21).

Assessing and planning

The student meets several times with Joe during the first fortnight, at his home, in a local bowling alley and in the office. She prioritises the building of their relationship and tries to get a sense of what he wants and where he would like to see himself in the future. She finds that she gets on well with him and that he has a good sense of humour. He enjoys the attention and as he finds she isn't judging or criticising what he says but just listening, he starts to talk more freely about his interests, music, sport, his life and worries. She uses the meetings to continue to focus on some of his behaviours and his readiness to change (Prochaska and Diclemente 1982). She gets a sense that he is at least thinking about trying to avoid offending behaviour. He is open about his 'messing about' with some friends at night and the trouble they sometimes cause and claims they don't really want to do anything seriously wrong and although his mum 'does his head in' at times, he does not want to cause her bother. He accepts that he needs to do something before things get out of hand.

The student senses that Joe is minimising or does not appreciate the effects of some of his actions on more vulnerable people within his community. She asks him to think about the effects on his grandfather if people were throwing stones and shouting outside his house at night. She sees a link between this and research-based findings which suggest some offending by young people is associated with a poor ability to foresee the consequences of behaviour in the longer term and limited appreciation of the feelings of others, including victims. She feels it is important and looks forward to doing victim awareness work with Joe in more depth. She is also able to get him to agree to participate in an educational participatory course with the fire brigade aimed at increasing young people's understanding of their work and the impact of attacks on their staff and vehicles.

When they talk about the reparation, Joe says he is embarrassed about what he might have to do, although he will do it rather than be taken to court. The student encourages him to think about things he likes or enjoys doing and that will be meaningful to him. Joe likes practical work and art.

Joe is more reticent in talking about his relationship with his mum. He expresses regret about upsetting her, but a home visit reveals ongoing difficulties and tensions in their relationship. The student is worried about this, more so about the potential for violence erupting in the family home. She encourages Joe's honest expression of frustration about his mum, but manages also to enable him to think about and have some appreciation of his mum's position. In discussion with Joe, his mum and her supervisor, it is agreed that some family work will be offered that will be overseen by the agency family work team.

The student produces an assessment and work-plan which meets agency standards. Joe is assessed as 'medium risk'. The following tasks are

stipulated: completion of a victim awareness programme including participating in the fire service course; to plan and consult on how he will do his
reparation; to participate in meetings with his mother to help improve their
relationship. In her evaluation of this work-plan, the student continues to
reflect on a range of values, knowledge and skill issues in her practice and
development. In relation to values and prejudice, she admits that before she
knew Joe she had been stereotyping him in her own head as a 'typical male
adolescent', someone who would not want to listen to her and even more
would not want to talk to her. This also involved elements of her own prejudice in terms of her attitudes to his class and religious background. She has
been able to work through this and now feels she sees him as an individual
person. Another value tension for the student centres on the nature of the
assessment process itself. In one sense, it is largely determined by the literature referred to earlier that identifies certain key criminogenic risk factors in
Joe's situation that need tackled. This seems to go against the importance of
person-centred approaches taught on her social work course. If Joe has little
say in what is agreed then how can it be called person-centred and how
much will he commit himself to it? The objective she feels, is to develop a
collaborative and open relationship with Joe. She is being up front with him
that her aim is to challenge, but also support and stand behind him in his
efforts to clear up 'the mess' he has caused in his local community and to
begin to identify and achieve his own more positive personal and social
goals.

Further evidencing of the NOS Key Roles

By this point, the student has gathered further significant pieces of relevant
evidence. These include the production of an agency assessment and
work-plan, additional agency records of several contacts with Joe (and his
mum), supervision minutes referring to these interactions, and written evaluations of some of this work. Within Key Role 1, as well as consolidating
further Units 2 and 3, her new evidence shows now that she has assessed
Joe's needs and recommended a course of action (Unit 3). In relation to Key
Role 2, she has additional evidence for Unit 5 and has also prepared, produced and evaluated a plan that addresses behaviour that presents a risk
(Units 6 and 9). The student also has evidence of Key Role 5 through the
production of the assessment and work-plan within the tight time scale
specified by the agency and recording various interactions (Units 14 and
16). Indeed her supervisor comments that she is particularly good at

recording things in a way that is accessible to Joe and his mum, something that does not always happen within the agency! Finally, in terms of her professional competence and Key Role 6, the student's work, and in particular her evaluations and discussion in supervision, shows how her intervention relates to up-to-date knowledge and research, meets agreed standards, addresses ethical dilemmas around her handling of power in terms of balancing Joe's rights and risks and is able to make a contribution to the promotion of best social work practice (Units 18, 19, 20 and 21).

Conclusion

The student's work continues. On the basis of her experiences to date, she is reasonably confident that she has made a small contribution towards his changing of the trajectory of Joe's life, moving away from a prescribed negative context to a more positive future (McAleece 2006). Of course, whether success or failure awaits Joe she is not sure. There is no ready-made guaranteed method of helping an individual change his or her offending behaviour, and precise knowledge of what seems to work best with specific kinds of offences remains limited.

Nevertheless, the student feels that her respect for Joe, of seeing him as a unique individual and not a problem to be solved, meshed with her growing understanding of the personal, social and cultural contexts of his offending, gives her a strong foundation upon which to go forward. The cement of this foundation and future work is the relationship that she has established with him. She is determined to nurture this as she takes him through the agreed intervention. It is this relationship that will help her to engage with Joe within his social context and face up to issues around power, risk, uncertainty, conflict, change, resistance and disadvantage. Her learning from this will be both fundamental and transferable. It is what she needs to build upon as she continues to face and meet the challenges of her ongoing professional training and development.

References

Bandura, A. (1986) *Social Foundations of Thought and Action*. Englewood Cliffs, NJ: Prentice Hall.

Banks, S. (2006) *Ethics and Values in Social Work*. Palgrave Macmillan.

Burnett, R. and Appleton, C. (2004) *Joined-up Youth Justice: Tackling Youth Crime in Partnership*. Lyme Regis: Russell House Publishing.

Campbell, C., Devlin, R., O'Mahony, D., Doak, J., Jackson, J., Corrigan, T. and McEvoy, K. (2006) *Evaluation of Northern Ireland Youth Conference System*. Research and Statistical Series Report No. 12. Belfast, Queens University: Northern Ireland Office.

Chapman T. (2000) *Time to Grow: A Comprehensive Programme for Working with Young Offenders and Young People at Risk.* Lyme Regis: Russell House Publishing.

Farrall, S. (2002) *Rethinking What Works with Offenders: Probation, Social Context and Desistance from Crime.* Willan Publishing.

Farrington, D.P. (1996) *Understanding and Preventing Youth Crime.* York: Joseph Roundtree Foundation.

Fox, D. (2005) *An Examination of the Implementation of Restorative Justice in Canada and Family Group Conferencing Approaches in the UK.* Birmingham: BASW.

Halpern, D. (2005) *Social Capital.* Cambridge: Polity Press.

Herbert, M. (2000) 'Children in Control.' In P. Canavan, P. Dolan and J. Pinkerton (eds) *Family Support: Direction from Diversity.* London: Jessica Kingsley Publishers.

Kemshall, H. (2002) *Risk, Social Policy and Welfare.* Buckingham: Open University Press.

Maguire, J. (2002) *Offender Rehabilitation and Treatment: Effective Programmes and Policies to Reduce Reoffending.* Chichester: Wiley.

Miller, R.W. and Rollnick, S. (2002) *Motivational Interviewing: Preparing People for Change.* London: The Guildford Press.

McCarney, W. (2004) 'International Developments in Youth Justice: A New Recommendation from the Council of Europe.' *Lay Panel Magazine 51*, 5.

Prochaska, J.O. and Diclemente, C. (1982) 'Transtheoretical Therapy: Towards a More Integral Model of Change.' *Psychotherapy, Theory, Resources and Practice 19*, 276–288.

Roberts, C. (2004) 'Offending Behaviour Programmes: Emerging Evidence and Indications for Practice.' In R. Burnett and C. Roberts (eds) *What Works in Probation and Youth Justice: Developing Evidence-Based Practice.* Cullompton: Willan.

Scottish Office (1998) Community Sentencing: The Tough Option *Section 2.2.1.* Edinburgh: The Scottish Executive.

Thompson, N. (2000) *Understanding Social Work: Preparing for Practice.* London: Macmillan.

Trotter, C. (1999) *Working with Involuntary Clients: A Guide to Practice.* London: Sage.

Whitehead, P. and Statham, R. (2006) *The History of Probation Politics, Power and Cultural Change 1876–2005.* Crayford: Shaw and Sons.

Youth Justice Board (2005) *Risk and Protective Factors.* London: YJB.

CHAPTER 8

Competence in Risk Analysis

Greg Kelly

Introduction

This chapter presents a model for the assessment of risk and its use on case material by a student social worker. The model was developed from Brearley's (1982) work in conjunction with a multi-disciplinary area child protection team for use in child protection cases. Its main distinguishing features from the Brearley work are the simplification of the language, the addition of a developmental perspective and focusing on the risk to be assessed. It has been used, evaluated and modified over six years by the Southern Health and Social Services Board in Northern Ireland. It uses a 'strengths' and 'weaknesses' approach, and its key elements can be applied to clarifying risk in other social work situations.

The issue at the heart of much child protection work is the estimation of risk associated with placing or leaving children in a particular situation. Risk in this sense means the danger of something going wrong, usually the children being abused or neglected or further abused or neglected. The public, political and professional pressures generated by a succession of child abuse inquiries (Dartington Social Research Unit 1995; Parton 2004) have led child care social work to be dominated by the fear of wrongly assessing risk. This preoccupation with the prevention of the negative, i.e. abuse or neglect, rather than the promotion of the positive – the support of vulnerable families – has long been recognised and criticised (Thorpe 1994). The Children Act 1989 (and the Children (NI) Order 1995) sought to redress the balance by emphasising the role of social services in supporting 'children in need' and making the grounds for court action more exacting. However successive governments across the UK have emphasised that they continue to see protection of children from abuse as a prime duty of the child care services. The legislation specifically requires and permits agencies to consider the likelihood of a child suffering harm in the future (Children Act 1989 Section 31 (2)). This formally places risk assessment at the centre of the responsibilities of social workers in child care and is reflected in the competences required by the National Occupational Standards (NOS) (Training Organisation for Personal Social Services 2004).

Limitations in prediction

All risk assessment involves trying to make an informed guess about what is likely to happen, i.e. to predict the likelihood of a particular outcome – usually undesirable. For example, will these children suffer further abuse if left with their parents? It is helpful to reflect on other unrelated areas of prediction, for example, in both economic and weather forecasting the deployment of enormous scientific resources leads to very modest and frequently mistaken forecasts. All the resources of the intelligence services of the Western powers failed to predict the sudden collapse of the Communist regimes of Eastern Europe in the late 1980s. In social work we are often dealing with volatile individuals under severe environmental pressure, often with poor personal resources and social support, and whom we may not know very well. This, and the limited assessment resources we may have, should make us cautious about our capacity to accurately assess risk. Humility, born of the inherent difficulty of the task, is invaluable.

Where possible we should have a contingency plan available and be honest enough to admit when our assessment of risk is inaccurate. This can be difficult when we are placed in the role of professional 'experts'. Decisions are often made by panels of 'experts', i.e. in case conferences. The development of user participation and negotiated agreements are recognition of the inadequacy of reliance solely on professional opinion. This co-operative approach is heavily emphasised in the National Occupational Standards. Risk assessment, therefore, should begin by seeking to engage the family, including (if age-appropriate) the children. This effort will not always be appreciated because the reason for the risk analysis is often a perceived inadequacy in the care children are receiving from the family. The potential for disagreement and conflict in child protection work remains high.

The capacity to work in this potentially conflictual arena is one of the keys to successful child protection work. Students need exposure to this dimension of practice, but as discussed in Chapter 5, such opportunities may be not be available, ironically, because of the risk associated with them. Students being placed in child protection work, need to gain experience in the assessment of risk in their allocated cases. They need good supervision as they try to cope with and minimise risk, and can benefit from shadowing other experienced colleagues undertaking this work. These are basic necessities for at least partial fulfilment of the requirement to develop beginning competence in Key Role 4 of the NOS: *To manage risk to individuals, families, carers, groups, communities, self and colleagues.*

Competence in the assessment of risk in child protection

In the following case a social work student, Graham, is working with a family when the agency receives a referral that the children may be at some risk of abuse or neglect. He is a mature student on the final placement of an undergraduate degree course. His previous placements and experience have been in the care of the elderly. He is confident and has shown a capacity to develop a good relationship with service users. He is supervised by an experienced practice teacher who is a member of the child care team for the area which specialises in family support and child protection. The area is a run down post-war housing estate on the outskirts of a large city.

Referral

The Wharton family were referred to social services by the health visitor, who was worried that the children were unkempt and suffering a succession of minor ailments, and that their mother Jean was beginning to neglect herself. The family were Jean (19), Mark (three) and Marie (eight months). Graham had visited the family only once when the local social services office received a referral from a neighbour. On that visit Graham had found Jean to be guarded and suspicious and this worried him, but she agreed that he would call again to discuss the possibility of day care so that she could return to work. Mark was small for his age, wore only a T-shirt, mostly stayed close to his mother but responded brightly to Graham when he asked him about his upcoming birthday. Marie was asleep in a pram. Graham called several times but got no reply, then a call came from a neighbour alleging that Jean Wharton's children had been left in the care of a young man unknown to the caller, that the children had been heard screaming, and this male stranger had been heard yelling at them. It transpired that this stranger, Michael Greer, was Jean's new boyfriend, and that he had been caring for the children three to four times a week while Jean was working in a local café.

The investigation

The visit following the referral was carried out by the student accompanied by his practice teacher, an experienced child protection worker. They agreed that the practice teacher would take lead responsibility with the adults and the student would attend to and observe the children. They arrived when Michael Greer was alone with the children, the children appeared to be very distressed, scantily dressed, and Mark had a bruise on his forehead. Marie cried ceaselessly; her nappy was unchanged; her legs were very inflamed; she appeared hungry. Mark seemed to remember Graham and was relieved at his attempts to engage him. He appeared wary of Michael. The practice teacher confirmed that the children had been left with Michael on a regular basis for three weeks and that he was, indeed, Jean's new boyfriend.

Michael said the bruise was caused by Mark slipping and hitting his head against a coffee table. Given Mark's stature and the height of the coffee table the practice teacher and student did not think this likely. He was anxious and aggressive, claiming that he was only doing Jean a good turn, enabling her to earn a few pounds. Records revealed that Michael is known to the social services and police. He was a persistent juvenile offender, who had committed offences of violence.

On a subsequent visit later in the day, Graham and his practice teacher met Jean Wharton. The house had been tidied; Michael was not there; the baby was asleep and Mark was in his mother's arms throughout the visit. The social worker, aided by Graham stated their concerns. Jean was aggressive and initially unco-operative. She said that she knew nothing good would come of social services visiting her. She denied that the children had been abused in any way but eventually agreed to a medical examination. Graham was surprised and frustrated that his efforts to offer support were met with so negative a reaction.

The two children were medically examined, accompanied by their mother. The paediatrician believed the bruise was non-accidental. He suggested that they were neglected to some extent, though their physical health was reasonable. Jean was shocked by the paediatrician's views, and denied any knowledge of Mark's injury. She insisted that Michael was not living with her now. She consented to Graham helping her make alternative child care arrangements to enable her to continue working. Otherwise she remained wary of social services and refused the offer of a family aide.

A case conference was held. Jean was invited to attend but was not at home when Graham called to accompany her. Supported by his practice teacher, Graham presented the information and the opinions formed during the investigation (see below). This work provided evidence of competence in NOS Key Role 1, particularly Units 1 and 2, and Key Role 2, particularly Unit 4, *Respond to crisis situations* and Unit 9, *Address behaviour which presents risk to individuals, families.* It taught him how difficult Key Role 1 Unit 4, *work with individuals and families to enable them to assess and make informed decisions about their needs,* could be in child protection generally. At the conference it was agreed that while care proceedings should not be instituted the children's names should be entered in the child abuse register and a full assessment completed.

Summary of background information emerging during assessment

The following information was gathered by Graham:

- Jean has been largely disowned by her family, though maintains intermittent contact with her mother located at the other end of town. Her father is dead. She had known Michael for only a few weeks. She admits their relationship can be stormy and that he isn't very good with the children. She said she asked him to meet with Graham but he refused.

- Jean's upbringing was characterised by poverty, violence, heavy drinking and criminal activity. Her father died when she was very young; her mother remarried, and her stepfather sexually abused her. He seldom worked, and periodically physically abused Jean's mother and all the children.

- Jean was the second youngest of six children. She was placed in care in a children's home when she was 15 after repeatedly running away from home. She appeared to find some stability there and remained for two years.

- When she left care she tried living again at home, but this was unsuccessful. She was seen by most of the family as the source of conflict, and it had the effect of uniting her mother and stepfather against her.

- There are two different fathers to the children; she has no contact with and receives no maintenance from either of them. She has been compelled in the past to seek refuge in women's aid.

- After the initial case conference Jean paid a neighbour to care for the children when she was working. She attended most, but not all, of the appointments made for her by her health visitor at the child development clinic. While remaining guarded she has co-operated with Graham in the assessment process. Mark's development continued to give some cause for concern, his speech appears slow, but Marie has achieved her developmental milestones.

Graham reported that Jean is hard-working and committed to the children. She appears of average intelligence, though semi-literate due to the social and educational deprivations in her upbringing. She has a good singing voice and was once a member of a church choir; she has not attended choir or church since Mark was born. She was emotional and volatile during the assessment period, and yelled at the children when she perceived them as defiant and troublesome. She became more accepting of social services' involvement and shared feelings about her past with Graham who she seemed to see as less threatening because he was a student. She would not talk about Michael, saying that he was only a friend now. The practice teacher believed that she was not entirely honest about this relationship. Social services continued to receive reports that he was in the house and a neighbour reported rows late at night.

Task

A review case conference is due two months after the original referral. The practice teacher asks Graham to prepare an analysis of the risks of Jean continuing to care for her children. The practice teacher introduces Graham to the Risk Analysis Model that the agency has adopted. This model and its application to the Wharton family are set out below. It is preceded by a summary of the knowledge, skills and values that make up competence in child protection in general and risk assessment in particular.

Knowledge

The purpose of developing models of assessment for practitioners is to distil current best practice and the knowledge that underpins it, and to make both readily available in a useable format. A model is rarely an exact fit for a 'live' case so an understanding of the underpinning knowledge can enable the worker to appropriately adapt the framework to suit the circumstances of the case. The knowledge base for risk assessment is similar to that set out in Chapter 5 for referral-taking. The literature on assessment associated with the *Framework for Assessing Children in Need and their Families* (Department of Health 2000) has much to offer. On particular issues Howarth (2000) and Calder and Hackett (2003) present a range of frameworks for assessing different 'risks', e.g. parental substance misuse, domestic violence, failure to thrive, neglect and physical abuse.

Values and ethics

The assessment of risk gives rise to difficult value issues. These are apparent in the emergence of lists of 'risk factors' to assist in the identification of parents more likely to abuse and neglect their children. Corby (1993) says there are many weaknesses and biases in the research that underpins these lists. Fundamentally they are too general and rarely specific enough for making decisions in relation to an individual child or family. A 'risk' factor such as 'parent previously abused or neglected as a child' may indicate a weakness or vulnerability to poor parenting capacity but actual evidence of poor parenting must be the only basis of intervention. The NOS sets out the values expected of professional social workers and all are relevant to the assessment process in child protection. As it sometimes involves the use of statutory powers and frequently involves a conflict between the worker, agency and family, it is particularly important for the worker to clearly set out their role and powers.

Skills

The skills of risk assessment are similar to those of social work assessment in general. Middleton (1997) defines assessment as 'the analytical process by which decisions are made... It is the basis for planning what needs to be done to maintain or improve a person's situation' (p.5). *The Child's World* (Department of Health 2000) sets out the phases of the assessment process in children's work:

> Referral / Request for Services – Initial Decision Making – Preparation and Planning for Assessment – Engagement of the Family and Children in the Assessment Process – Gathering Information –

Exploring Facts and Feelings – **Giving meaning to the situation – reaching an understanding of what is happening, strengths, difficulties and impact on child(ren) – analysis of children's needs and parenting capacity – professional judgement: Is this a child in need or at risk? – Identification of where intervention is required** – Decision on Action plan – Record of Decisions and Rationale – Inform child, family, other agencies of decisions and plan – Implement Plan – Review. (p.47)

The steps in **bold** are those that the following risk analysis framework aims to assist with, thus the worker needs to have deployed their skills and organisation particularly in relation to establishing a relationship with the child (where possible) and the family, and gathering information.

Risk Analysis Model

Core features and functions

The Risk analysis Model is designed for use in situations where there are serious concerns for children's welfare or safety. Its main use is when investigations lead to multi-disciplinary case planning, or an initial case conference. It may also be useful in subsequent case conferences or reviews. The purpose is to assist in the structuring of decision-making. The model is not designed for decision-making in emergency intervention, but rather for medium to long-term decision-making, with due time for deliberation. It helps participants clarify the issues in relation to the protection of children, to address the key questions in decision making, e.g. 'what is the problem and how serious is it?' It enables the professionals and those caring for the child(ren), to be clearer about their concerns, specifically whether or not abuse or neglect will continue or recur. The development of a non-technical language has improved the model and made it useful in sharing and discussing issues with parents and a wide range of professional staff.

Multi-disciplinary perspectives

A potential problem (and strength) in analysing risk is that numerous professionals provide different expertise, on for example, physical, emotional, psychological abuse-development. Different professionals may identify different dangers and/or factors that can contribute to or lessen these dangers. It is not the purpose of this model to try to summarise or arbitrate between these, but rather to provide a vehicle for discussing them. The model's

insistence that the risk and the factors contributing to it are clearly identified facilitates such discussion. It is each professional's responsibility to be
competent in current practice, including the essential knowledge base,
within his or her discipline.

Completing the analysis

Following the initial case conference Graham was tasked with completing
his analysis with particular reference to the care and protection of the children. He used the *Framework* document (DoH 2000) concentrating on the
Parental Capacity and Family and Environmental Factors sections. The children's principal needs at this stage were seen to be adequate basic care and
protection from possible abuse. Graham used the knowledge he has accu-
mulated about the family (see above) to complete the Risk Analysis Model.
He presented it to the subsequent conference, accompanied and supported
by his practice teacher. Jean Wharton again did not attend. The model is
explained and set out below. This is followed by Graham's use of it (supervised by his practice teacher) to analyse the risks posed to the Wharton
children if they are to remain with their mother.

Key questions in risk analysis

The Risk Analysis Model proceeds by asking the workers to consider a
series of questions. These are now listed and discussed.

1. WHAT IS THE NATURE OF THE ABUSE OR NEGLECT THAT MIGHT OCCUR
OR CONTINUE?

Different professionals may have differing perceptions of the nature of the
neglect or abuse in a particular situation. These differences need to be aired
and, insofar as is possible, the precise nature of the problem agreed.

2. HOW SERIOUS ARE THE CONSEQUENCES OF IT OCCURRING FOR THE
CHILD, FOR THE CHILD'S FAMILY AND FOR THE AGENCIES INVOLVED?

This is an invitation to discuss and agree on how serious the alleged or
actual incidents of abuse were for the child (primarily) but also for the family and to note any particular issues for the agencies involved.

3. PREVIOUS INCIDENTS OF ABUSE OR NEGLECT?

Detail any previous incident of abuse or neglect or any record of the current caretakers having abused or neglected other children. Children are more at risk in the care of those who have previously abused or neglected children. This also needs to be incorporated in the 'strengths and weaknesses' table below and taken account of in the estimation of the likelihood of abuse or neglect. No previous allegations in a long career of parenting should normally be seen as a 'strength'.

4. WHAT IS THE SITUATION FOR WHICH THE RISK IS BEING ANALYSED?

Risk analysis is only valid for the situation for which it is carried out. If the child moves to another situation with a different caretaker the nature and the degree of risk will be different. Set out details of where the child is to be cared for and by whom. Mention other individuals in the environment who might pose a risk to the child or who may protect the child.

5. WHAT IS THE TIME FRAME FOR WHICH THE RISK ANALYSIS IS BEING CARRIED OUT?

The situations of children and families are fluid. The longer children are subject to elements of risk the more likely they are to be harmed. Therefore each risk analysis has a limited life span and a date should be set for review. A review will be deemed urgent when professionals agree that the risk is high (see question 11).

The 'strengths and weaknesses' table

The framework then invites workers to explore the following areas in tabular form:

- strengths, weaknesses
- growth/change
- help/services.

6. WHAT ARE THE STRENGTHS IN THE SITUATION BEING ANALYSED?

What makes the occurrence or continuance of abuse less likely? Parents, extended family and community should be considered, but strictly in relation to the abuse or neglect under consideration. A supportive extended family that provides good care and childminding will be a 'strength' in many situations, but it may be of little use in protecting a child from a devious sex abuser. Here too the emphasis must be on the current situation but consideration should also be given to factors from the caretaker's past where there is evidence that past experiences are strengthening current coping capacity, for example, a parent who has 'coped' for a number of years prior to the current concerns.

7. WHAT ARE THE WEAKNESSES IN THE SITUATION BEING ANALYSED?

What factors make the occurrence or continuance of abuse more likely, i.e. what are the 'weaknesses' or vulnerabilities in the arrangements for the care and protection of the child? These are usually inadequacies in the care provided by the child's family or in the protection afforded to the child. There may also be weaknesses in the services available to the family or in the family's willingness to co-operate. The emphasis should be on the current situation and the physical and emotional care being provided for the child. However, consideration should also be given to factors from the past where there is evidence that these are making current coping more difficult. For example, the fact of parent(s), themselves, having been abused or neglected in childhood would be included if it was thought to be having an effect on their capacity to care for and provide for their children. As indicated under question 3 above, the responsibility of the parents / caretakers for previous abuse or neglect to this child or other children should be given particular consideration.

8. WHAT ARE THE PROSPECTS FOR GROWTH AND CHANGE IN THE SITUATION?

Is there evidence of growth and positive change in the circumstances that have surrounded the abuse or neglect or is there evidence of deterioration in the situation? A risk analysis is an attempt to forecast how a situation will develop in the future; clearly the capacity for improvement or deterioration in the current conditions is central to any such assessment. A key indicator of the likelihood of change is the parent's attitude to the abuse; an acknowledgement of the difficulties and a preparedness to work towards change would normally be seen as lessening the risk; a denial would be seen as increasing it. However, care needs to be taken not to discriminate against parents solely on the basis of their taking a different view of the abuse or alleged abuse from the social worker or other professionals. Co-operation also needs to be viewed in the context of the seriousness of the abuse or neglect, some incidents of physical or sexual abuse or neglect are so serious that compulsory protective action may need to be taken despite evidence of co-operation from parents.

9. WHAT HELP AND SERVICES CAN BE OFFERED TO BUILD ON STRENGTHS AND COMBAT WEAKNESSES?

At all stages in the analysis of risk, the availability of and the family's use of help and support should be considered. Inquiry reports and research repeatedly confirm that abuse and neglect have their origins in poor or inadequate parenting. Offering support services will be an outcome of most child protection investigations. Clearly a positive response from parents to such services is helpful but we need to be aware of the danger of discriminating against parents solely on the basis of their not co-operating with services and the danger of superficial co-operation hiding deeper resistance.

10. WHAT IS THE LIKELIHOOD OF ABUSE OCCURRING OR RECURRING?

The previous four questions on strengths and weaknesses (in tabular form in Table 8.1) lead ultimately to this most crucial consideration. The table is not to be used as a means of numerically totting up strengths and weaknesses. One weakness (e.g. alcoholism) in a family can generate numerous strengths and one strength (e.g. a strong partner relationship) can overcome many weaknesses. Professionals are invited to consider the balance of strengths and weaknesses, the evidence of the caretakers' capacity to grow or change and the availability of services that might help the family. The table must be supported by more detailed reports wherein the summary statements will be substantiated. On the basis of a rounded overall judgement, an assessment may then be made of the likelihood of abuse or neglect occurring or reoccurring. This may appear, and often will be, somewhat subjective. The function of this question and indeed the whole exercise is to encourage staff, parents and children (age permitting) to voice their opinions on the situation being analysed, to encourage discussion and deliberation as to the best way forward. In all but the most serious situations these decisions are and will continue to be made on the basis of discussion and negotiation.

Level of risk?

In the light of the information summarised in response to questions 1 to 10 a judgement of the level of risk in the current situation may be made. The level of risk is a compound of two elements:

1. How serious is the abuse or neglect that it is feared might occur or reoccur? This should be detailed in the responses to questions 1 and 2 (above).

2. How likely is its occurrence or reoccurrence? This is gauged from the study of the 'strengths and weaknesses' table as detailed under question 10.

In considering these two over-arching elements, it is worth bearing in mind that a minor incident of abuse (e.g. bruising as a result of smacking) that is very likely to recur might be graded low risk, whereas a serious sexual assault, which was considered possible but not likely, might be regarded as medium or even high risk.

Risk may then be categorised as 'very low', 'low', and 'medium', 'high or very high' (question 11). It is evident that the two elements could have a whole range of mixes from the high likelihood of the occurrence of serious abuse – 'very high' risk, to the low likelihood of the occurrence of a mild form of abuse – 'very low' risk.

The workers involved in preparing the risk analysis will have a view on the level of risk in a situation but the final say on the degree of risk should be made as result of the discussion at the case conference or case planning meeting. There will invariably be a degree of subjectivity in judgements of this nature (both in categorising the seriousness of the abuse and estimating the likelihood of its occurrence). The purpose of the Risk Analysis Framework is to help make these judgements explicit and open them up to discussion.

The Risk Analysis Model is designed as an aid to decision-making in situations where child abuse or neglect is a risk. A key concept in risk management is the acceptability of risk, i.e. having identified the risks, are they acceptable to those responsible for the decision, or more acceptable than the risks associated with alternative courses of action available (question 12)?

Is this level of risk 'acceptable' to the case conference or more 'acceptable' than the risks associated with the alternative courses of action available?

On the basis of the level of risk identified should the child's name be placed on the Child Protection Register?

The criteria for registering a child's name on the Child Protection Register are that 'there must be one or more identifiable incidents which can be described as abuse' and 'professional judgement is that further incidents are likely'. One would expect then that in situations where the level of risk was assessed as 'high' or 'very high' children would be registered, 'medium' risk might depend on the case circumstances and 'low' and 'very low' would not be registered.

Application of Risk Analysis Model to the Wharton family (Key Role 4 Unit 12, National Occupational Standards)

1. DESCRIBE THE ABUSE OR NEGLECT THAT HAS OCCURRED OR THAT IS FEARED MAY OCCUR

At referral Mark (aged three) had suffered a suspected non-accidental injury, a bruise to his head. A full medical examination revealed no other evidence of physical abuse, and there is no evidence of subsequent abuse. Mark is small for his age but just within the normal range.

Mark and Marie showed some signs of neglect, Mark was poorly clad and Marie had a bad nappy rash and spent long periods of the day in her pram when her mother was working and she was being cared for by Michael, Jean's boyfriend at the time.

2. COMMENT ON THE SERIOUSNESS OF THE ACTUAL OR ALLEGED ABUSE / NEGLECT FOR THE CHILD, THE CHILD'S FAMILY AND THE AGENCIES INVOLVED

The general circumstances that the children were found in on the day of the referral from a neighbour were very worrying. The children were distressed and hungry. Mark had sustained a bruising injury to his head; Marie appeared to have been lying in an unchanged nappy for some hours. They were being cared for by Michael Greer who appeared ill-equipped for the task. Extended exposure to this standard of care would pose a serious risk to the children.

Social and health visiting services were working with the family at the time of the referral, but while they were concerned, neither had seen the poor standard of care evident on the investigation of the referral.

3. DETAIL PREVIOUS INCIDENTS OF ABUSE OR NEGLECT INVOLVING PROPOSED CARETAKERS

There had been no previous referrals for abuse or neglect in relation to Mark and Marie. The health visitor made a referral one month prior to the referral made by the neighbour. It expressed concern about Jean's care of herself and the children but made no allegations of abuse or neglect.

Michael Greer has a criminal record for violence but not to children and not domestic violence.

4. DESCRIBE THE SITUATION OR PLACEMENT FOR WHICH RISK IS BEING ANALYSED

This analysis is to consider the risk associated with Mark and Marie remaining at home with their mother. The position of Michael Greer is uncertain. Jean has told social services that the relationship is over but he sometimes calls to see her and social services have had reports that he has been at the house late at night.

Currently the children are being cared for by Jean except when she is working (20 hours a week) when they are cared for by a neighbour who is seeking registration as a childminder.

5. WHAT IS THE TIMEFRAME FOR WHICH THE RISK ANALYSIS IS BEING CARRIED OUT?

Date Risk analysis agreed: *25th March 2007*

Date Risk analysis to be reviewed: At the next review case conference (if the children are placed on the child abuse register) *or* within three months time as part of the ongoing family support work.

Table 8.1: The strengths and weaknesses table

| 6. Strengths
What factors in current situation make abuse less likely? | 7. Weaknesses
What factors in current situation make abuse more likely? | 8. Growth and Change
What are prospects for improvement or deterioration? | 9. Help/services
What help/services may encourage change; is it likely to be accepted? |
|---|---|---|---|
| Jean's care of children for over three years; no concerns raised until this year.

Protective of her children since allegations.

Mother-children 'attachment' evident. She has organised a reliable, experienced local woman to care for children while she's working.

She has responded positively to crisis caused by allegations.

No further signs of abuse or neglect.

She has a job and is keen to work and support her family.

She has co-operated with health and Social Services Department; has begun to form working relationship with student social worker. | Jean does not have support in her parenting role: no contact with extended family; poor experiences of being parented.

She has had difficulty accessing good child care facilities.

Has very limited financial resource.

Tends to form unstable partner relationships with men who have offered little or nothing as parents.

She has only begun to make supportive contacts within the community.

Has left children in care of Michael Greer when it was evident that he was incapable of caring for them. | Jean was initially resistant to evidence that children had shown signs of abuse and neglect but has now accepted it and expresses determination that it will not happen again.

She has mostly co-operated with social and health services although she does miss appointments and remains suspicious of social services.

The children have generally shown signs of being better cared for. Marie's nappy rash has not recurred and Mark is bright and responsive. | Jean is isolated within the community and from her family. I (student social worker) have explored usefulness of re-establishing contact with her mother. She prefers to do this herself.

We have discussed support that Homestart can offer and she is considering a self-referral.

She has been resistant to suggestions of work being done jointly with her and Michael Greer at the Family Centre. |

Continued on next page

Table 8.1 continued

6. Strengths What factors in current situation make abuse less likely?	7. Weaknesses What factors in current situation make abuse more likely?	8. Growth and Change What are prospects for improvement or deterioration?	9. Help / services What help / services may encourage change; is it likely to be accepted?
She is intelligent, and appears able to learn quickly. She is trying to develop a wider social / support circle in the area. She has been asked to sing at local social functions and church services.	The relationship with Michael Greer presents a number of difficulties: in addition to having a criminal record for violence, he offers children poor and possibly abusive care. He will not co-operate with social services. The relationship with Jean has been conflictual. Jean maintains the relationship is over but he has been seen at the flat. The children are young and vulnerable; need consistent child care from their mother or substitute competent carers with whom they can form stable relationships.	Jean maintains that she is only 'friends' with Michael Greer but he remains a visitor to her flat and Jean accepts there have been rows between them. Michael Greer refuses to co-operate with social services.	She has also refused the offer of a family aide.

10. IN THE LIGHT OF THESE FACTORS HOW LIKELY IS IT THAT ABUSE OR NEGLECT WILL OCCUR OR REOCCUR IN THE SITUATION UNDER ANALYSIS:

(a) Very likely   (b) Likely   (c) **Not very likely**

(d) Unlikely   (e) Uncertain   (f) Cannot make an estimate

The last 2 (e) and (f) categories may indicate the need for further analysis.

Comment on issues in relation to likelihood of occurrence / recurrence

Jean Wharton has had many disadvantages to cope with in her life and these may be factors in the instability of the relationships she has had with partners and the lack of support she has from family. This has meant that she has been parenting her two babies largely unaided. There has never been any suggestion that she has intentionally abused or neglected them. She has left the children in the care of Michael Greer who was a dangerous and neglectful carer. She has not left them with him since and has been shocked by what has happened. The continuing concerns are set out above, particularly the nature of her relationship with Greer and his refusal to work with social services. As far as can be ascertained the children now have little contact with Greer and the care provided for them both by their mother and the childminder is satisfactory.

11. CONSIDERING THE LIKELIHOOD OF FURTHER ABUSE AND /OR NEGLECT OCCURRING (RESPONSE TO QUESTION 10) AND THE RESPONSES TO QUESTIONS 1 AND 2 (ON THE SERIOUSNESS OF THE FEARED ABUSE NEGLECT) ABOVE, INDICATE THE LEVEL OF RISK ASSOCIATED WITH THE SITUATION UNDER REVIEW:

Very high	High	Medium	**Low**	Very low	Unable to estimate

Comment on issues in relation to level of risk

In addition: the level of risk currently is low for the reasons set out in response to question 10 above. The worry is that Jean may again be involved with an unstable/unsuitable partner (in terms of his danger to the children) or that the relationship with Michael Greer may again pose a danger. It is hoped that the continuing involvement of social and health visiting Services and a relationship with a Homestart volunteer would help monitor and mitigate any such developments.

12. IS THIS LEVEL OF RISK ACCEPTABLE (OR MORE ACCEPTABLE THAN THAT ASSOCIATED WITH THE AVAILABLE ALTERNATIVE COURSES OF ACTION) TAKING ACCOUNT OF SAFEGUARDS / SERVICES THAT ARE OR WILL BE IN PLACE (CIRCLE ANSWER)?

 Yes   No   Unable to decide

Comment on the acceptability of the risk

The circumstances that gave rise to the abuse/neglect have now improved. This has largely been due to the efforts Jean has made in response to the situation. She is well motivated to try to maintain this improvement and the services and supports set out should be of assistance to her going forward.

13. ON THE BASIS OF LEVEL OF RISK IDENTIFIED, SHOULD THE CHILD'S NAME BE PLACED ON THE CHILD PROTECTION REGISTER (CIRCLE ANSWER)?

Yes   No   Unable to decide

Comment on decision in relation to registration

Mark and Marie's names had been added to the Register at the initial case conference. The review case conference needs to consider whether they should remain registered.

Conclusion

Graham found the Risk Analysis Model to be a useful framework for summarising and discussing the issues in the Wharton family. He introduced it at an early stage to Jean and over several visits found that it did help focus on her needs and the needs of the children. He was frustrated by her tendency to insist that 'That is all in the past'. However, she understood the 'strengths and weaknesses' approach and, while unwilling to discuss Michael Greer, did not object to the references to him in the analysis. Graham learnt much from the experience not least that the measured use of statutory responsibility can be a stimulus for change. He found it hard to adjust from a value base that was very heavily reliant on developing an open and trusting relationship with service users to one where he was obliged to become at times vigilant and suspicious about what Jean was telling him. He found discussions with his practice teacher helpful in this area, particularly 'un-packing' the NOS value statements on the 'role and purpose of (his) contact' and being clear about the 'powers, including legal powers in a way that can be understood by all'. In thinking about the services that might help the Wharton family he had to continually remind himself of the importance of involving Jean and exploring options with her despite her suspicion of him and hostility towards social services.

References

Brearley, C.P. (1982) *Risk and Social Work.* London: Routledge and Kegan Paul.

Calder, M. C. and Hackett, S. (2003) *Assessment in Child Care, Using and Developing Frameworks for Practice.* Lyme Regis: Russell House Publishing.

Corby, B. (1993) *Child Abuse, Towards a Knowledge Base.* Buckingham: Open University Press.

Dartington Social Research Unit (1995) *Child Protection and Child Abuse: Messages from Research.* London: HMSO.

Department of Health (2000) *The Child's World, Assessing Children in Need; Trainer Manual.* London: Department of Health.

Howarth, J. (ed.) (2000) *The Child's World, Assessing Children in Need.* London: Department of Health.

Middleton, L. (1997) *The Art of Assessment.* Birmingham: Venture Press.

Parton N (2004) 'From Maria Colwell to Victoria Climbié: Reflections on Public Inquiries into Child Abuse a Generation Apart.' *Child Abuse Review 13*, 2, 80–94.

Thorpe, D. (1994) *Evaluating Child Protection.* Buckingham: Open University Press.

Training Organisation for Personal Social Services (2004) *National Occupational Standards.* London: TOPSS.

CHAPTER 9

Competence in Health Care

John McLaughlin

Introduction

Social workers in the hospital setting in the UK have long been recognised as having made a valuable contribution to providing a sensitive and holistic response to the needs of sick and disabled patients and their families at times of transition and crisis. Following the establishment of the National Health Service, health-related social work developed and changed in response to the evolving policy and legislative agendas. The traditional counselling or casework role, an original (and highly effective) aspect of hospital-based social work, gradually gave way to the priority of discharge planning. By the 1980s, the shift in government policy towards the rationing of health care and the introduction of cost-containment strategies in the UK resulted in reduced bed numbers and a consequent drive within the NHS to speed up patient throughput and reduce lengths of stay in hospital. Because of their skills in interdisciplinary working and their established links with community services, hospital social workers were viewed as being particularly well equipped to help patients cope with their illness and its effects as well as facilitating their transition to the community with all the necessary supports (Bywaters 1991; Rachman 1995). Early research studies of hospital social work (Connor and Tibbitt 1988; Social Services Inspectorate (SSI) 1993) highlighted not only the effectiveness of their contribution to service provision but also the valuable role they played in addressing the social, emotional and material needs of patients and families during the hospital discharge process.

The NHS Community Care Act and the equivalent policy document for Northen Ireland, *People First* (Department of Health and Social Services (NI)

1990) heralded a major transition for front-line workers in health and social services by introducing numerous reforms, including new arrangements for community care assessments. Within these reforms, and the 'new managerialism' (Lymbery 2005) which they promoted, effective hospital discharge procedures are crucial to the wellbeing of service users, and necessitate social workers (care managers) assuming new responsibilities for assessing complex individual needs and arranging 'care packages'.

Hospital placements offer social work students excellent learning opportunities. They represent an important interface between institutional care and care in the community. They facilitate the development of assessment skills which are sensitive to the needs of patients and carers. They enable students to demonstrate core competences in the provision of social work services.

This chapter explores the process of care management and the single assessment process in the hospital setting. It focuses on a student's practice in undertaking a community care assessment of an older patient who has suffered a stroke. The chapter also highlights how the final year student addresses the challenges of providing a person-centred and competent response to the patient and his family at a time of crisis and transition.

Case study

Jim Brown (76) and his wife Peggy (73) live in a two-storey terrace house in an inner city area. They have one daughter, Betty (47), who lives nearby and is separated. She has no family.

Before retirement, Jim worked as a labourer and enjoyed reasonable health. However, two years after he retired he suffered a small heart attack and developed breathing difficulties. Weekends are a special time for Jim when he meets up with his friends at the local pub to have a drink and play darts. He also enjoys gardening. Jim's wife, Peggy, worked until retirement as a dinner lady in the local primary school. Although she suffers from quite severe arthritis in her hips, Peggy has managed to get around reasonably well. Lately, however, her condition has worsened and she now uses a walking stick when climbing the stairs. Peggy also suffers from mild angina, which becomes more severe when she is required to walk any distance or when she is worried or upset. Jim and Peggy are visited regularly by their daughter Betty with whom they have a close and caring relationship. Betty separated from her husband three years ago and lives alone in a council house. Since the break-up of the relationship, Betty has become heavily dependent on alcohol and is now attending Alcoholics Anonymous (AA). She is presently unemployed and suffers from periodic bouts of depression. The AA meetings, which she attends three evenings a week, are a great source of support for her.

Last week Mr Brown was admitted to hospital where he was diagnosed as having suffered a stroke. He has lost the power on the right side of his body and is experiencing loss of sensation in his limbs. Since his admission, Mr Brown has been receiving intensive nursing care and remains quite weak and traumatised. His speech is slurred and hesitant but he is still able to make himself understood. It is anticipated that he will continue to receive care and treatment from the multi-disciplinary team on the ward for another three to four days and once medically stable he will be transferred to the rehabilitation unit within the hospital.

The knowledge base

When older people are admitted to hospital it is normally in situations of crisis, for example, the traumatic onset of illness, a severe fall in the home, respiratory difficulties or strokes. The major disruption to family systems as a result of illness and the disabling consequences of such traumatic events requires a competent and skilled response from the hospital social worker to help support and reassure both patient and family (Holiman, Dziegielewski and Datta 2001). Students will be required to draw on a range of knowledge in the course of their practice learning opportunity in the hospital and the following key areas provide a preliminary frame of reference.

Legislation relevant to people with physical disabilities and older people

- The definition of disability (National Assistance Act 1948 [s29])

- Gathering and dissemination of information (Chronically Sick and Disabled Persons Act [CSDPA] 1970 [s1]) and Disabled Persons (Services, Consultation and Representation) Act 1986 [s9]

- Assessment of needs (CSDPA 1970 [s1]; DPA 1986 [s4] (a) (b), [s8]; and NHS and Community Care Act 1990 [s47])

- Provision of services in the community (National Assistance Act 1948 [s29]; as extended by CSDPA 1970/DPA 1986/NHS and Community Care Act 1990 Part III)

- Provision of residential accommodation (National Assistance Act 1948 [s21])
- Residential care and nursing homes (Registered Homes Act 1984)
- Rights to involvement in assessment and advocacy (Community Care (Direct Payments) Act 1996)

Carers' legislation

- Carers (Recognition and Services) Act 1995
- Carer's independent right to assessment (Carers and Disabled Children Act 2000)

Policy, procedures and guidance

The following key documents are relevant to health care social workers:

- Griffiths Report (1988) *Community Care: Agenda for Action*
- *Caring for People: Community Care in the Next Decade and Beyond* (Department of Health (DoH) 1989)
- *Modernising Social Services: Promoting Independence, Improving Protection, Raising Standards* (DoH 1998)
- *No Secrets: Guidance on Developing and Implementing Multi-agency Policies and Procedures to Protect Vulnerable Adults from Abuse* (DoH 2000a)
- *National Service Framework for Older People* (DoH 2001)
- *The Single Assessment Process* (DoH 2002a)
- *Fair Access to Care Services: Guidance on Eligibility Criteria for Adult Social Care* (DoH 2002b)
- *Intermediate Care: Moving Forward* (DoH 2002c)
- Hospital department's policy and procedures on assessment and care management and the Single Assessment Process (SAP). (These arrangements may vary both within and between agencies, according to local circumstances.)

Additionally, students will need to:

1. know the process of care management and the organisational arrangements necessary to implement that process

2. be always aware of the primary goal: to tailor services to individual needs

3. realize that assessment is only one of the seven core tasks that cumulatively constitute the process of care management (Social Services Inspectorate 1991, p.9).

Figure 9.1 illustrates that process.

The Single Assessment Process

The Single Assessment Process (SAP) (introduced in the NHS Plan (DoH 2000b) and reaffirmed in the *National Service Framework for Older People* (DoH 2001)) is an integral part of the care management process which has expanded the assessment process within care management. Step 6 of the SAP has four types of assessment:

Figure 9.1: Process of care management

1.   Contact assessment – recording of basic personal information.

2.   Overview assessment – 'more rounded' assessment by health and social care professionals.

3.   Specialist assessment – may be triggered by an overview assessment and will involve a multi-professional assessment to explore specific needs.

4.   Comprehensive assessment – offered to service users with complex needs who are likely to require intensive domiciliary care packages or who may require nursing care.

Under the *Fair Access to Care Services* initiative (DoH 2002b), social services are now required to place service users who have had a community care assessment of need into four bands of risk: *critical, substantial, moderate* and *low*. The various levels of dependency/impairment of the service user are then matched with the four bands of risk in respect of the service user's level of ability or impairment across a range of domains (e.g. mobility, level of self-care, daily living skills).

Medical conditions and their psycho-social implications

Students on hospital placements should know about the effects (physical/social/emotional) of particular conditions and their implications for patients and carers (Wright and Arraras 2002). Literature on strokes is particularly relevant to the case which follows, and is adequately addressed (e.g. Hinds 2000; Kelson 2000). Although there is no formal requirement to be knowledgeable about the clinical aspects of particular conditions, it will be important for students to understand, for example, the nature of the illness or disease and the general treatment, management and types of support needs the patient and family may require during the rehabilitation period. In addition, knowledge of the social model of disability (Oliver 1996) can inform the student on the importance of promoting a holistic and partnership approach to patient care as well as challenging oppressive practice within an environment where the medical model perspective is dominant.

Self-knowledge

Working with sick and disabled people in a hospital setting can be emotionally demanding. It can be helpful, therefore, for the student to discuss their experiences of illness, disability and any bereavements or losses with their practice teacher and explore these as openly as possible. This type of exploration, within a supportive and permissive environment, can help reduce any anxieties the student might be feeling about having to deal with these issues in practice and therefore reduce the possibility of them becoming 'blocked' in sensitively engaging with vulnerable older people experiencing profound ill health.

Methods and theories for practice

Assessment of need within the care management process is now a core task for hospital based social workers. They do however have many other responsibilities, some of a more therapeutic nature, that require substantial levels of knowledge, skills and expertise. In addition to the more commonly used theories and methods within the hospital setting – e.g. task-centred work (Doel 2002), crisis intervention (O'Hagan 1991), advocacy (Payne 1995), counselling (Egan 2001) – knowledge of other critical theoretical perspectives will be important, for example, on disability theory and perspectives (Priestly 2003), social gerontology perspectives (Phillipson 1998), ageing and life course perspectives (Hockey and James 1993), and social work with older people (Lymbery 2005).

Skills

The following are some of the key skills that are relevant to hospital social work:

- Interviewing skills: ability to ask appropriate questions; communicate clearly and effectively

- Counselling skills: ability to actively listen and use open questions; ability to use skills such as reflecting, clarifying and summarising

- Multi-disciplinary work: understanding the differing perspectives of other professionals; share knowledge appropriately; work collaboratively

- Advocacy skills: representing the interests of others when they are unable to do so themselves

- Problem-solving skills

- Writing: ability to write clear, concise and accurate records that can be shared with service users (plus: keep records updated)
- Self-organisation
- Time management
- Work under pressure/understand and manage stress.

Values and Ethics

Qualified social workers must demonstrate ethical practice. To be competent in accordance with the National Occupational Standards (in Northern Ireland these standards are incorporated within a Framework Specification document, Department of Health, Social Services and Public Safety 2003), social work students must demonstrate that they have achieved competency whist adhering to values and principles stated in the new Code of Practice for Social Care Workers (Training Organisation for Personal Social Services 2004). The Code has identified a number of key value requirements which must be demonstrated during the practice learning opportunity. The following are relevant to the Brown case:

- Awareness of your own values, prejudices, ethical dilemmas and conflicts of interests and their implications for your practice

The student needs to explore her attitude to older people and how ageist assumptions based on negative stereotypes can marginalise older people and contribute to oppressive practice. The student should acknowledge each family member's right to express preferences for services which will promote autonomy and personal empowerment. Effective negotiation skills will therefore be required to address and resolve competing priorities and preferences among the range of key stakeholders involved in the case as well as between the patient and family members.

- Listening to, respecting, promoting and balancing the views and wishes of individuals, families...

The student needs to acknowledge and respect the identified needs of Mr and Mrs Brown and their daughter and to ensure that their expressed views and preferences are accurately represented and supported during the period of hospitalisation as well as throughout the care management and single assessment process.

Setting the context

The case has been allocated to the student, Helen Johnson, by her practice teacher, who works in the medical ward where Mr Brown is a patient. The student has been on placement for two weeks but has not yet had the experience of being involved in a complex care management case. Her practice teacher believes this case would offer her valuable practice learning opportunities and enable her to demonstrate a range of professional competences. Although there is a range of care management models currently in operation throughout the various local authorities in the UK (SSI 1991), it will be assumed that the hospital-based care manager is a professionally qualified social worker who has responsibility for managing the community care budget for residential and nursing home care as well as domiciliary services. Her role therefore involves the 'commissioning' of assessments from the range of hospital-based professionals but she has no direct contact with patients until after uni-disciplinary assessments have been completed. It will also be assumed that stroke patients with complex needs are transferred to the rehabilitation unit within the hospital. Furthermore, in order to enable the student to gain experience of inter-professional collaboration, arrangements have been made between the practice teacher and the relevant community-based teams for the student to take responsibility for managing the discharge planning process and to co-work the case with the community-based social worker, when Mr Brown returns home.

The Single Assessment Process: Contact Assessment

The ward staff nurse has interviewed Mr and Mrs Brown in accordance with the guidance on the implementation of the stages of the SAP. She has noted their concerns about their ability to cope when Mr Brown returns home. She has also explained the *single assessment process* to the family and has agreed to make a referral to the hospital-based social worker for a more thorough assessment. On the basis of 1. initial contact, 2. assessment information, and 3. the severity of Mr Brown's stroke, the medical and nursing staff on the ward believe that the health and social care needs (domains of need) seem to be sufficiently complex to require a more rounded *overview assessment* by the multi-disciplinary team.

Determining level of assessment following referral

Determining the level of assessment within the SAP equates with stage 2 of the care management process. Social work practice at this preliminary phase necessitates good preparation on the student's part and sensitive guidance, support and direction from the practice teacher. Evidence collated at this important preparatory phase will assist hospital-based students to fulfill the majority of the requirements of Key Role 1 and related Units 1, 2 and 3.

KEY ROLE 1: PREPARE FOR AND WORK WITH INDIVIDUALS, FAMILIES, CARERS, GROUPS AND COMMUNITIES TO ASSESS THEIR NEEDS AND CIRCUMSTANCES

Unit 1   Prepare for social work contact

Unit 2   Work with individuals, families, carers, groups and communities to help make informed decisions

Unit 3   Assess needs and options to recommend a course of action

Contact Assessment

The Contact Assessment form provides the student with brief details of Mr Brown's admission, diagnosis, medical history, the family's social situation and perception of needs and the reason for referral. The form also notes that Mr Brown's illness precludes a thorough exploration of his views and feelings until such time as he feels able to respond to such queries.

Overview Assessment

During the *Overview Assessment* phase, it will be important for the student to establish contact with and engage the patient and relatives in order to understand and assess their needs and wishes, which are likely to alter or change over time (Coulshed and Orme 1998). This early contact with family and carers can help them to 'tell their story', and provides the student with an opportunity to reassure them that they will not be left to manage the situation on their own. Good inter-disciplinary liaison and communication with the hospital team will be essential at this time and provides the student with opportunity to demonstrate competence for Key Role 5 Unit 17, *Work in and across multi-disciplinary and multi-organisational teams, networks, systems and agencies to contribute to the integration and effectiveness of services.*

In preparation for the first meeting with Mr Brown, the student, with the help of the practice teacher, begins to understand the immense physical impact of a stroke and the emotional trauma of the condition for Mr Brown. She also 'tunes-in' to her own feelings about the visit and about dealing with possible communication difficulties. Initial visits should be brief and focused, as early days are traumatic and stressful for older people who are profoundly ill. Rehearsal of anxieties can be a great help to students preparing for new situations and should be seen as an integral part of interview preparation (Douglas and McColgan 1995). Assessment is not simply a technical exercise but an ongoing process that requires good interpersonal and interviewing skills.

First contact

On her visit to Mr Brown on the side ward, the student introduces herself and explains the purpose of her visit:

STUDENT: Hello, Mr Brown. My name is Helen Johnston. I'm a
           student social worker based in the hospital. Sister Jones
           asked me to call with you to see if social services could
           be of any help to you and your wife when you leave
           hospital.

Mr Brown raises his left arm slowly as if to say 'hello' and utters a few slurred words that are difficult to understand. The student picks up Mr Brown's frustration and tries to ease his possible embarrassment:

STUDENT: Just take your time, Mr Brown. I'm sure this is very
           frustrating for you…there's no rush.

After spending some time with Mr Brown discussing his admission to hospital and his home situation, an early rapport between the student and patient is established and she agrees to return at visiting time to met Mr Brown's wife and daughter.

The ability to form and develop working relationships with the patient and his family in this early phase of relationship-building should be a key objective for the social work student in order to promote user and carer-centred practice. It reassures patients and families that support will be available throughout this critical stage of hospitalisation. The use of process recordings of initial interviews between the student and patient or family can provide important evidence to demonstrate the competence requirements for Key Role 1 as well as Unit 19 of Key Role 6, *Work to agreed standards of social work practice and ensure own professional development.*

Plan of first meeting with Mrs Brown and Betty

Planning for first meetings with relatives requires both mental preparation and a clear understanding of the purpose of the meeting. Because of the trauma likely to be experienced by family members, emotions and anxieties are likely to be close to the surface. Tuning-in to how Mrs Brown and Betty might be feeling at this time, and role playing the first encounter with the practice teacher, can help reduce the student's own level of anxiety; both may enhance her understanding and increase her confidence.

The student reviews the literature on user and carer involvement in the discharge process (Key Role 6 Unit 18, *Research, analyse, evaluate and use up-to-date knowledge of best social work practice*). She learns how carers are often not consulted or kept informed (Holzhausen 2001) and of their need to be supported through the process (Hill and MacGregor 2001). An interview plan similar to that outlined in Box 9.1, focusing on working in partnership with relatives, is a useful tool in helping the student mentally prepare for the first meeting. It may be used as evidence of competence in preparing for social work contact and involvement. A practice teacher's written assessment of student competence during preparatory sessions (e.g. role plays) as well as documented evaluations of direct observations of practice can also serve as useful evidence of competence for the requirements of Key Role 1 (Units 1, 2 and 3) as well as Key Role 3 Unit 11, *Prepare for, and participate in decision-making forums and assist others (where appropriate) to do so as well*.

Box 9.1: First meeting with Mrs Brown and daughter – Overview Assessment

1. Preparation for interview: Establish 'preliminary empathy': how Mrs Brown and Betty might be feeling at this time of crisis. What are the student's own feelings/concerns about interviewing them? Anticipate possible family needs. Rehearse information giving. Study hospital policy and procedures on single assessment process/care management.

2. Multi-disciplinary liaison: Establish contact and communicate with appropriate ward staff. Agree to complete Overview Assessment form following interview across relevant 'domains'.

3. Introductions: Introduce self as student social worker. Full name. Mention earlier contact with Mr Brown.

4. Outline of meeting: Explain referral source and purpose of visit. Encourage relatives to share details about patient's admission. Acknowledge the stress and trauma of Mr Brown's admission for family. Use skills of listening, reflecting, clarifying, paraphrasing etc; open questions; empathy.

5. *Information gathering:* Encourage/enable relatives to identify concerns about rehabilitation and post-discharge periods. Check family and accommodation details; responsibilities; perceived limitations/constraints/risks/strengths.

6. *Information giving:* Explain: hospital assessment principles of needs-led assessment; single assessment process/care management. Reassure that Mr Brown will not be discharged until a satisfactory package of care services has been agreed. Inform family of financial assessment details.

7. *Next meeting:* Agree to keep in touch to arrange another meeting at hospital's rehabilitation unit.

The first meeting with Mrs Brown and Betty has enabled the student to form an early working relationship and has identified some of their post-discharge concerns. Three of the main issues discussed were:

1. Betty's concern about how her mother will cope with Mr Brown's complex needs.

2. Betty's willingness to contribute to her father's care at home.

3. Betty's own need to attend AA meetings three times a week.

Ongoing assessment

After reviewing the single assessment process with the family, the student agrees to arrange another meeting with them in the rehabilitation unit to further explore their needs and the level of support they will require when Mr Brown returns home. Because recovery from stroke is a long-term process, multi-disciplinary assessments of the patient's progress and rehabilitation potential are necessarily ongoing to enable effective monitoring and evaluations of the patient's functional abilities and changing levels of dependency (e.g. transferring from bed to chair). The preliminary Overview Assessments from the physiotherapist, occupational therapist and doctor indicate that while Mr Brown's medical condition has stabilised, ongoing assessment of his impaired physical functions and mobility will be necessary during his four-week rehabilitation programme to determine whether a comprehensive assessment will be required.

Throughout the acute phase of Mr Brown's treatment the student has stayed in regular contact with the patient and family, and has provided them with emotional support and facilities to talk about their fears and anxieties for the future. The student has also spent time with Mr Brown to enable him to verbalise his feelings about the stroke and its emotional impact on his life. She has reassured the patient and family about her continued involvement and support during Mr. Brown's period of rehabilitation. Process recordings which 1. reflect and critically analyse the interpersonal skills and knowledge used to provide ongoing support to patients and their families, and 2. which demonstrate learning outcomes, are useful pieces of evidence to demonstrate competence for Key Roles 1, 3 and 6.

Rehabilitation unit – Comprehensive Assessment

Since his transfer to the rehabilitation unit a week ago, Mr Brown has continued to make steady but slow progress with his mobility and requires the assistance of two people to transfer from bed to chair. Following a pre-discharge home visit by Mr Brown to assess his functional abilities and level of risk, the care manager has received the completed Overview Assessments from the multi-disciplinary team and has decided that due to the complex level of need in the case and the 'substantial' degree of risk involved, a comprehensive assessment is warranted. The practice teacher and care manager agree that the student will be the key worker in the case.

The student arranges a meeting with Mrs Brown and her daughter. The purpose is *assessing need* and *care planning*, in accordance with stages 3 and 4 of the care management process. The discussion will focus primarily on their needs and on their concerns about post-discharge care arrangements, but will also explore how they may contribute to the eventual care plan.

Meeting with Mrs Brown and her daughter

In preparation for the meeting, the student has undertaken the necessary tuning-in and the session is observed by the practice teacher with Mrs Brown's and her daughter's permission. The student provides the following account of the meeting.

STUDENT NOTES

I started the meeting by welcoming Mrs Brown and her daughter and thanked them for coming. I then explained the purpose of the meeting and suggested that it might be helpful to further explore and agree specific concerns about Mr Brown's eventual discharge. As they updated me on Mr Brown's progress, I maintained good eye contact and periodically used affirmative and supportive statements when progress in Mr Brown's condition was mentioned. As the interview progressed, I got the impression that both women were feeling a bit more relaxed, as they talked in quite positive terms about Mr Brown's condition and his slow but steady progress. They expressed some concern however about the level of help he would need at home and the fears they had of 'something going wrong'. I feel I conveyed empathy in this early phase by actively listening and reflecting back on both their satisfaction at Mr Brown's progress but also their concerns in case anything went wrong.

In the next phase of the interview, I sensitively encouraged Mrs Brown and her daughter to identify the precise concerns they had about Mr Brown returning home. I used a combination of open and closed questions to elicit the necessary information. The concerns are as follows:

MRS BROWN

1. Getting Mr Brown in and out of bed in the mornings and at bedtime

2. Tending to his personal hygiene/toileting (toilet and bathroom are upstairs)

3. Lighting the fire, shopping, laundry, supper (Mrs Brown has arthritis in hip; husband used to attend to these things)

DAUGHTER

1. Worried about her mother not managing the care demands of Mr Brown

2. Fear of the stress of the situation triggering her depression

3. Concerned about not being able to attend the AA meetings. May revert to drinking

We then went on to discuss possible areas where each of them felt they could contribute to the care plan:

MRS BROWN

1. Preparing light breakfast

2. Afternoon snack

DAUGHTER

1. Live with parents in meantime

2. Prepare evening meals

3. Shopping at weekends

In the course of the meeting, the student explores several support networks with the relatives and provides literature on local stroke support schemes, the Stroke Association and Carers UK. Information is also provided on Attendance Allowance and the contact details given for the local Welfare Rights Service with a view to the family having their entitlements to benefits fully assessed. In a subsequent supervision session with the practice teacher, the interview with Mrs Brown and her daughter was analysed and evaluated. The student's strengths (e.g. communication and enabling skills) and shortcomings (lack of information on carers' right to assessment) were identified. An exemplar such as the summary analysis of the above interview can be submitted along with a critical self-evaluation as evidence to demonstrate competence in relation to Key Roles 1, 3, 5 and 6 and associated units.

Stages 3 and 4 of the care management process are concerned with assessing need and care planning, and seek to provide a holistic view of the person's physical, social and emotional needs in which a range of other professionals are involved. Through the use of the exchange model of assessment (Smale et al. 1993), the student has worked in an empowering way with Mrs Brown and her daughter by keeping them central to the decision-making process.

Care package

In undertaking assessment of stroke patients, the student should remain sensitive to the patient's needs and wishes and work at their pace. Through a number of phased and time-limited sessions, the student has appreciated Mr Brown's eagerness to return home to continue his rehabilitation programme and has agreed to liaise with the occupational therapist to arrange for his bed to be moved downstairs and for a commode to be delivered to his home. In addition, the community stroke rehabilitation team, as part of the local intermediate care scheme, will provide rehabilitation in Mr Brown's own home during the week.

A subsequent meeting with all of the family to explore their preferred care package of domiciliary support, highlighted the need for Betty to be enabled to attend AA meetings three times a week (Mon/Wed/Fri). In collaboration with the care manager and the multi-disciplinary team members, it has also been agreed that a personal carer will visit in the mornings at 8.30am to help get Mr Brown get up, get dressed, and ensure personal hygiene; in the evening they will assist the family with bedtime preparations. A support worker from the local care attendant scheme will visit the family between 8.30pm and 10.30pm three nights a week to enable Betty to attend AA meetings.

The student role in contributing towards the formulation of an agreed care plan has required her to work in partnership with the family which has involved undertaking financial and risk assessments (Key Role 4 Unit 12, *Assess and manage risks to individuals, families, carers, groups and communities*) as well as holistic assessments of need. The assessment and care planning role has also provided the student with opportunities to work collaboratively with the multi-disciplinary team (Key Role 5 Units 16 and 17) and to contribute to the final care plan and multi-disciplinary pre-discharge meeting at which monitoring and review arrangements are discussed and agreed.

Critically reflective self-evaluations of the learning outcomes in the application of knowledge, skills and values in these challenging areas of professional practice can provide quality evidence to demonstrate competence in respect of the requirements for Key Roles 2, 3, 4, 5 and 6 and associated Units. Similarly, in relation to the implementation, monitoring and review of the care plan post-discharge, the student can provide a range of evidence of the tasks involved in stages 5, 6 and 7 of the care management process. The opportunity of co-working the Brown case with the community-based social worker following discharge can also enable the student to provide appropriate critical reflection and analysis of the interpersonal and organizational challenges involved in supporting and sustaining the Brown family through the process of change (Key Role 3 Units 10 and 11) as well as the monitoring and review of service provision (Key Role 2 Unit 7, *Support the development of networks to meet assessed needs and planned outcomes*).

Conclusion

Hospital placements present students with a range of personal, professional, organisational and inter-professional challenges as well as confronting them with the distressing consequences of illness and disability. On one level, social work practice in this setting is about managing 'systems' in a competent manner. On another, skilled professional practice is concerned with responding to human need and vulnerability in a sensitive and compassionate way. Effectively integrating these dimensions is the challenge facing the social work student.

The student in the Brown case has responded to a range of challenges at each stage of the care management process and has turned these into opportunities for demonstrating competent practice. Supervision sessions have also enabled her to critically evaluate her work in a challenging yet permissive and supportive environment. Although community care assessments in the hospital setting can be prescriptive and bureaucratic, there is undoubtedly scope for social workers to incorporate more therapeutically oriented approaches into their practice which can provide a compassionate and helping response to vulnerable older people who are experiencing profound ill health.

It may prove instructive for students to recognise that 'competent practice' is indicated only when practice requirements are consistently demonstrated throughout the placement. Professional development is a continuous and cumulative process and competence therefore should not be seen as being 'achieved' at any one point in time, or even over a series of assessment events during placement. Competence 'achieved' is not an absolute indication of ability or 'know how' but should rather be viewed as a new milestone in the overall process of consolidation and professional development. Students on hospital placements committed to undertaking the necessary practice preparations and who consistently and reflectively integrate professional knowledge, skills and values into their work can greatly enhance their potential in demonstrating and maintaining competent social work practice in the health care field.

References

Bywaters, P. (1991) 'Case Finding and Screening for Social Work in Acute General Hospitals.' *British Journal of Social Work 21*, 1, 19–39.

Connor, A. and Tibbitt, J. (1988) *Social Workers and Health Care in Hospital.* Edinburgh: HMSO.

Coulshed, V. and Orme, J. (1998) *Social Work Practice: An Introduction.* Basingstoke: Macmillan.

Department of Health and Social Security (NI) (1990) *People First: Community Care in Northern Ireland for the 1990s.* Belfast: HMSO.

Department of Health (1989) *Caring for People: Community Care in the Next Decade and Beyond,* Cmnd 849. London: HMSO.

Department of Health (1998) *Modernising Social Services: Promoting Independence, Improving Protection, Raising Standards,* Cmd 4169. London: Stationery Office.

Department of Health (2000a) *No Secrets: Guidance on Developing and Implementing Multi-agency Policy and Procedures to Protect Vulnerable Adults.* London: HMSO.

Department of Health (2000b) *The NHS Plan: A Plan for Investment. A Plan for Reform.* London: DoH.

Department of Health (2001) *National Service Framework for Older People.* London: Stationery Office.

Department of Health (2002a) *The Single Assessment Process, Guidance for Local Implementation.* London: DoH.

Department of Health (2002b) *Fair Access to Care Services: Guidance on Eligibility Criteria for Adult Social Care,* local authority circular LAC (2002) 13. London: DoH. Available at: www.doh.gov.uk/scg/facs/lac200213.htm

Department of Health (2002c) *Intermediate Care: Moving Forward.* London: DoH.

Department of Health, Social Services and Public Safety (2003) *Northern Ireland Framework Specification for the Degree in Social Work.* Belfast: DoH, SS and PS.

Doel, M. (2002) 'Task-centred Work.' In R. Adams, L. Dominelli and M. Payne (eds) *Social Work: Themes, Issues and Critical Debates.* 2nd edn. Basingstoke: Palgrave/Open University Press.

Douglas, H. and McColgan, M. (1995) 'Preparation for Contact: An Aid to Effective Intervention.' *Journal of Staff Practice and Development 4,* 1, 53–64.

Egan, G. (2001) *The Skilled Helper: A Problem-Management and Opportunity-Development Approach to Helping,* 7th edn. Pacific Grove: Brooks/Cole Publishing.

Griffiths, R. (1988) *Community Care: Agenda for Action (The Griffiths Report)* . London: HMSO.

Hinds, D.M. (2000) *After Stroke: The Complete Step-by-step Blue Print for Getting Better.* London: Thorsons.

Hill, M. and MacGregor, G. (2001) *Health's Forgotten Partners? How Carers are Supported Through Hospital Discharge.* London: Carers UK.

Hockey, J. and James, A. (1993) *Growing Up and Growing Old: Ageing and Dependency in the Life Course.* London: Sage.

Holiman, D., Dziegielewski, S. and Datta, P. (2001) 'Discharge Planning and Social Work Practice.' *Social Work in Health Care 32,* 3, 1–19.

Holzhausen, E. (2001) '"You Can Take Him Home Now". Carers' Experience of Hospital Discharge.' London: Carers National Association.

Kelson, M. (2000) *Care After Stroke: Information for Patients and their Carers.* London: Royal College of Physicians.

Lymbery, M. (2005) *Care Management and Professional Autonomy: The Impact of Community Care Legislation on Social Work with Older People.* London: Sage.

O'Hagan, K. (1991) 'Crisis Intervention in Social Work.' In J. Lishman (ed.) *Handbook of Theory and Practice for Social Work.* London: Jessica Kingsley Publishers.

Oliver, M. (1996) *Understanding Disability – From Theory to Practice.* Basingstoke: Macmillan.

Payne, M. (1995) *Social Work and Community Care.* Basingstoke: Macmillan.

Phillipson, C. (1998) *Reconstructing Old Age: New Agendas in Social Theory and Practice.* Basingstoke: Macmillan.

Priestly, M. (2003) *Disability: A Life Course Approach.* Oxford: Polity.

Rachman, R. (1995) 'Community Care: Changing the Role of Hospital Social Work.' *Health and Social Care in the Community 3,* 163–172.

Smale, G., Tuson, G., Biehal, N. and Marsh, P. (1993) *Empowerment, Assessment, Care Management and the Skilled Worker.* London: HMSO.

Social Services Inspectorate (1991) *Care Management and Assessment: Practitioner's Guide.* London, DoH SSI/SWSG.

Social Services Inspectorate (1993) *Social Services for Hospital Patients II: The Implications for Community Care.* London: DoH.

Training Organisation for Personal Social Services (2004) *National Occupational Standards.* London: TOPSS.

Wright, S. J. and Arraras, J. I. (2002) *The Psychology of Chronic and Life-Threatening Illness.* Buckingham: Open University Press.

CHAPTER 10

Competence in Working with Families

Dorota Iwaniec

Introduction

Numerous Department of Health publications on requirements of current social-work training emphasise that students should, first, acquire essential knowledge, second, develop skills to transfer that knowledge into competent practice, and to practise in a manner which is fair and respectful to the service user. Values, knowledge and skills, therefore, have to be learnt to achieve competence in practice. Working with children and their families is a challenge to all practitioners, as it requires an accumulation of knowledge about parenting, children's developmental needs and factors associated with the family environment (economic and living conditions, family and child care law, social policies, rules and regulations, availability of resources and multi-disciplinary working, to mention just a few). This chapter will deal with the case of a student who has been given the task of carrying out a comprehensive assessment on a failure-to-thrive (FTT) child, based on the Framework of Assessment (Department of Health (DoH) 2000), incorporating and adhering to National Occupational Standards (NOS). (In Northern Ireland, the Key Roles are interpreted within a Framework Specification document, DHSSPS 2003). The case will be presented briefly from the referral point and taken through the stages of assessment and analysis of information.

Case study

Natasha (two years old) was referred to Social Services by the consultant paediatrician because of failure to thrive and concerns about her wellbeing and general development. It was Natasha's second hospitalisation for growth-failure, and no physical reason was found for her poor growth and development. She looked small for her age and was extremely thin. Her weight was almost continuously under or on the second centile, and her appearance was quite striking. She presented as lethargic, withdrawn, apathetic, pale and sad, and her developmental attainments were poor. Natasha's mother was described as being a bit like her daughter – small, sad, and unconnected with the environment, lacking physical and emotional energy. The father, who was a long-distance lorry-driver, spent little time with his family, and while at home he took care of Natasha and she related to him in a better way. The paediatrician and the GP were concerned about the quality of physical and emotional care provided for Natasha, and especially worried about the ability of her parents to meet her developmental needs. The case was allocated to a final-year student on placement with the child care team.

The knowledge base

This case necessitates learning what constitutes failure to thrive, how it manifests itself, what the indicators are, and when it is considered serious enough for the professionals to get involved. Knowledge-based preparation for assessment is essential, not only for competent investigation but also for ethical reasons. The worker has to know what he/she is looking for, and avoid misjudgement and misinterpretations. Once reasonably familiar with the failure-to-thrive problem the student has to determine how to conduct assessment and to know what methods, frameworks or instruments to use. The knowledge base underpinning appropriate assessment in general is outlined in the NOS (Training Organisation for Personal Social Services (TOPSS) 2004), but more specifically, as applied to failure to thrive, using the DoH *Framework* (Iwaniec 2004; Iwaniec, Sneddon and Allen 2003). The student needs to learn the relevant obligations of the 1989 Children Act, agency regulations and procedures, and to become acquainted with available resources in the area.

As FTT is fundamentally about inadequate growth and development, comprehensive knowledge of child development is imperative. Growth-faltering may have multi-factorial aetiology which needs to be explored in order to devise appropriate intervention. Children may fail to thrive because of:

- illness

- not being given sufficient food

- acute feeding difficulties (including oral-motor dysfunction)

- parent's poor understanding of their child's nutritional and nurturing needs

- neglect, rejection, abuse, parental poverty, mental illness, substance abuse, immaturity, social isolation, or learning disabilities. There is seldom one factor which determines FTT.

FTT is normally diagnosed within the first two years of life, although its effects and consequences can be observed much later. Estimates of prevalence have varied from as many as 10 per cent of the deprived children in out-patient clinics in both urban and rural areas (Skuse, Wolke and Reilly 1992) to 1 per cent of all paediatric hospitalisations. Most children who fail to thrive come into a category of non-organic failure to thrive. They are physically healthy, but their environment and quality of parenting may be inadequate and stressful.

Failure to thrive is generally defined in terms of growth. When children are undernourished they fail to gain weight, and after a while their growth in height also falters. On the growth-chart they drop below the second percentile of weight and height, and can remain there for a long time. The effect of early malnutrition may be extensive, given the rapid period of growth, particularly brain growth, which occurs during the first five years of life (Wynne 1996). If appropriate intervention does not take place at an early stage, failure to thrive may lead to many serious problems including abuse or even death.

Using the Framework of Assessment

The DoH (2000) assessment framework is multi-dimensional, exploring parenting capacity, children's developmental needs, and family and environmental factors. Ecological theory is adopted, postulating that children's development is influenced by the quality and capacity for parenting which, in turn, is influenced by the characteristics of their families, social network, neighbourhoods, communities, and the interrelations among them (Bronfenbrenner, 1993).

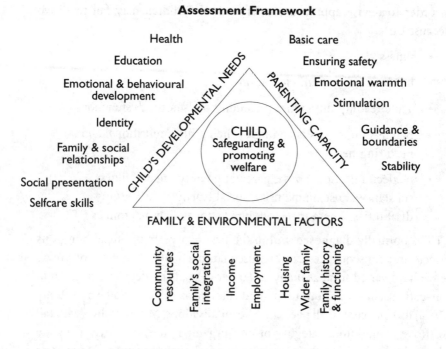

Figure 10.1: Framework of Assessment (Source: Dott 2000)

The philosophy of the new framework aims to redirect assessment focus from the risk and blame culture to the developmental needs of children, and the ways of meeting these needs in the families and communities in which they live. The 'wait-and-see' approach needs to be avoided when dealing with cases where evidence suggests a poor prognosis for change in parenting, e.g. chronic alcohol abuse, mental illness, immaturity, etc., thus promoting quicker decision-making to avoid further deterioration and increase in difficulties which may result in significant harm. Students must become well informed as to what stands in the way of optimal development, addressing each case individually. For example, a child might be developmentally delayed and failing to thrive because of a mother's depression (as illustrated in Natasha's case) which will diminish the mother's energy and drive to interact with and attend to the child's basic needs. Or it could be parental unawareness of such needs, unwittingly impairing the child's potential, but it also might involve neglect due to rejection. The reasons for poor developmental outcomes have to be identified during the assessment stage, so that the right decisions are made for both child and family.

The child has to be seen in the family and community context. A family does not operate in a vacuum; it belongs to a certain community, culture, and social structure that influences behaviour, attitudes, customs and beliefs. The *Framework of Assessment* is, quite rightly, based on ecological theory, taking into consideration all aspects of the child's life in the family context. Ecological perspectives are in tune with the philosophy of social-work education and requirements of TOPSS professional standards.

Skills

The skills required in undertaking comprehensive assessment are numerous and complex. The student has to be able to communicate, listen, ask relevant questions in a simple and easy-to-understand way; to be able to observe and interpret behaviour and interactions within the family; to empathise; to be patient and sensitive to the parents' predicament; to check accuracy as to what the parents have said; to interview in an orderly and prepared way, collecting and presenting the evidence; to write reports; to update files and create new files; to use suitable instruments for data-collection; and to check and discuss emerging issues with the supervisor. A social worker beginning her career working with children and families must learn how to work directly with children using various means appropriate to each case: it is essential to be able to communicate, to encourage and to put a child at ease during interviews in order to elicit the required information so that problems may be identified and resolved. The use of drawings, storytelling, projective techniques or different types of play therapies will be needed to work with children at different developmental stages. Skills in how to measure and interpret developmental attainments by using appropriate developmental charts or protocols for collecting data are essential, as is the ability to observe and analyse the behaviour of the child and its parents. The student has to understand growth-charts (i.e. weight, height, head circumference) and consult with health visitors or GPs on how to interpret a child's growth. Throughout assessment, guidance from supervisors is essential, especially for students and newly qualified workers.

Values

The student must balance the needs and predicaments of both parents and children, but also has to be constantly aware that the welfare of the child is paramount and that advocacy on behalf of the child is part of the protection and ethics of social work practice. Judgements about families should be based on evidence, and not on personal prejudices and first impressions. Listening to what parents are saying and acknowledging and recognising parental difficulties both facilitate mutual problem-solving. Enabling parents to express their fears, worries and concerns, without risk, is crucially important.

   The student at the outset seeks collaborative and open partnership with parents, based on trust and mutual respect. She should understand parental rights and responsibilities, and be able to demonstrate that parental participation is vital in any decision-making. A good working relationship with the family is a key factor for the appropriate outcome, even if the child has to be removed from home. In some instances parental attitudes and behaviour may have to be challenged, even to the point of issuing an ultimatum and carefully explaining the consequences. Natasha's mother did initially realise that she needed help for depression; that it was impacting adversely on her care of Natasha, and that professionals needed to act on Natasha's behalf immediately. Such challenges require sensitivity and skill in enabling the mother to comprehend the gravity of the situation.

National Occupational Standards
Of the six Key Roles in the NOS, 1, 3, 4 and 6 are particularly relevant. The student will attempt to partially fulfil the requirements of each of them in her assessment and work with the family.

Methods, content and process of assessment
Comprehensive assessment is usually based on:

1.   carefully planned semi-structured interviews with parents and children

2.   engagement with children in accordance with age

3.   direct observation of parents and children interaction

4.   observation of living conditions and social milieu

5.   examination of existing files and recording

6.   information from other professionals and agencies knowledgeable about the family.

An important task is to identify parental strengths and limitations, and their capacity, willingness and ability to work towards identified goals. Resources and support-systems also need to be identified. The student will be guided by the *Framework Assessment* (DoH 2000). She will be supervised and helped in preparation, and such preparation will be considerably enhanced if she has had the opportunity to watch her supervisor conduct an assessment. She should anticipate the possibility of a difficult interview, due to a parent's defensiveness, aggression, reluctance to talk, refusal to get engaged or fear of being judged as bad or incompetent (or both). Demonstrative respect, plain speaking, honesty and warmth, however, can reduce tensions and improve co-operation considerably.

Competences required during the initial stage of assessment

First contact and interview is crucially important. This case has been referred by a GP and a paediatrician, and the student may say something like:

> Your GP and Dr Green, the paediatrician, asked me to see you. Dr Green was a bit worried about Natasha's low weight (which has been observed for a long time), poor speech and the fact that she has only now started to walk. It would appear that Natasha needs to do a bit of catching up with talking, walking, playing, and putting on weight by eating more. Before we can do anything to help you both I need to see you three or four times to find out more of what these problems are, and then discuss with you what will be the best way of helping Natasha and you. You may want to tell me about other things bothering you as well.

The student expands on the reasons for the referral, on why assessment is taking place, how it is going to be conducted, what information will be required, how the information is going to be obtained and from whom, and what is going to happen at the end of the assessment.

The student should ask to be introduced to Natasha, should chat and play with her for a few minutes, should have a general warming-up conversation with the parents, and then should ask the parents what are their major worries and concerns, encouraging them to express themselves in their own way. It is advisable to make a list of the stated problems and issues, prioritising them according to parental perception as to what are the most difficult areas to cope with. Listed problems should be defined and clarified at this stage. Since the referral expresses concerns about Natasha, and both parents are anxious to hear about them, an initial interview should focus on her. The following problems were identified. Natasha presented:

- some eating problems, faddiness, refusal to eat, lack of interest in food, and unpredictability in showing hunger
- frequent appearances of withdrawal and lack of desire to engage in any activities
- tendencies to excessive sleeping
- stubbornness and irritability.

Eating problems were identified as most worrying, and the parents associated them with poor weight-gain and withdrawn or irritable behaviour. They were not able to see that limited and poor quality interaction, as well as lack of attention to nutritional and nurturing needs, also triggered reasons for Natasha's failure to thrive. The student should examine in depth Natasha's physical and nutritional care and the quality of parent-child interaction, emotional care, safety, and stimulation. In other words the student has to assess parenting capacity as stated in the *Framework of Assessment* (DoH 2000), remembering to take the child's age into consideration.

Parenting capacity

The checklist in Table 10.1 (Iwaniec 2004) can be used to assess physical and nutritional care of the child. It rates the quality of basic care provided for the child based on direct observation, food-intake recording and interview data. The higher the score, the greater the cause for concern for the child's welfare.

Assessing emotional care of a child

A child needs physical and emotional care in order to develop healthily and normally. The absence of such care can bring about anxiety, fretting and disruption of biological functions in the child. Infants and small children deprived of warmth, parental care and lack of responsiveness to their emotional needs may develop profound depression or acute withdrawal with subsequent lack of appetite, loss of weight and serious developmental delays (Iwaniec 1995, 2004). Some parents of FTT children are unable to tune into their children's emotional needs for various reasons. In the case of

Table 10.1: The quality of nutritional and physical care of a child

Section A	Most of the time (1)	Sometimes (2)	Not very often (3)
Nutrition			
Is the child regularly fed?			
Is the child given enough food for their age?			
Is the child being picked up when fed?			
Is the child encouraged to eat by being prompted and praised?			
Is food presented in an appetising way?			
Is the food suitable for the child's age?			
Are the signals of hunger or satiation properly interpreted?			
Is the manner of feeding comfortable and anxiety free?			
Is there availability of food?			
Is the child handled patiently during feeding/eating?			
Is the child encouraged to eat?			
Is there reasonable flexibility in feeding/eating routine?			
Physical care			
Is there awareness of child being too thin, small or unwell?			
Is the child's medical care being seen to, such as: medical examinations, vaccination, eye and hearing tests etc.?			

Continued on next page

Table 10.1 continued

Section A	Most of the time (1)	Sometimes (2)	Not very often (3)
Is medical advice sought when the child is unwell?			
Is there recognition and concern about the child's wellbeing?			
Is the child appropriately dressed for the weather?			
Is the child changed and clean?			
Are medical or other health or welfare agency appointments being kept?			
Do the parents administer required medication for the child?			
Is the safety of the child observed?			
Is the child supervised and guided?			
Is the child protected from a smoking environment and other unhealthy substances?			
Total for Section A			

Source: Iwaniec, D. (2004)

Natasha, her mother had post-natal depression, which was not fully assessed or treated at the time, and which almost certainly adversely impacted on the general care of Natasha. The quality of emotional care is often revealed in direct observation. Interviews with parents can verify what one is observing, and provide explanation for it. Table 10.3 provides a useful framework for exploring emotional care.

Parent-child relationship and interaction

Equally important is assessment of the parent-child interaction, which, as a rule, will provide information as to what kind of relationship parents might have with their child. The quality of interaction of FTT children and their

Table 10.2: Parental attitudes and behaviour regarding feeding and food

Section B	Most of the time (3)	Sometimes (2)	Not very often (1)
Does the caregiver appear angry during the feeding/eating period?			
Is there evidence of frustration during the feeding/eating period?			
Is the child punished for not eating?			
Is food withheld as a means of punishment?			
Does the caregiver restrict the child's intake of food to prevent possible obesity?			
Does the caregiver restrict the child's intake of food and variety of food due to fabricated illnesses, allergies, etc.?			
Are the caregiver's attitudes to food and eating negative (e.g. dislike of food, preoccupied with healthy food, strictly vegetarian or vegan?)			
Has the caregiver shown tendencies to anorexia, bulimia or other eating problems?			
Total for Section B			

Source: Iwaniec, D. (2004)

parents tends to be poor, infrequent, and of short duration. Some FTT children appear to be nervous and apprehensive when in the parents' company, which indicates painful and anxiety-provoking interaction and poor relationship. Tables 10.4 and 10.5 enable workers to explore these crucial matters.

Table 10.3: Emotional care

Emotional needs	Some defining criteria
Affection	Physical contact, praise, touching, holding, comforting, making allowances, being tender, showing concern, communicating
Security	Continuity of care, predictable environment, consistent controls, settled patterns of care and daily routines, fair and understandable rules, harmonious family relationships
Responsibility	Discipline appropriate to the child's stage of development, providing a model to emulate/imitate, indicating limits, insisting on concern for others
Independence	Providing opportunities for child to act and decide independently, in accordance with age and ability
Responsiveness	Prompt, consistent, appropriate actions to meet the child's needs
Stimulation	Encouraging curiosity and exploratory behaviour, by praising, by responding to questions and play, by promoting training/educational opportunities and new experiences

Source: Iwaniec, Herbert and Sluckin (2002)

Ensuring safety

Failure to thrive may be the consequence of chronic neglect, or physical or emotional abuse. This is more likely when FTT has persisted over a long time, and social work and medical intervention have not produced the desired change. A vicious circle can take root in which the short stature and psychosocial underdevelopment of the FTT child can lead to rejection and further neglect. The child may be intentionally deprived of food as a punishment, or beaten at the slightest provocation. Older children may attempt self-harm, with knives or sharp objects, or they may eat non-food items, which can upset or harm the digestive system. The student has to be alert to all possibilities, including fabrication of illnesses, or active inducement of illness (e.g. giving a child a laxative to induce diarrhoea). Alternatively, the student must ensure she does not rush to unfair conclusions.

Stimulation

FTT children often have developmental delays which indicate poor stimulation and socialisation. The parent–child interaction check list will help to

Table 10.4: Interaction between caregiver(s) and child

Father's/mother's reactive and proactive behaviour	Often	Seldom	Almost never
Are the parents:			
talking to the child?			
looking at the child?			
smiling at the child?			
making eye contact (loving)?			
touching (gently)?			
holding (closely, lovingly)?			
playing?			
cuddling?			
kissing?			
sitting the child on the lap?			
handling the child in a gentle way?			
giving requests (as opposed to commands)?			
helping the child if it is in difficulties?			
encouraging the child to participate in play and other activities?			
being concerned about the child?			
picking the child up when it cries or when it is hurt?			
answering the child's questions?			
not ignoring the child's presence?			
emotionally treating the child the same as other children?			
handling children consistently?			

Source: Iwaniec, D. (1995)

elicit information about frequency and intensity of parental involvement. Natasha, for example, was seldom picked up, spoken to or played with. She spent a lot of time in social isolation, which impeded her psycho-motor

Table 10.5: Interaction between child and caregiver(s)

Child's reactive and proactive behaviour	Often	Seldom	Almost never
Is the child:			
playing freely?			
laughing/smiling?			
running?			
talking freely?			
coming for help?			
coming for comfort?			
cuddling up to mother/father?			
responding to affection?			
responding to attention?			
at ease when he/she is near the child?			
joining in activities with other children?			
not frightened when approached, or corrected by mother/father?			
eating/feeding satisfactorily?			
asking for food – indicating hunger?			
at ease during feeding/eating time?			

Source: Iwaniec, D. (2004)

development. The student observed that her mother's interactions with her were usually silent, and limited to occasional bathing, changing and feeding.

Assessing a child's developmental needs

From birth, infants can signal information about their needs. When parents perceive the signals accurately and respond emotionally appropriately, the child is more likely to develop normally. Trust, confidence and security will be enhanced by these emotional interactions, and crucial attachments will take root. In a well-functioning attachment-system the caregiver is sensitive and emotionally and psychologically available to give comfort, support and contact as well as opportunities for environmental exploration. The opposite experience will induce a sense of anxiety and insecurity, with children lacking confidence in their carers' ability to respond to them, unconfident about their world in general. The total dependency of infants makes them vulnerable and fragile. When their basic needs are not met, their physical, cognitive and emotional development is quite likely to be arrested, and they often present distorted attachment-behaviour. Research on attachment of FTT children to their mothers suggests that a considerable number of children are insecurely attached (Crittenden 1990; Ward, Lee and Lipper 2000; Iwaniec 2004). The ability of such children to form meaningful and warm relationships with peers will be adversely affected (Iwaniec 2000).

Assessment of children's attachment to their parents is a very important task that the student must undertake. There are many check lists and protocols that may be used as a guide. Table 10.6 provides an example of attachment classification, carer's behaviour and the effect on a child (Iwaniec 2004).

Child health

FTT can be caused by physical illness. Natasha was admitted twice to hospital, but no organic cause was found for her poor growth. (Only 5 per cent of children fail to thrive because of illness, which can be exacerbated by problematic parenting.) Natasha consistently remained under the second percentile in weight, height and head-circumference, and her wellbeing was causing concern. At the stage of psychosocial assessment the student must obtain information regarding the child's growth from the GP, health visitor or hospital (if the child was seen by the paediatrician) to learn as many facts as possible.

Feeding/eating

The most common factor in FTT is the feeding/eating behaviour of children and parental interaction during the management of the feeding process. Sustained feeding difficulties can lead to serious under-nutrition and problematic parent-child interaction. Additionally, early feeding and caring difficulties can disrupt the formation of a secure attachment of children to parents and bonding of parents to children.

During the assessment, attention should be given to the following: asking parents to record daily intake of food for a week; observing two to three feeding times – videotaping each session if possible. Parent-child

Table 10.6: Types of attachments, parental behaviour and child's reactions (outcomes)

Types of attachments	Carer's behaviour	Effect on child's developmental outcomes
Securely attached children	Sensitive; responsive to signals of distress; warm, reassuring; supportive; encouraging; patient; comforting; available; concerned; engaging; protective	Self-confident; high self-esteem; social leaders; empathic; popular; show good developmental attainments; open; trustful; sociable; skilful in interacting with others; adaptable; mature; emotionally stable; friendly
Avoidant/anxious	Hostile; rejective; critical; persistent rebuffing; unsupportive; unresponsive to signals of distress; uncommunicative; avoiding physical contact with a child	Unselective attachment; treats parents and strangers alike; over-friendly with strangers; poor self-confidence; poor concentration span; disruptive; destructive; developmentally delayed; difficulty in building relationships with peers; attention-seeking
Anxious/ambivalent	Neglectful; unsupportive; disorganised; insensitive; dismissing; chaotic	Apprehensive; confused; passive; detached; withdrawn; developmentally retarded; poor self-confidence; chronic doubts; poor socialisations
Disorganised/ disoriented	Unpredictable; frightening; frightened; changeable; secretive	Confusion; anxiety; undirected expression of fear and distress; dazed or disoriented facial expression; emotional and thought conflicts; disorganised behaviour; apprehension

Source: Iwaniec, D. (2004)

interaction should also be observed to determine parental feeding-styles and the child's reactions, and the amount of food and types of food consumed.

Table 10.7 describes different parental feeding styles and children's reactions to feeding (Iwaniec 2003).

Developmental delays

The child's early experiences can have long-lasting effects on its later development. FTT children reveal poor developmental outcomes, particularly for mental abilities (Reif *et al.* 1995). Nearly all of a child's brain-growth and synoptic connections occur by the age of two, but if the protein and calories are not present to support that growth it cannot occur (Iwaniec and Sneddon 2002). Corbett, Drewett and Wright (1996) found that even in relatively mild FTT there are long-term adverse cognitive deficits. IQ can be reduced by 10–20 points, which is reversible if positive changes occur in the child's life or if appropriate intervention and treatment takes place.

Family and environmental factors

Comprehensive assessment must consider the family and its environment as a whole. This includes

- parental history and upbringing
- current social life and integration within the community
- education
- economic factors like income and employment
- availability of child care facilities and other resources.

Parental history and functioning

Stress is common within FTT families. It may be caused by parental illness, divorce, separation, depression, conflict between parents, social isolation and lack of support. Parent's childhood experiences are often reflected in their child-rearing practices. The student's exploration revealed that Natasha's mother had been emotionally abused by her parents; she felt rejected all her life. She lacked self-confidence and her self-esteem was low. She demonstrated little affection and engagement with Natasha. In contrast, Natasha' father had had a loving childhood. He maintained contact with his parents and siblings. It became increasingly obvious to the student

Table 10.7: Interactions between child and carer during feeding

Carer's feeding style	Behaviour of carer	Reaction of child
Forceful, impatient and angry	Rushing child to eat, getting frustrated and angry, screaming, shaking, smacking, frequent force-feeding, anxious	Refusal to eat, crying, choking, vomiting, stretching out, fearful and apprehensive, uneasy when in the carer's company. Little intake of food
Unconcerned and neglectful	Failure to respond to child's signal of hunger and distress. Fed irregularly and in a haphazard way. Not appropriate food given. Seldom picked up when fed	Lethargic, withdrawn, sleeps a lot. Little movement, seldom heard. Looking detached and sad. Little intake of food.
Not persistent and passive	React to stress with high anxiety. Tend to get depressed and helpless. Low self-esteem. Give up easily, unable to cope and to exert authority	Strong-willed, persistent, irritable, getting their own way, manipulating, miserable. Persistent refusal to eat, to swallow and chew. Little intake of food
Determined and coaxing	Preoccupied with feeding. Generally resourceful, patient, try different ways to manage, try different food. Anxious about child's poor growth	Long feeding periods, faddiness, spitting, storing food in mouth, heaving, refusal to chew. Stubborn and difficult to distract. Little intake of food
Preoccupied with weight, restrictive of food intake	Restricting intake of food, putting child on low calorie diet. Diluting formula to prevent weight acceleration. Anxious about excessive weight gain	Child appears to be always hungry, looking thin and undernourished. There are no eating problems as such. Food is simply not available. Little intake of food

Source: Iwaniec, D. (2003)

that the parents' contrasting responses to Natasha mirrored their very different upbringings, attitudes and parenting skills. Natasha's father worked full-time and was seldom at home. He was not fully aware of the developing crisis, and reasoned that whatever problems his wife was having were temporary, and due to Natasha being a particularly difficult child. The parents quarrelled on this matter, and relationships became very strained. There were quarrels and disputes between the parents as to how to handle the child, and this seriously affected the couple's relationship.

Summary of data analysis deriving from assessment

Once the assessment is completed the student has to analyse the data, draw conclusions and make suitable recommendations. The results of assessment have to be discussed with the parents in a manner which is not anxiety-provoking, but looks for solutions. The conclusions are:

- The quality of physical and emotional care of Natasha was poor, leading to failure to thrive.

- Post-natal depression had been an earlier contributory factor. Mother was then unaware of Natasha's emotional needs, and unable to respond emotionally appropriately. Nutritional provision and feeding of child was inadequate, and the consequential reactions of child (unable or unwilling to eat) wrongly interpreted by mother.

- There was social isolation, and a reluctance to ask for help because it was feared that Natasha might be taken into care.

- Father's long absences precluded him gaining sufficient understanding of the problem, and contributing to its solution.

Attaining National Occupational Standards

The application of assessment tools and frameworks contributes towards fulfilling NOS requirements. This final section of the chapter provides brief extracts from a student's evidence.

STUDENT NOTES

Key Role 1

The three Units of the first Key Role are:

1.   *Prepare for social work contact and involvement.*

2. *Work with individuals, families, groups and communities to help them to make informed decisions.*

3. *Assess needs and options to recommend a course of action.*

I (i) did extensive preparatory work before seeing the family; (ii) read several papers on FTT and discussed it with my supervisor; (iii) studied comprehensive assessment (DoH 2000), relevant sections of the Children Act 1989 and the agency's child-protection manual; (iv) prepared evidence-based check lists and questionnaires; (v) encouraged the parents to participate in and collaborate with the assessment process; (vi) represented their views, fears, needs and circumstances; (vii) observed my supervisor doing assessments; (viii) role played the task in college; (ix) consulted with colleagues and other professionals; (x) used the supervisory process extensively; (xi) upheld social work values and ethics.

Preparation of various check-lists and questionnaires was of immense value to both parents and myself. It focused their attention and stimulated worthwhile discussion about children's needs, positive parenting, and what stands in the way of bringing up children. I shared the results with both parents after discussing my analysis with the supervisor. I believe I have done so in a way which was respectful, not judgemental, and honest. I engaged them in the discussion of planning intervention in a collaborative way. I also found it helpful liaising with the health visitor and dietician regarding assessing nutritional and health issues and visiting the local Family Centre to see how staff work with children like Natasha. I believe I have carried out a comprehensive assessment competently in a manner which promotes social work values and ethics.

Key Role 3 (Units 10 and 11)

Support individuals to represent their needs, views, and circumstances.

Research, supervision and continuous study convinced me that comprehensive assessment of FTT children could be anxiety-provoking for the parents and inhibit them from expressing themselves and their needs. The mother's illness and the father's long absences from home exacerbated this problem. The primary objective at all times was to identify risk factors in the child's home environment without creating fear and anxiety or assuming that there was deliberate neglect. Mother appeared guarded in her responses, and often responded monosyllabically. However, I believe I succeeded in substantially minimising her fear and distrust, and she became open and co-operative, shedding a great deal of light on why Natasha was failing to thrive. I shared the assessment with the parents at all stages, and facilitated their realisation that both Natasha and they needed help. I explored the parents' backgrounds and their present relationships in respect of their caring for Natasha. I was especially sensitive about the risk of undermining mother's morale further, and sought to highlight her many strengths. After numerous joint and separate interviews, mother agreed to be helped by psychiatric services, to get involved with the locality's mother's group, and to have some personal counselling to address her childhood history. I supported the father in making an application for a change of job, so he could spend more time with his family.

Key Role 4

Management of risk to individuals, families, carers, groups, communities, self and others.
This case was heavily risk-laden: risk to Natasha, risk of parents losing their child, risk of a marriage disintegrating, risk of me exacerbating the problem. In retrospect I believe that I carried out the assessment in a way which minimised these risks but, simultaneously, enabled the parents to accept that Natasha urgently needed help. In addition to the numerous instruments of assessment that I was using (Tables 10.1–7), the parents provided important information upon which competent decision-making could be made, including whether or not to convene a case conference, which may have decided on registering Natasha 'at risk'.

Key Role 6

Demonstration of professional competence in practice
I believe I demonstrated professional competence in applying skills and social work values. I have re-examined all aspects of my preparation for assessment (see extracts from Key Role 1 above). I used my supervisor's knowledge, experience, and support to evaluate my assessment findings (Unit 18.2), and valued being instructed and directed to relevant areas of study to enhance my knowledge and confidence when dealing with similar cases in the future (Unit 18.2a,b,c,d). I increasingly realised the importance of the requirement Unit 18.2a and b: they necessitate the identification of (a) sources of knowledge that can inform best practice and (b) areas of practice that require more in-depth and up-to-date knowledge. This dis-

cernment of knowledge was instrumental in precluding precipitate conclusions or blaming either parent for Natasha's FTT (O'Hagan and Dillenburger 1995). It also fulfilled certain requirements relating to social work values and ethics, encouraging rigorous analysis, objectivity and self-reflection.

Supporting evidence of competence

There is ample evidence that an assessment of Natasha was carried out competently and ethically. The student supervisor observed two sessions and discussed each part of the assessment with the student. She also checked the suitability of assessment instruments and discussed available literature during supervision sessions. The student was instructed in how to take notes during the actual assessment process, check its accuracy with the parents, and then write a substantial report backed up by empirical evidence.

Conclusion

Competence-led assessment should be based on 1. knowledge, 2. skills, 3. values and ethics. This chapter gives some indication of the scope and challenge of each of these constituents in effective assessment. The challenges in each of them are formidable. Comprehensive assessment should be seen as a key aspect of social work intervention, because its outcomes determine action for good or ill for the child and family as a whole. The methods, processes, instruments and social work skills necessary for comprehensive assessment are fully supported by the requirements of the National Occupational Standards. Indeed, comprehensive assessment, successfully carried out, will fulfil many of these requirements, and make a valuable contribution towards the student attaining the standards as a whole.

References

Bronfenbrenner, U. (1993) *Parenting – An Ecological Perspective.* Hillsdale, NY, and London: Erlbaum Associates.

Corbett, S.S., Drewett, R.F. and Wright, C.M. (1996) 'Does a Fall Down a Centile Chart Matter? The Growth and Developmental Sequelae of Mild Failure to Thrive.' *Acta Paediatrica 85*, 1278–1283.

Crittenden, P.M. (1990) 'Internal Representational Models of Attachment Relationships.' *Infant Mental Health Journal 11*, 3, 259–277.

Department of Health (2000) *Framework of Assessment of Children in Need and their Families.* London: HMSO.

Department of Health, Social Services and Public Safety (2003) *Northern Ireland Framework Specification for the Degree in Social Work.* Belfast: DHSSPS.

Iwaniec, D. (1995) *The Emotionally Abused and Neglected Child: Identification, Assessment, and Intervention.* Chichester: John Wiley & Sons.

Iwaniec, D. (2000) 'From Childhood to Adulthood: A 20-year Follow-up Study of Children who Failed to Thrive.' In D. Iwaniec & M. Hill (eds) *Child Welfare Policy and Practice: Current Issues Emerging from Child Care Research.* London: Jessica Kingsley Publications.

Iwaniec, D. (2003) 'A Framework for Assessing Failure-to-thrive.' In M.C. Calder and S. Hackett (eds.) *Assessment in Child Care – Using and Developing Frameworks for Practice.* Lyme Regis: Russell House Publishing.

Iwaniec, D. (2004) *Children Who Fail to Thrive.* Chichester: John Wiley & Sons.

Iwaniec, D. and Sneddon, H. (2002) 'The Quality of Parenting of Individuals who had Failed to Thrive as Children.' *The British Journal of Social Work 32, 3, 283–298.*

Iwaniec, D., Herbert, M. and Sluckin, A. (2002) 'Helping Emotionally Abused and Neglected Children and Abusive Carers.' In K. Browne, H. Hanks, P. Stratton and C. Hamilton (eds) *Early Prediction and Prevention of Child Abuse: A Handbook.* Chichester: John Wiley & Sons.

Iwaniec, D., Sneddon, H. and Allen, S. (2003) 'The Outcomes of a Longitudinal Study of Non-organic Failure to Thrive.' *Child Abuse Review 12, 216–226.*

O'Hagan, K. and Dillenburger, K. (1995) *The Abuse of Women Within Child Care Work.* Buckingham: Open University Press.

Reif, S., Beler, B., Villa, Y. and Spirer, L. (1995) 'Long-term Follow-up and Outcome of Infants with Non-organic Failure to Thrive.' *Israel Journal of Medical Sciences 31, 8, 483–489.*

Skuse, D., Wolke, D. and Reilly, S. (1992) 'Failure to Thrive: Clinical and Developmental Aspects.' In H. Remschmidt and M.H. Schmidt (eds) *Developmental Psychopathology.* Lewiston, NY: Hagrefe & Huber.

Training Organisation for Personal Social Services (2004) *National Occupational Standards.* London: TOPSS.

Ward, M.J., Lee, S.S. and Lipper, E.G. (2000) 'Failure to Thrive is Associated with Disorganised Infant-mother Attachment and Unresolved Maternal Attachment.' *Infant Mental Health Journal 21, 6, 428–442.*

Wynne, J. (1996) 'Failure to Thrive – An Introduction.' *Child: Care, Health and Development 22, 4, 219–221.*

CHAPTER 11

Competence in Mental Health Social Work

Jim Campbell

Introduction

Working in the field of mental health offers many challenging, yet rewarding, opportunities for social work students. As other chapters in this book
have discussed with reference to different client groups, it is an area of practice which is constantly being shaped by often competing social, political
and legal discourses. The last decade has witnessed many changes to the
contextual background of mental health social work, including substantial
shifts from institutional to community based forms of care and treatment;
more serious acknowledgement of the rights of service users and carers by
professionals; attempts by policymakers to make services more joined
up and flexible (Department of Health (DoH)1990, 1999, 2006) and the
review and reform of mental health law in each of the jurisdictions of the
United Kingdom. The six Key Roles described in the National Occupational Standards (NOS) for social work need to be understood with these
contexts in mind. The following chapter describes and analyses how a
Bachelor in Social Work (BSW) level 3 student social worker deals with a
new referral and engages with a family over a three-month period. This
account will be supported by reference to literature on knowledge, skills
and values. In the concluding section of the chapter you will read about how
the student reflected upon her use of NOS key roles and units in a way
which does not lose sight of the complexity, personal anxiety and human
fragility which often characterises interactions in this field (Golightly
2006).

Case study

The student is one month into her first placement and has managed to settle well into a newly formed community mental health team (CMHT) which consists of her supervisor (a senior social worker) three community psychiatric nurses (CPNs), an occupational therapist (OT) and a part-time psychiatrist. Previously she has carried out some relatively uncomplicated assessments with clients. Her supervisor feels that she is now ready to become involved in a more complex work. The team have received a written referral from the local psychiatric hospital. The referrer, a hospital social worker, provides the following information:

Shauna Jackman (33) and her cohabitee John Burnside (35) live in a local authority terrace in a run-down inner city area covered by the CMHT. She has a teenage daughter, Patricia (14) from a previous marriage. Shauna has a long history of mental disorder which began with an acute psychotic episode following the birth of Patricia. Since then she has had numerous admissions to psychiatric hospital, over half of which have been on a compulsory basis. The original diagnosis of schizophrenia has been occasionally questioned by psychiatrists, but remains. For the last five years Shauna has received visits from her community psychiatric nurse (CPN) who administers a long-acting depot injection, designed to counteract delusional thoughts of persecution, and to monitor the use of oral tranquillisers. Her situation is reviewed by psychiatrists at an outpatient clinic on a monthly basis. John, who has a low-paid cleaning job, struggles to hold the family together, particularly at times of crisis when Shauna's mental state deteriorates. He has a caring relationship with Patricia but feels guilty that he cannot provide her with enough money to meet her needs as a teenager. There is little support from any extended family. Last week Shauna was discharged from psychiatric hospital after another compulsory admission. The admission followed a period when she became increasingly disturbed, expressing suicidal thoughts and believing that persons unknown were constantly watching her. Hospital staff feel that a social worker should be involved to ensure follow-up care as well as an assessment of the family current circumstances.

Preparing to visit the family

The student is initially concerned about her capacity to work with Shauna and her family. She has had limited teaching on mental health social work;

this is the first time she is facing someone who has a serious mental illness and who is at apparently at risk. She must consider the depth of the client's human distress and its impact on the worker's awareness of 'self' (Bower 2005). Professionals often use exclusionary knowledge and discourses (O'Hagan 1996; Rogers and Pilgrim 2005, pp.122–3) to avoid thinking about the possibility that they themselves are vulnerable to stress and mental ill-health. This in turn can adversely affect the quality of the helping relationship. The student begins her preparation by thinking through her worries: what she will find when she makes her first home visit; will Shauna continue to have bizarre, delusional thoughts and what does this mean in terms of risk? How does she manage the needs of her client Shauna whilst dealing with any problems which John and Patricia might have? Her supervisor encourages her to gather further information from the referrer, and research literature on helping people with mental health problems in general, and schizophrenia in particular.

Although the student is apprehensive about starting these tasks, she is reassured by a telephone call she has with the referral agent. He tells her that Shauna has recovered well from her latest crisis, is coping at home, but needs support to prevent a relapse. He explains that Shauna has never engaged in any dangerous behaviour towards others, it is just that when she becomes unwell she 'loses contact with reality', stops eating and drinking and finds it hard to deal with everyday activities. There is a predictable pattern which begins with disorder of thought and gradual loss of interest, leading to ideas of suicide.

Psychiatric discourses tend to be underpinned by medical terminology and assumptions about the predictive quality of the science. It is very important that the student is aware of the predominance of this view and its position in the mental health system. They will find themselves using the medical model because it provides a convenient epistemology which supports practice judgements and establishes them as part of the multidisciplinary team (Pritchard 2006; Tilbury 1993). The student, however, becomes aware of the possibility that too close an attachment to this perspective may lead to a simplistic assessment of Shauna's social and mental health problems. The reason for her involvement is to bring a social work perspective to the situation, one which borrows from a range of academic disciplines. The medical model is a significant, but not comprehensive, guide to understanding disturbed mental states, and alternatives to this approach should become part of the student's practice repertoire (Bentall

2003). Rogers and Pilgrim (2005) argue that we need to use sociological and psychological theories to deconstruct common sense views on mental illness and health. The student therefore begins to consider whether at least some aspects of Shauna's thoughts, feelings and behaviour are conditioned by the role of 'being a patient', or perhaps it could be that the way she acts is socially learned (Sutton 1994). Finally, she has read that there are a range of discourses supported by service users which are increasingly challenging conventional views on mental health, highlighting what has become known as the 'recovery model' (Wallcraft 2005). The recovery model challenges the assumption that service users are not well equipped to understand their own mental health or are unable to deliver services for themselves. What many 'experts by experience' want is to have their views of care and treatment to be valued and to have more control of mental health services (Read and Reynolds 1996). Shauna and her family may well have suffered many losses as a result of her mental health problems, including the impoverishment of social and personal relationships, but the student realises that she should refrain from making generalised assumptions about this family's experience of mental illness. A critical awareness of these social contexts will be invaluable for her as she prepares for her first visit. As a way of 'tuning in' to the needs of the family members, the student has made the following notes about issues she will have to deal with.

STUDENT NOTES

SHAUNA:

- Can she talk of her experiences of breakdown and compulsory admission to hospital?

- Can she be allowed to express her feelings about loss of role as a wife and mother?

- What are the effects of stigma on her identity and personal confidence?

- What are the risk factors which will need to be recognised?

JOHN:

- Can he express anger about the role and expectations of caring for the family?

- Has he had an opportunity to talk about losses in his life?
- Are his views different to those of Shauna?

PATRICIA:

- In what way has her childhood and adolescence been affected by the disruption?
- Has she been given appropriate care and support?
- Are her social networks adequate?

Making contact

The student is conscious of the need to adhere to a sound value base. Mental health professionals are now required to listen to the views of service users and carers (Braye 2000; Ramsey *et al.* 2001). The student should avoid reinforcing or replicating poor experiences Shauna may have had in previous contacts with mental health services. For example her recent detention in hospital may well have damaged her self-esteem and trust of professionals. There is a real possibility that she will perceive anyone associated with mental health services as a sinister, controlling threat to her personal freedom and the wellbeing of her family.

The manner in which the first contact is carried out may influence the outcome of any interventions. It is imperative therefore, that the client knows why, and for what reasons, they are being contacted and who the person is who will be visiting them. A well-planned and thoughtful approach which respects the client's rights will often enhance future relationships. The student has been advised to write to Shauna to help her understand the purpose of the intervention and give her the opportunity to accept or reject the help that is being offered. The student has constructed the following introductory letter in language which is, she hopes, uncomplicated and understandable.

Dear Ms Jackman

I am a student social worker based with the community mental health team in London Road. My work address is on the top of this letter along with my telephone number. I am writing to you because your hospital social worker, Mr Smith, has asked me to call with you to see if there is anything I can do to help now that you have returned home. If you think it is suitable I can call on you next

Friday at 2.00pm, then we can talk about ways in which I might be able to help you and your family. If you would prefer to meet me in my office that can be arranged, or if you do not wish me to visit, or you want more information, you can contact me either by telephone or letter.

Yours sincerely

Three days later, Shauna's partner John telephones to say they are glad that someone is visiting. He is worried that a relapse will occur if they do not receive support. This is a relief to the student – she remembers from last year's teaching that clients who are accepting of social work interventions will be easier to engage – but feels rather uneasy because it was John and not Shauna who contacted her. Dealing with the conflicting needs of service users and their carers is not uncommon in the field of adult services (Braye and Preston-Shoot 1995). She hopes that offering to visit Shauna's home and speak directly to her in the first interview will make it feel more secure and less threatening for the client.

Preparing the groundwork

Research suggests that an effective therapeutic milieu between professionals and clients is a good precursor to positive outcomes (Rippon 2005). An empathic approach which communicates a caring and committed style will lay the foundation for future work, particularly in helping the family to re-establish their lives following the hospital discharge. Because of the debilitating nature of schizophrenia – often including disorders of thought or negative symptoms of reduced motivation and loss of affect – there is a need to move at Shauna's pace and engage the family in managing levels of harmful stress (Leff and Vaughan 1998). She may have had bad experiences in communication with professionals in the past, and her capacity to under-stand the student's role may be limited by her disturbed mental state and/or the side effects of psychotropic medication. The student, therefore, intends to describe the purpose of her involvement in language which is nonthreat-ening, jargon-free and which makes sense to the client. She is keen to demonstrate empathy through the use of skills in active listening and clari-fying. These skills can also be used to communicate with various parts of the family system (Dallos and Boswell 1993).

First meeting

The student visits the couple when Patricia is at school. Her anxieties slowly dissipate as she begins to make sense of the situation. Fears that Shauna may somehow be out of touch with reality and at risk are misplaced. Although her speech is slowed down and there is a passivity about her manner and presentation, she provides the student with important information about her life and aspirations. She talks about her worries if and when the voices return – they usually tell her that she is a bad mother and that she has let everyone down. She stresses that she wants to do her best for her family and to live a normal life. She knows that taking her prescribed medication is important in keeping her well, but the side effects – dry mouth, loss of libido, difficulty in mixing in the community – often get her down and sometimes make her life a misery. The student listens carefully, resisting the temptation to fill the space when there are occasional silences – the use of non-verbal cues to actively listen to service users at the early stage of the intervention is a key skill which cannot be underestimated.

John is asked to explain how the student might be able to help. He loves his partner but has become increasingly frustrated with the lack of support by mental health services: it needs a crisis before anyone responds, and then it's too late, the family are once again disrupted, because Shauna is hospitalised. This resonates with the student's reading about mental health services being underfunded and poorly delivered. This often implies that the service user's basic need of consistent, reliable access to professionals in whom she trusts cannot be fulfilled.

This first meeting enlightens the student on the complex nature of serious mental illnesses. Neurological processes are affecting the way Shauna presents herself to the world. Sometimes she seems to lose concentration and the manner in which she explains things has a disjointed feel about it. Yet there remains a warmth and insight about the way her family understand the challenges they face, which is both a source of relief and encouragement to the student. The student believes that social and psychological processes also need to be considered. Herein lies the potential for her to make a difference to the lives of these people. In her report to her supervisor she highlights the following issues, based on this first assessment:

1. Shauna needs more time to talk about her experiences and worries about becoming so ill that she needs hospitalisation.

2. She feels that she lacks the drive to socialise and her lifestyle is limited because of impoverished social networks.

3. She worries about the effect that her mental health problems have on her family.

4. John needs help and support in caring for his partner and stepdaughter.

5. Patricia's views need to be sought.

6. It is important to engage with other relevant professions to ensure a consistent and safe service.

Planning and delivering services

Having established a working relationship, the student needs to demonstrate that she can deliver services which match the needs of her clients. Because the needs of the family are complex the student should be prepared to become both a manager of and negotiator for resources, as well as being a counsellor – someone who can be consistently available to the individuals as needs arise. For these reasons the student has decided to use a systems-based approach (Parker and Bradley 2003, pp.86–87). She draws the ecomap in Figure 11.1 to help her explore what now appears to be a complex set of personal, familial and society relationships in this situation.

The student begins by assessing Shauna's needs in more depth. She uses a non-directive, non-judgemental, counselling style of interviewing to help Shauna express emotions of loss, grief and guilt about the problems of the past and her hopes for the future. The past may have included psychiatric experiences that left her stigmatised and degraded, subjected to stereotypical ideas about her loss of role as a mother and carer for her child. Women are often disadvantaged by the psychiatric system in these ways (Prior 1999, Chapter 5). Shauna should be allowed to revisit this past and its consequences.

The student considers other helpful therapeutic approaches. For example, cognitive behavioural and family based models of intervention can prevent relapse (Iqbal and Birchwood 2000). In both of these forms of intervention the student needs to be convinced that there is an agreement with the client and/or family about the nature of the problems, and that there is a commitment to the fulfilment of agreed tasks.

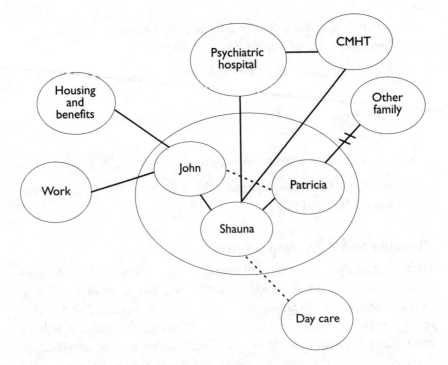

Figure 11.1: Ecomap

Once problems are recognised by clients and practitioner it is possible to address 'blockages' in the system. The painful slowness of Shauna's thought process and intermittent fears of persecution, John's struggle to provide for his partner and stepchild, the possible shame and frustration which Patricia may harbour about her mother's mental illness – these are all changing personal and social circumstances, to be sensitively considered in each contact with the family members. The student has advisedly taken a pragmatic, realistic approach to her work with the family – she only has a few months to go on placement, so it is a question of establishing trust and using non-directive approach to assess, plan and set limited objectives. To be overambitious and yet end the placement without the family perceiving worthwhile results would be disastrous.

Accessing resources

The student's assessment of the family's needs is a crucial factor in any negotiations for resources. People with mental health problems, as with other client groups (Bateman 2006; Craig 2002), have multiple disadvantages in terms of access to employment, benefits, education and other social resources. In using her systems-based model the student visualises points in social and economic networks where she can target and make interventions practical, yet meaningful; in doing so she feels she can advocate for the family. She carries out an audit of their income and housing needs, and learns from Citizen's Advice that the family are entitled to extra housing benefit (because of John's low income) and disability living allowances (based on Shauna's health and social care needs). She helps the couple complete the paperwork, and is confident that such benefits will impact positively on the family as a whole. She seeks out local organisations which may help people with mental health problems re-engage with community networks – the student believes that this may be an answer to Shauna's feelings of social isolation and loss. The student uses her contact with the team's OT to investigate possible day care, educational or occupational facilities in the catchment area.

The children of people with mental health problems

The student is concerned about how Patricia is coping. Patricia is always at school or with friends when the student visits. Her mother is worried that Patricia often comes home late, occasionally near midnight. Golightly (2006) suggests that children of mentally ill parents are more likely to suffer from social isolation, school problems and psychological disturbance. Patricia may well have been traumatised by the series of crises caused by her mother's mental illness, or stigmatised by what she has witnessed both at home and in her regular visits to hospital. With the parent's permission, the student seeks to explore these issues with Patricia, at a time and location she (Patricia) regards as suitable (Crawford 2006).

They meet in a local coffee shop after school. It soon emerges that no one has bothered telling Patricia how and why such mental health problems arise in families, nor that there are positive and worthwhile ways in which the situation can be helped. The student gives Patricia basic information about schizophrenia and about the role of professionals in the care and treatment of people with mental health problems. She offers Patricia the opportunity of meeting up with other young people who have shared similar experiences. They agree to meet again, when Patricia has had time to digest this information.

Maintaining contact with other professionals

The student recognises the importance of being fully engaged with the other professionals who are involved with Shauna and her family. Service users and their carers often complain about having to repeat the same information to different professionals, or that they are unsure of the different roles that they may play. The CPN who visits the family updates the student on her work with Shauna, and believes that progress is being made. The student telephones the hospital social worker, the original referral agent, and then the psychiatrist who sees Shauna on an outpatient basis every month. They are appreciative of the student's efforts. In consultation with her supervisor, the student has written a summary report on her involvement to date which has been circulated to the multi-disciplinary team. The student believes she has managed to positively affect some aspects of the system described in her ecomap.

Managing potential risk

Three weeks before the end of placement the student noticed that Shauna was agitated and finding it difficult to focus on a discussion about Patricia's attendance at school. Shauna had seen a school report which highlighted absences which neither she nor John had been aware of. Shauna also discloses that the voices had returned and were beginning to tell her that she was unworthy. The student is very concerned by these developments. Was Shauna's mental state beginning to deteriorate? Was this a prelude to another suicide attempt? Were there indications here of a depressed mood, or conversely, overactive or bizarre thought processes? Whatever was happening, the student had a pervasive sense of risk, for both Shauna and her family.

The student has read and learnt much about risk management in mental health. In each of the UK jurisdictions, laws have been enacted for the dual purpose of upholding the rights of patients and their nearest relatives, but also to allow doctors, social workers and nurses to compulsorily admit clients to hospital when the risks to them and others warrants it (DoH 1983; DHSS (NI) 1986; Scottish Executive 2003). The Approved Social Worker (ASW) (or Mental Health Officer in Scotland) have significant powers in this respect (Huxley and Kerfoot 1994; Manktelow *et al.* 2002; Ulas and Connor 1999). There are, however, structural inequalities in implementing mental health laws, often leading to the unfair treatment of cultural minority groups and women (Hatfield *et al.* 1996; Hatfield, Huxley and Mohamad 1997). Recent reviews of these laws suggest that 'capacity' condition will be used in the assessment of risk, and new forms of community-based coercive powers will be introduced (Bean 2001; Campbell *et al.* 2006).

This learning creates moral dilemmas for the student. She aspires to a profession which yields substantial power which, if misused, can lead to discrimination and injustice. She is determined to hold on to a sound value base regardless of her apprehensions. The student follows her supervisor's advice and returns the following afternoon to explore ways of further assessing and hopefully minimising the risk. The issue of risk assessment in the mental health field is complicated even for the most experienced practitioner. There are numerous ways of judging risk (Hawton *et al.* 2005; Pritchard 1999). Actuarial approaches, informed by epidemiological studies, suggest that some groups of people may be more vulnerable than others – for example those who have attempted suicide in the past, or who have experienced recent losses, or clients with some co-morbid conditions. Clinical assessments may identify other factors, a change of personality or appearance, depressed mood and/or suicidal or violent ideation. Environmental contexts may contribute to, for example, an absence of social networks, and easy access to alcohol or drugs. While exploring such possibilities, positive factors also need to be considered. John and Patricia are genuinely concerned about Shauna, they never leave her alone for long periods; there are regular visits by professionals; past relapses have been relatively predictable and she is still happy to attend a local day centre for two days per week. Such factors help the student to focus on a strengths-based approach at this particular time of crisis (Ramon 2006). She tests out some of her concerns with Shauna and John. The following is a series of excerpts from a process recording subsequently used by the student in supervision:

The student sits on a sofa beside the client in her living room, facing her with an open and attentive posture.

STUDENT: Hello Shauna, you seem very low today. (*open, but probing question*)

Shauna stares at the student.

Student waits, and resists the temptation to break the silence with another question.

SHAUNA: (*In a low, stumbling voice*) I'm not feeling well at all.

STUDENT: Is it possible for you to tell me in what way do you not feel well?

SHAUNA: The voices have returned.

STUDENT: (*Worried about the implications for Shauna's wellbeing; pauses, uses non-verbal cues and an empathic tone of voice, then replies*) It must be difficult for you when this happens – what do they say? (*reaching for feelings, then closed question*)

SHAUNA: That I am a bad mother.

STUDENT: It must be terribly hard for you to listen to this message. (*again, reaching for feelings*)

SHAUNA: I feel awful.

STUDENT: (*After a pause uses a statement*) Shauna…I want you to know that I am here to help you in any way I can…do you understand? (*clarifying*)

SHAUNA: Yes…you have been very good to us, but sometimes things get me down.

Shauna gradually becomes more willing to communicate. It emerges that she had a row with Patricia two days ago, and since then Patricia has come home late from school.

STUDENT: You seem to be saying that when this happens between you and Patricia things get you down, is that right? (*reflecting back and summarising*)

SHAUNA: Yes, it makes me feel that I have done something wrong, that's what the voices say, and maybe they are right, what do you think? (*client seems to have moved from a passive to more engaged style*)

STUDENT: It must be hard for you if that's what they are saying…but *I* know you're doing your best for Patricia.

SHAUNA: (*Silent, sad pause.*)

At this point the student knows that eventually she needs to check with Shauna about whether she has any suicidal ideation. This seems to be an appropriate time.

STUDENT: You've told me that in the past when such things happened that you got so down you felt like harming yourself, or that you had lost the will to live. (*paraphrasing*)

SHAUNA: Yes,…that's happened all right, but no…it's just…Patricia…she worries me…

The student continues to explore Shauna's concerns about Patricia, occasionally clarifying how she feels about herself. Shauna has not mentioned thoughts of suicide, and at one point says that she needs to tidy the house up before her husband comes back from work. The student is relieved on hearing this, but knows the potential for crisis remains. She waits until John arrives. He confirms that Patricia's behaviour remains a major concern for them. They approve of the student speaking to Patricia again.

Following this meeting a number of strategies are agreed upon:

1. enlightening Patricia about her unintentional exacerbation of her mother's predicament (this elicits remorse and new commitment from Patricia)

2. consultation with the CPN (this leads to an adjustment to the medication regime which has made Shauna more lethargic and prone to depressive episodes)

3. an immediate out-patient review for Shauna by her psychiatrist. The student will accompany Shauna to ensure that the psychiatrist is made aware of pertinent home and family circumstances.

Endings

The student reflects on many of her changing perceptions and feelings during her work. The apprehension and sense of foreboding which characterised the first weeks were gradually replaced by a growing confidence in her own skills, in working with both family and professionals. She understands now how the social work role often entails working with ambiguities and contradictions. However much she wanted to be available for the family, for example in accessing resources, the risk factor compelled her to consider the possibility (and necessity) of control and coercion. But she was honest with her clients about this eventuality.

A crucial and neglected aspect of the mental health social work role is the challenge of ending relationships in a manner conducive to the healing process. The student explained to the family during initial contacts that her placement was limited. In the final month, she checked that the application to uptake benefits was progressing and that a local voluntary agency would consider Shauna for membership of a group for women with mental health problems. She prepared comprehensive reports of all her contacts with the family, making these available for her supervisor and the referral agent, and stressing her view that there was a need for a another worker to be involved.

Attaining National Occupational Standards

The following extracts from the student's commentaries link her work with the National Occupational Standards.

STUDENT NOTES

I arrived at my placement with some teaching on mental health social work. The NOS have been useful in getting me to see how the social work task and process is structured, but they nevertheless hold the temptation of pigeon-holing everything into the Key Roles and Units. We and our clients are complex beings, and we need to see interventions in terms of fluid, sometimes unpredictable events.

Key Role 1: *Prepare to work with individuals, families, groups and communities to assess their needs and circumstances.* Preparation enabled me to fulfil a number of units:

1. reading important literature and mental health legislation (Unit 1.1)

2. liaising with the referral agent and continuously seeking advice from my supervisor (Unit 1.2)

3. clarifying my role at the outset, through discussion and letter (Unit 2.1)

4. facilitating the family in their decision on whether or not they wished to accept me (Unit 2.4).

Although I was not entirely clear about the meaning of assessment (Unit 3), I learnt that it is a multi-dimensional and interdisciplinary process – involving work with the individual, family and other professionals to arrive at a comprehensive and consensual view of what the problems might be.

Key Role 2: *Plan, carry out, review and evaluate social work practice*
This was broadly covered in the account described above. My response to Shauna's worries, and the assessment that I carried out, partially fulfilled the

requirements of Units 4 (*Respond to crisis situations*); Unit 9 (*Address behaviour which presents a risk to individuals, families, carers, groups and communities*); Units 12 (*Assess and manage risk to individuals families, carers, groups and communities*) and 13 (*Assess, minimize and manage risk to self and colleagues*).

The interrelationships between assessing and managing risk (Key Role 4: *Manage risk to individuals, families, carers, groups, communities, self and others*), often in a crisis situation, is complicated and anxiety-provoking; often I depended on my supervisor and multi-disciplinary colleagues for advice (Unit 17: *Work within multi-disciplinary and multi-organisational teams, networks and systems*).

I used a systems approach to work to fulfil parts of Key Role 3: *Support individuals to represent their needs, views and circumstances,* and to access resources and make connections with community based services (Unit 7.2: *Work with individuals, families, carers, groups, communities and others to initiate and sustain support networks*). This also involved me being an advocate for the family (Unit 10.3: *Advocate for, and with, individual families, carers, groups and communities*).

In terms of Key Role 5: *Manage and be accountable with supervision and support, for your own social work practice within your organization,* I made professional judgements based on a sound knowledge base (Unit 14.2) and developed important skills in using supervision (Unit 14.4: *Use professional and managerial support to improve your practice*). Finally I believe I *demonstrated professional competence in social work practice* (Key Role 6) *particularly in terms of considering the values underpinning social work practice* (Unit 19.3) and in dealing with some of the ethical dilemmas arising (Unit 20.2). My objective was to offer family members a voice and choices in the decision-making process although I was conscious at the same time that I might have some part to play in taking Shauna's liberty away.

Conclusion

This account of social work interventions within a family where there are serious mental health problems describes and analyses the complexity of this type of work. The student was faced with a wide range of tasks and professional responsibilities, some of which can be matched across to the relevant National Occupational Standards. A number of key messages about competent practice in the mental health field emerged in this chapter. All too often in this area the rights of service users and carers are barely recognised and understood, it was therefore crucial that the student was aware of the need to both understand the causes of such discrimination, and that interventions should be built upon a sound, reflective value base. It is this value base that was tested when a crisis arose. The student was able to use her knowledge of risk assessment, the law and multidisciplinary working to help Shauna and her family when they needed her most. Of course mental social work is much more than responding to crises. It involves building relationships, becoming an advocate and being prepared to be flexible in developing opportunities at the level of the individual, family and community. The student has been given a broad range of learning opportunities to develop her skills of assessment, planning and delivering services, supported by her supervisor and interdisciplinary colleagues. There is a lot to learn in mental health social work. This is a good beginning.

References

Bateman, N. (2006) *Practising Welfare Rights*. Abingdon: Routledge.

Bean, P. (2001) *Mental Disorder and Community Safety*. Basingstoke: Macmillan.

Bentall, R.P. (2003) *Madness Explained: Psychosis and Human Nature*. London: Penguin.

Bower, M. (ed.) (2005) *Psychoanalytic Theory for Social Work Practice: Thinking Under Fire*. London: Routledge.

Braye, S. (2000) 'Participation and Involvement in Social Care: An Overview.' In H. Kemshall and R. Littlechild (eds) *User Involvement and Participation in Social Care: Research Informing Practice*. London: Jessica Kingsley Publishers.

Braye, S. and Preston-Shoot, M. (1995) *Empowering Practice in Social Care*. Buckingham: Open University Press.

Campbell, J., Brophy, L., Healy, B. and O'Brien, A.M. (2006) 'International Perspectives on the Use of Community Treatment Orders: Implications for Mental Health Social Workers.' *British Journal of Social Work 36*, 7, 1101–1118.

Craig, G. (2002) 'Poverty, Social Work and Social Justice.' *British Journal of Social Work 32*, 6, 669–682.

Crawford, K. (2006) *Social Work and Human Development: Reflective Reader*. Exeter: Learning Matters.

Dallos, R. and Boswell, D. (1993) 'Mental Health.' In R. Dallos and E. McLaughlin (eds) *Social Problems and the Family*. London: Sage.

Department of Health (1983) *Mental Health Act 1983*. London: HMSO.

Department of Health (1990) *The Care Programme Approach*, HC (90) 23. London: HMSO.

Department of Health (1999) *National Service Framework for Mental Health*. London: DoH.

Department of Health (2006) *Reviewing the Care Programme Approach 2006: A Consultation Document*. London: DoH.

Department of Health and Social Services (Northern Ireland) (1996) *Mental Health (NI) Order 1986*. London: HMSO.

Golightly, M. (2006) *Social Work and Mental Health*. Exeter: Learning Matters.

Hatfield, B., Mohammad, H., Rahim, Z. and Tanweer, H. (1996) 'Mental Health and the Asian Communities: A Local Survey.' *British Journal of Social Work 26*, 3, 315–336.

Hatfield, B., Huxley, P., and Mohammad, H. (1997) 'Social Factors and Compulsory Detention of Psychiatric Patients in the UK.' *International Journal of Law and Psychiatry 20*, 3, 389–397.

Hawton, K., Sutton, L., Haw, C., Sinclair, J. and Deeks, J.J. (2005) 'Schizophrenia and Suicide: A Systematic Review of Risk Factors.' *British Journal of Psychiatry 187*, 1, 9–20.

Huxley, P. and Kerfoot, M. (1994) 'A Survey of Approved Social Workers in England and Wales.' *British Journal of Social Work 24*, 3, 311–322.

Iqbal, Z. and Birchwood, M. (2000) 'Psychological Interventions for Mental Health Problems.' In D. Bailey (ed.) *At the Core of Mental Health: Key Issues for Practitioners, Managers and Mental Health Trainers.* Brighton: Pavillion.

Leff and Vaughan (1998) *Expressed Emotions in Families.* New York: Guildford.

Manktelow, R., Hughes, P., Britton, F., Campbell, J., Hamilton, B. and Wilson, G. (2002) 'The Experience and Practice of Approved Social Workers in Northern Ireland.' *British Journal of Social Work 32*, 4, 443–461.

O'Hagan, M. (1996) 'Two Accounts of Mental Distress.' In J. Read and J. Reynolds (eds) *Speaking Our Minds: An Anthology.* Basingstoke: Macmillan.

Parker, J. and Bradley, G. (2003) *Social Work Practice: Assessment, Planning, Intervention and Review.* Exeter: Learning Matters.

Pritchard, C (1999) *Suicide – the Ultimate Rejection: A Psychosocial Study.* Buckingham: Open University.

Pritchard, C. (2006) *Mental Health Social Work: Evidence based Practice.* Abingdon: Routledge.

Prior, P. (1999) *Gender and Mental Health.* Basingstoke: Macmillan.

Ramon, S. (2006) 'Risk Avoidance and Risk Taking in Mental Health Social Work.' In L. Sapouna and P. Herrman (eds) *Knowledge in Mental Health: Reclaiming the Social.* New York: Nova.

Ramsey, R., Gerada, C., Mars, S. and Szmukler, G. (2001) *Mental Illness: A Handbook for Carers.* London: Jessica Kingsley Publishers.

Read, J. and Reynolds, J. (1996) (eds) *Speaking Our Minds: An Anthology.* Basingstoke: Macmillan.

Rippon, S. (2005) 'Interventions in Mental Health: Promoting Collaborative Working and Meaningful Support.' In T. Ryan and J. Pritchard (eds) *Good Practice in Adult Mental Health.* London: Jessica Kingsley Publishers.

Rogers. A and Pilgrim, D. (2005) *A Sociology of Mental Health and Illness.* Maidenhead: Open University Press.

Scottish Executive (2003) *The Mental Health (Care and Treatment) (Scotland Act) 2003.* Edinburgh: Scottish Executive.

Sutton, C. (1994) *Social Work. Community Work and Psychology.* London: BPS.

Tilbury, D. (1993) *Working with Mental Illness.* Basingstoke: BASW.

Ulas, M. and Connor, A. (1999) *Mental Health and Social Work.* London: Jessica Kingsley Publishers.

Wallcraft, J. (2005) 'Recovery from Mental Breakdown.' In J. Tew (ed.) *Social Perspectives in Mental Health: Developing Social Models to Understand Work and Stress.* London: Jessica Kingsley Publishers.

CHAPTER 12

Competence under Child-care Legislation, Policy and Theory

Joe Duffy and Stan Houston

Introduction

The National Occupational Standards for Social Work (Training Organisation for Personal Social Services (TOPPS) 2002) are centred on the need for a quality social work service at both qualifying and post qualifying levels (Trevithick 2005). They provide a benchmark for best practice by specifying competence requirements which must be fulfilled. Of particular relevance to this chapter, the standards emerged during a period of significant change in child care policy and legislation. The Labour government made its intentions clear in this respect in 1997, but it is fair to say that the more radical reforms it introduced were influenced and speeded up by various research projects and reports and inquiries, most notably Lord Laming's (2003) investigation into the death of Victoria Climbié. This chapter will focus on key aspects of child care research, policy and legislation that have prefaced or coincided with the introduction of the National Occupational Standards (NOS). It will then present a case study in which a student in a child care placement works within the new policy and legislative frameworks, and seeks to achieves competence in accordance with the NOS.

Background to the National Occupational Standards

Social work and social work education in the UK have undergone radical change during the past decade. The changes have been influenced by a myriad of policy and legislative measures, reflecting policy paradigms such as state paternalism, defence of the birth family and parent's rights (Harding 1997). The government's *A Quality Strategy for Social Care* (Department of Health (DoH) 2000a) heralded the necessary and consequential changes to social work training, including the registration of all social care staff. In 2002 it published *Requirements for Social Work Training* (DoH 2002) which introduced the new degree in social work, in which the core objective was attainment of National Occupational Standards (TOPSS 2002). Social work students now have to complete 200 days of assessed practice learning, in two practice settings, with at least two service user groups (DOH 2002). The standards incorporated a Statement of Expectations from service users who participated in their formulation. This was highly significant in helping agencies and their staff determine the type and quality of services required. Levin comments that 'the thrust of all the new arrangements is that service users and carers get high quality social work services in terms of both processes and outcomes' (2004, p.8). Just as important, social work students would now see 'service users and carers as active participants in service delivery rather than as passive recipients' (p.9).

The Key Roles of the NOS

The Key Roles of the NOS give cognisance to the now widely accepted international definition of social work:

> A profession which promotes social change, problem solving in human relationships and the empowerment and liberation of people to enhance well-being. Utilising theories of human behaviour and social systems, social work intervenes at the points where people interact with their environments. Principles of human rights and social justice are fundamental to social work. (International Association of Schools of Social Work and the International Federation of Social Workers 2001, in Department of Health, Social Services and Public Safety (DHSSPS) 2003, p.12)

The Key Roles are closely linked and are designed to represent the holistic nature of social work practice. Key Roles 1–4 cover the practice of social work, and Key Roles 5 and 6 refer to the social worker as an accountable and professionally competent practitioner. Values and ethics permeate all six key roles.

Research, policy and legislation

Changes in child care social work training have been influenced by many factors; some of the most significant include research (DoH 1995), government guidelines (DoH 2000a) and Child Abuse inquiry reports (Laming 2003). The Department of Health's *Messages from Research* (DOH 1995) confirmed the well-grounded suspicion that 'the majority of referrals did not involve serious child abuse but rather involved concerns that children may be at risk of harm' (Hayes 2006, p.103). Corby compared the child protection system to 'a giant sieve taking in a broad spectrum of referrals about the care of children' (2000, p.57). Twenty-four per cent of the referrals resulted in child protection conferences and in just over half of these conference-recommended child protection registration.

These findings have led to a significant refocusing in child protection work. The previous blanket response to child abuse referrals was replaced by 1. identifying and targeting children judged most in need of protection from serious forms of abuse, 2. using more comprehensive, broadly based assessments of such children and their families. Great effort is made to ensure that all families mentioned on a referral are not exposed to rigorous and distressful child protection investigations. Corby says that 'child protection professionals need to be less concerned with externally identified abuse and more focused on tackling the psychological impact of being a child in need' (2000, p.58).

This refocusing is also reflected in the *Framework* document (DoH 2000b) and in the *Working to Safeguard Children* guidelines (DoH 1999). In the former, child care workers are provided with comprehensive frameworks enabling them to more accurately assess children who are in need, or subject to significant harm, and it identifies a wide range of services that can meet the needs of such children and their families. The *Framework* document 'emphasizes the holistic assessment of children in need and their families in contrast to focussing narrowly on investigation and protection' (DoH 2000a, p.76).

In response to the Laming (2003) Report, the government's *Every Child Matters* (Department for Education and Skills 2003) identified five key outcomes for children and young people: being healthy; staying safe; enjoying and achieving; making a positive contribution and economic wellbeing (Doyle 2006). The Children Act 2004 implemented many of the proposals of *Every Child Matters*, and provided a legislative framework to encourage integrated planning, commissioning and delivery of services, with great emphasis on monitoring and evaluating quality). The Children (Leaving Care) Act 2000 focused on the vulnerability and disadvantage faced by many young care leavers in relation to homelessness and low educational attainment. It amended some sections of the Children Act 1989 by requiring personal advisers to develop pathway plans for eligible 16–17 year olds who are leaving care.

Nearly all recent government publications relating to child care and child protection emphasise that competence should be based, in so far as is possible, on evidence-based practice. They do not denigrate or preclude the necessity of common worker attributes such as intuition, empathy and courage in child protection work, but they consistently promote the use of 'current best evidence about the effects of particular interventions on the welfare of individuals, groups and communities' (Macdonald 2002, p.123). Although all the above examples of new child care policy and legislation indicate a *state paternalist* approach to social policy, the fact remains that the hopes they espouse for improved quality of services for children and their families can only be fulfilled, ultimately, through competence practice at the front line.

The Human Rights Act

Increasingly, there is an international context that governments must consider in formulating child care legislation, and in determining competence in practice. The Human Rights Act (1998) became law in all parts of the UK in October 2000. It owes much to the European Convention on Human Rights (ECHR). It obligates health and social services trusts with ensuring that their actions are at all times compatible with human rights requirements. This is a formidable task in child protection work, which is one of the most obvious arenas of conflicting rights, as Henricson and Bainham articulate: 'Concerns have been increasingly voiced by family lawyers about a possible contradiction between the welfare principle, which makes children's interests paramount, and the commitment to the human rights of parents and other family members under the act' (2005, p.3).

The following child protection case will elucidate further on some of these issues. It will highlight an integrated approach, and demonstrate competence in accordance with 1. the Key Roles of the NOS, and 2. policies and legislation already discussed.

Finding practice on placement to demonstrate competence

Social work education revolves around the successful integration and demonstration of academic learning in practice placements. As O'Hagan suggests in Chapter 1, what matters essentially in this endeavour is the expression of competent practice in a range of different contexts. In child and family social work, this demonstration of competence is enmeshed, as we have argued earlier, in a legal and policy framework. So students on placement in child care settings, need to pay attention not only to the requirements of the National Occupational Standards, but also how they are contextualised within agency imperatives as defined by statute, policy and procedure. Moreover, students are required to have knowledge of contemporary academic discourses, research findings and debates that feed into particular areas of practice, and their accompanying value dilemmas and operational exigencies.

The student

We will now attempt to ground these reflections in a case study centring on Paul, a first year student on a social work degree programme. Paul's occupation background is in sharp contrast to his current vocational interest in social work. A city trader in London for over five years prior to entering social work education, he became disillusioned with the materialistic and individualistic emphasis of his role. However, some relief from this oppressive work context was realised in out-of-hours volunteer work with refugees – a focus that had been kindled by what he saw as the xenophobic trends within the media and society at large towards this section of the community. Critically, though, the final decision to pursue social work training was made only after experienced a period of stress-related illness. The time spent off work enabled him to reflect on key priorities in his life. What appealed to him about social work as a career option was its holistic value base and the space it afforded to work with the person in a social context.

Mid-way through the first academic term at college, Paul was inspired by a taught module on the application of ecological and systems theories in social work practice (Jack 2000). An assignment on the subject further helped him to understand the relevance of ecological thinking and intervention, particularly in relation to young people 'in need' within the community. The legal and policy context of social work also became significant. The objectives in the seminal work *Every Child Matters* (DfES 2003), could be realised, he believed, through a perspective that was wide-ranging, that took account of child development and optimal child outcomes in terms of concentric circles of influence surrounding the young person. Bronfenbrenner's (1979) articulation of these social influences was, for Paul, a credible platform within the broad church of ecological theory from which he could link a number of academic discourses in social work to practical field work. Hill's (2002) more practical application of ecological theory using a variety of social network assessment tools provided Paul with a conceptual framework and armoury of techniques that could be applied to concrete situations involving children or young people 'in need'.

The placement

Paul's placement was located in a statutory fieldwork team specialising in services to young people in accordance with the Children Act (1989) definition of children 'in need'. The work was also governed by the Children Act (2004), with its emphasis on integrated working in children's services. The central thrust of the team's approach was to offer family support services to young people and their families, enabling them to resolve presenting difficulties or cope with problematic situations in ways that enhanced their resilience and adaptation to stressful situations. From background material on the team's role and function, Paul also learned that the team could be involved in situations where young people had to be accommodated or received into care under the relevant provisions of the Children Act (1989). Such situations might need to be invoked when young people were deemed to be at risk either through their own actions or the actions of significant others in their lives.

Drawing on his knowledge of the re-focusing debate and the landmark *Messages from Research* (DoH 1995), Paul understood that the risk in this context would have to meet a certain threshold of concern (again defined by the relevant legislation). Moreover, attempts at family support would either have failed or would be deemed to be inappropriate. Given that the team also dealt with young people in the care system, the Children (Leaving Care) Act 2000 was highly relevant.

College and placement objectives

One of the key requirements of this placement was to undertake a piece of social intervention based on the preceding assignment and its underpinning knowledge base, write it up, reflect on it and subsequently return to a recall day mid-term when the intervention and reflection on it would be presented within a small group to staff and fellow students, enabling feedback and further learning to occur.

The wider all-pervasive objective, of course, was fulfilling the six Key Roles of the NOS. Paul immediately saw that many of the requirements underpinning them were based on an ecological perspective. Key Role 1 for instance, emphasised working with individuals, carers and communities to assess their needs and circumstances. This emphasis was also germane to the second Key Role (*Plan, carry out, review and evaluate social work practice, with individuals, families, carers, groups, communities and other professionals*); its Unit 7 explicitly required the implementation of support for the development of networks to meet assessed needs and planned outcomes. In fact, the emphasis on informal networks throughout the role specification seemed to be incontrovertible.

Placement preparation for case allocation

Paul shadowed social workers on the team and observed interventions with a range of different families (Key Role 5 Unit 14.4). Combined with supervision and the reading of summaries of research on effective, preventive services, he learnt that responses in family support work should aim to:

1. Work in partnership with young people and families.

2. Provide a clear focus on the wishes, feelings and needs of family members.

3. Reflect a strengths-based perspective which reinforces and builds resilience.

4. Strengthen informal networks of support.

5. Be accessible and flexible.

6. Involve young people and their families in the planning, delivery and evaluation of interventions.

7. Promote social inclusion and avoid the misuse of power with particular reference to issues such as gender, ethnicity, disability and the differences between urban and rural communities.

All of these aims, if achieved, would fulfill the requirements of many of the specifications of the NOS, and would also adhere to the values and ethics underpinning them.

Case study

Paul's discussion with his supervisor and reading of the file (Key Role 1, Units 1.1, 1.2, 1.3) elicited the following facts: Abul is 15. He and his parents arrived in London from Pakistan approximately one year prior to the referral to social services. His father, a doctor, had obtained a work permit in the United Kingdom for three years allowing him to practice in palliative care. His mother, a qualified nurse, had secured part-time work in a nearby hospital. The referral, from Abul's head teacher in the local comprehensive school, had raised numerous concerns. First, Abul had a very poor record of attendance. This was having a substantive adverse effect on his academic performance. The staff unanimously felt he was a highly intelligent lad with much potential, particularly in music, drama and English. Second, staff observed that he was basically, a loner; his emotional expression was largely negative; he seldom smiled or engaged in camaraderie. He seemed dejected and/or depressed. Occasionally, he would erupt in aggressive outbursts in class. Recently, one of these outbursts had led to a physical altercation with another boy resulting in Abul's temporary suspension from school. Third, Abdul's parents regarded their son's behaviour as incomprehensible, and felt increasingly helpless in changing it. They deeply regretted his not taking the opportunities afforded him in attending this particular school.

Paul undertook a literature review on research into effective family support interventions in cultural minority groups (Key Role 6 Unit 18). Chand and Thorburn's (2005) meta-analysis of practice effectiveness suggested that effective services depended primarily on comprehensive assessments carried out by experienced, knowledgeable and culturally sensitive staff. Such assessments needed to be holistically framed taking account of the three domains of the Assessment Framework (DoH 2000b): (a) the child, (b) the parents and (c) social networks. This research also concluded that it was not the technique or model that was important but rather the nature of the relationship between the family members and the worker; empathy, listening skills and reliability were perceived as important from the families' point of view.

Paul reflected on the concept of *cultural competence*, which McPhatter (1997, p.169) defines as 'the ability to respond to the unique needs of individuals and families by integrating cultural knowledge and awareness into interventions and thus support and sustain clients within their appropriate cultural context'. He became aware of the linkage between culturally inappropriate intervention and the tendency to view minority cultures and communities as being fixed over space and time and removed in some way from majority cultures (Husain 2006). Paul did not merely have to acquaint himself with knowledge of Abul's culture (Smith 1998); he also needed to explore the extent of his own cultural competence. In the context of family support in the UK, culturally competent practice required him to work on three related components: cultural knowledge, cultural awareness and cultural sensitivity.

Initial impressions

The case file study, research and literature readings, and discussion with his supervisor indicated that Abul may be a child 'in need' in accordance with the definition in the Children Act (1989). If the situation remained unchanged, i.e. his increasing alienation with the school and family, then his health and development were likely to be significantly impaired. The indicators pointed to the need for intervention and support. Yet the legislation highlighted another challenging need: to work in partnership with young people and their families. Abul's voice had to be heard (Children Act 1989; UN Convention on the Rights of the Child 1989), and, should he so choose, his rights to privacy would have to be respected (Article 8 of the Human Rights Act 1998).

Contact with subject and family

After careful preparation in supervision, and face-to-face discussion with the head teacher (Key Role 1 Unit 1.2), Paul made contact with the family, with the principal purpose of beginning assessment. He carried with him, for easy reference and constant reminder, the seven aims of the team's mission statement (Key Role 5 Unit 14.1) (see the aims above: they are mirrored throughout the six Key Roles practice specifications).

He was aware of the importance of building trust, listening and showing empathy to all family members, while taking a social history and gathering information about the context surrounding Abul's behaviour. He was also sensitive to the importance of a needs-led approach as being the best way of helping families experiencing difficulty (Gardner 2003; Parton

1997). He chose the Smale *et al.* (1993) *exchange model of assessment* which focuses upon service users as capable of defining their own needs (Coulshed and Orme 2006, p.33) and upon their social context, influencing the dynamics and relationships within families.

Paul explained the purpose of his involvement and the statutory nature of his responsibilities in line with the Children Act. He also spoke of the multi-disciplinary nature of social work intervention in situations like this, and of the value of working closely with other professionals (e.g. in school).

Abul's parents said that the move to England from Pakistan was intended to make life better for everybody. They felt let down and embarrassed by Abul's behaviour; it was not how he behaved in Pakistan.

Abul seemed agitated by these comments; he avoided eye contact with his parents. Paul asked him directly: 'Do you understand why your parents feel let down Abul?'

What then emerged from Abul's responses and emotional reaction was an impression of an isolated youth, estranged from his family and wider social context. The transition from Pakistan to England, had, it seemed, evoked in him feelings of loss, confusion and anger. He said he hated school and found it hard to make friends. He also said that he assaulted another pupil who had racially abused him.

Abul's parents were shocked by these disclosures and were disappointed that he hadn't told them. Abul however made it clear that they hadn't always been around for him. He emphasised that his experiences of schooling in Pakistan were very different from what he was experiencing in England; he said that he wouldn't return there.

Still adhering to the Smale model of assessment, Paul identified the following tasks, which if carried out, would fulfil a number of Key Role requirements:

1. Liaising with the school to ensure that Abul was not subject to abuse. (Key Role 2 Unit 10: *Advocate on behalf of clients.*)

2. Exploring and enhancing (or adding to) whatever networks and social supports Abul may have. (Key Role 2 Unit 7.1: *Examine support networks...that can be accessed and developed.*)

3. Working with Abul and his parents to encourage more open communication about issues and expectations in terms of Abul's current situation and worries. (Key Role 4 Unit 12.2: *Balance the rights and responsibilities of individuals, families, etc.*)

Supervision (Key Role 6 Unit 19.5)

Paul shared the outcome of initial contact with his supervisor. He referred repeatedly to the Assessment Framework (DoH 2000b) as his principal guide. He also quoted Hill's statement: 'network relationships are of central significance in social work, because they make up the immediate environment in which service users lead their daily lives. They play a vital role in the production, maintenance, prevention, alleviation and resolution of problems' (2002, p.237).

Paul critically reflected on his work and on his own cultural background (Key Role 6 Unit 19.4). He was acutely conscious of the power and authority bestowed on him by the state and how this might be perceived by and within a family from a cultural minority in these times of religious and cultural tensions and controversies within the population as a whole (Key Role 6 Unit 20.1).

Hill's (2002) paper encouraged him explore Abul's social network (Key Role 2 Units 7.1, 7.2, 7.3). Hill writes 'network relationships are of central significance in social work, because they make up the immediate environment in which service users lead their daily lives. They play a vital role in the production, maintenance, prevention, alleviation and resolution of problems' (p.237). Hill cautions about the need to avoid simplified assumptions, particularly with regard to the influence of culture on network patterns. In this respect the key factors to take cognisance of were:

> (1) religious and cultural traditions e.g. kinship patterns; (2) the attitudes of other people and in particular the implications of racism; (3) the effects of migration on network contacts and the relative importance of links with people back home; and (4) proximity to others of the same background, religion and/or locality of origin. (p.243)

Paul also considered relevant Thompson's (1993) three levels of oppression characterised by the Personal, Cultural and Structural (NOS knowledge base for Unit 1: discrimination and oppression, 2e).

Strengthening the worker-client relationship

All this preparatory thinking and ongoing literature search for meaning and application were contributing towards fulfilling the requirements of Key Role 1 in particular and its various Units and specifications of practice. Paul, however, was very much aware that central to any future progress in the case would be his relationship with Abul. 'Network assessment' had to be completed not in a step-by-step mechanistic manner but, rather, as part of a continuing relationship of trust between the worker and client. Paul attempted to build up his relationship with Abul by getting to know him more through leisure pursuits and social activities. Parallel with this objective, he sought to maintain close contact with Abul's parents and the school head teacher (Key Role 7 Unit 7.2), to provide regular feedback, and to remain attentive to their concerns.

Second home visit

DESCRIPTION OF PRACTICE – HOME VISIT WITH ABUL AND COMPLETION OF ECOMAP

Paul visited Abul at home and made the customary enquiries about how things had been since the last contact. Abul told Paul that relationships have been strained at home with his parents still seeming quite agitated towards him and growing impatient with the fact that he was still out of school. Paul told him, as proposed at the first meeting, that he had discussed the situation with Abul's Head of Year, Mr Abbott, who was keen to discuss the issue with Paul himself, and who assured Paul that Abul would not be treated like this again (Key Role 4, ii.4, 12.1).

Paul then explained to Abul that the purpose of this visit was to get to know him better and find out what supports were available to him given that the family's move from Pakistan was tumultuous. In this way, Paul was indicating his intentions to use the techniques in a collaborative way as a prompt for systematic discussion.

Paul's first major step in network assessment was to construct an ecomap with Abul. As Hill explains, this comprises a symbol for the key person which is then placed in the centre of a blank page. Significant people in the person's life are then placed in other shapes (such as circles, squares or triangles) and lines drawn to connect them with the central person and each other. Distance is a key factor in all of this. For instance, people who are deemed to be loosely associated with the key person will be placed in shapes that are far away from him or her on the page. Activities can be included as well as people to enlarge the range of information elicited.

Paul encouraged Abul to take responsibility for drawing the ecomap on a laptop computer (Key Role 1 Unit 2.4). Abul proceeded to draw a circle in the middle of a page to represent himself. He then connected his circle closely to his parents with a *dotted line* indicating the current fractured state of the relationship between them. He also showed that he had one close friend in school, Imran, and one friend who lived nearby, Faruk, who he occasionally socialised with. He also elaborated further on his interest in music, drama, art and soccer but was unable to identify any leisure outlet for developing these interests further. He said that he kept in touch with friends in Pakistan through his computer. In addition, what also emerged was a large extended family of uncles, aunts and cousins with whom he had little contact or connections even though there were cousins who are close in age to him.

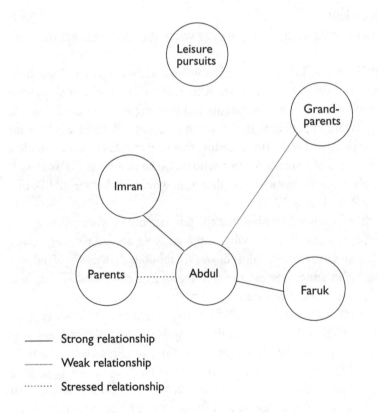

Figure 12.1: Paul's ecomap

Exploring the client's perceptions of their social network

The ecomap was a source of much interest and discussion. Abul realised now that he was quite isolated and Paul recalled Dolan's view that 'a perceived presence of a responsive support network was central to enhancing children's and parent's resiliency and mental health' (2006, p.197) More precisely, the four forms of support that are targeted are: tangible support ('are there friends you can depend on to help you if you really need it?'); emotional support ('do your relationships with your friends provide you with a sense of acceptance and happiness?'); esteem support ('do you feel your talents and abilities are recognized by your friends?') and advice support ('is there a friend you could trust to turn to for advice, if you were having problems?') (p.197).

Paul explored this matter fully with Abul during a further visit. He linked this to an exploration of how Abul perceived his parent's challenges in attempting to establish themselves in a new country, to integrate socially, economically, culturally within the community. Abul slowly began to acknowledge that in his preoccupation with his own difficulties, he had not considered theirs.

Paul ensured, however, that he did not minimise the importance of Abul's sense of isolation and alienation. But he managed to shift the focus from these to Abul's reputed interests and potential in music, art and drama, and on the opportunity to exploit these within available outlets within the community. Such activities held the prospect of greatly enhancing his social life and integration. Abul agreed to a final visit whereby Paul would meet with Abul and his parents to share and discuss the outcome of the work that Paul and Abul had been working on together (Key Role 5 Unit 16.4).

Case study – Reflection stage

From earlier supervision sessions with his practice teacher, Paul had learned that reflection was a process of describing what one had done and its results, how it had been achieved and lastly, why it had been undertaken in that particular way. Inherent in all of this was the question of what might have been done differently. These reflective steps were integral to Key Role 6 and its requirement under Unit 18.2 *to use professional and organizational supervision and support to research, critically analyse, and review knowledge based practice.*

For Paul the use of network tools had proved invaluable. Critically, they enabled Abul's view of his situation to emerge in line with rights-based legislation. For example, Paul's practice showed compliance with Article 8 of the Human Rights Act (1998), the right to respect for private and family life. However, in writing up his reflective notes for the college recall day, it became apparent that perhaps his work to date had not sufficiently engaged Abul's parents and significant others in his life. In this context, it occurred to him that perhaps a family group conference (involving the extended family) might have been employed alongside the one-to-one work with Abul. Once again, the Key Roles within the NOS were helpful in pointing out the need for this extra dimension to his work. For instance Key Role 1 Unit 2.2 stipulated the need to *work with individuals, families, carers, groups and communities to identify, gather, analyse and understand information.*

Paul concluded that although there was a large extended family of uncles, aunts and cousins, geographically concentrated nearby, Abul did not feel that they were readily or helpfully accessible. Paul believed that there was lack of connectedness within these family network affiliations and crucially, an increasing gulf of misunderstanding between the family's cultural convictions and Abul's interests. There was a need to strengthen alternative social (peer) networks for Abul, both within the school and the community. He was a clever and gifted lad, and needed encouragement and support in finding outlets for his many talents. Setting these findings alongside the outcome of the social provisions scale, what concerned Paul most was Abul's perception that emotional and esteem support was in limited supply – even from his parents.

Application of the social provision scales model had enlightened Paul about Abul's social life. The lack of engagement however, with parents and other significant family members remained a matter of reflection, in which Paul considered numerous alternative ways that objective may have been achieved (e.g. family group conference). He also contemplated in reflection the possible usefulness of theories of loss and change in understanding and empathising with the parents' move from Pakistan, and the severance with so much (and so many) that were undoubtedly important to them. The Key Roles within the NOS were helpful in pointing out the need for this extra dimension to his work.

Clearly identifiable areas of work had been delineated at the outset:

1. Abul's perception of his immediate networks not being readily or helpfully accessible.

2. A lack of connectedness within these family network affiliations.

3. An emerging gulf between the family's cultural convictions and Abul's interests and rights.

A reasonable beginning had been made in each of these areas, but much more had to be done, monitored and evaluated.

Conclusion

This chapter includes both an overview of the prevalent policy and key legislative landscape that accompanies child care social work and examples of how relevant social work theory is applied to the practice learning context. What emerges from the practice example provided is the complementary way in which the National Occupational Standards merge with social work theory, policy and legislation to create opportunities for social work students to demonstrate competent practice in their work and reflections. Such professional competence, however, will depend not only on the willingness of students to engage proactively and critically with their learning and experiences but also to appreciate the influence of social work ethics, values and skills on their practice. In this way, the student is enabled to effectively make connections between the NOS and their resonance in terms of generating opportunities for the demonstration of competence in both the practice and theoretical domains of social work training.

References

Bronfenbrenner, U. (1979) *The Ecology of Human Development: Experiments by Nature and Design.* Cambridge, MA: Harvard University Press.

Chand, A. and Thornburn, J. (2005) 'Research Review: Child and Family Support Services with Minority Ethnic Families: What can we learn from Research?' *Child and Family Social Work 10,* 169–178.

Corby, B.C. (2000) *Child Abuse: Towards a Knowledge Base,* 2nd edn. Buckingham: Open University Press.

Coulshed, V. and Orme, J. (2006) *Social Work Practice,* 4th edn. Basingstoke: Palgrave Macmillan.

Department for Education and Skills (2003) *Every Child Matters,* Command Paper 5860. London: HMSO.

Department of Health (1995) *Child Protection – Messages From Research.* London: HMSO.

Department of Health (1999) Working Together to Safeguard Children: A Guide to Inter-agency Working to Safeguard and Promote the Welfare of Children. London: DoH, HO, DEE.

Department of Health (2000a) *A Quality Strategy for Social Care.* London: DoH.

Department of Health (2000b) *Framework for the Assessment of Children in Need and their Families.* London: Stationery Office.

Department of Health (2002) *Requirements for Social Work Training.* London: DoH.

Department of Health, Social Services and Public Safety (2003) *Northern Ireland Framework Specification for the Degree in Social Work.* Belfast: DHSSPS.

Dolan, P. (2006) 'Assessment, Intervention and Self-appraisal Tools for Family Support.' In P. Dolan, J. Canavan and J. Pinkerton (eds) *Family Support as Reflective Practice.* London: Jessica Kingsley Publishers.

Doyle, C. (2006) *Working with Abused Children,* 3rd edn. BASW Practical Social Work. Palgrave: Macmillan.

Gardner, R. (2003) *Supporting Families: Child Protection in the Community.* Chichester: NSPCC and Wiley.

Harding, L. (1997) *Perspectives in Child Care Policy,* 2nd edn. Harlow: Longman.

Hayes, D. (2006) 'Rebalanced and Refocused Social Work Practice?' *Child Care in Practice 12*, 2, 97–113.

Henricson, C. and Bainham, A. (2005). *The Child and Family Policy Divide. Tensions, Convergence and Rights.* Joseph Rowntree Foundation. Available at: www.jrf.org.uk

Hill, M. (2002) 'Network Assessments and Diagrams: A Flexible Friend for Social Work Practice and Education.' *Journal of Social Work 12*, 2, 233–254.

Husain, F. (2006) 'Cultural Competence, Cultural Sensitivity and Family Support.' In P. Dolan, J. Canavan and J. Pinkerton (eds) *Family Support as Reflective Practice.* London: Jessica Kingsley Publishers.

Jack, G. (2000) 'Ecological Perspectives in Assessing Children and Families.' In J. Horwarth (ed.) *The Child's World – Assessing Children in Need.* London: Jessica Kingsley Publishers.

Laming, H. (2003) *The Victoria Climbié Inquiry.* London: Stationery Office.

Levin, E. (2004) *Involving Service Users and Carers in Social Work Education.* Bristol: Social Care Institute for Excellence.

Macdonald, G. (2002) 'The Evidence-based Perspective.' In M. Davies (ed.) *The Blackwell Companion to Social Work,* 2nd edn. Oxford: Blackwell.

McPhatter, A.R. (1997) 'Cultural Competence in Child Welfare: What is it? How do we achieve it? What happens without it?' *Child Welfare 76*, 1, 255–278.

Parton, N. (1997) 'Child Protection and Family Support: Current Debates and Future Prospects.' In N. Parton (ed.) *Child Protection and Family Support: Tensions, Contradictions and Possibilities.* London: Routledge.

Schon, D. (1993) *The Reflective Practitioner.* New York: Basic Books.

Smale, G., Tuson, G., Biehal, N. and Marsh, P. (1993) *Empowerment, Assessment, Care Management and the Skilled Worker.* London: National Institute for Social Work Practice and Development Exchange, HMSO.

Smith, L. (1998) 'Concept Analysis: Cultural Competence.' *Journal of Cultural Diversity 5*, 1, 4–10.

Thompson, N. (1993) *Anti-Discriminatory Practice.* London: Macmillan.

Training Organisation for Personal Social Services (TOPSS) (2002) *The National Occupational Standards for Social Work.* Leeds: TOPSS.

Trevithick, P. (2005) *Social Work Skills – A Practice Handbook,* 2nd edn. Maidstone: Open University Press.

List of Contributors

Beverley Burke is Senior Lecturer in Social Work at Liverpool John Moore's University, teaching on the BA in Applied Social Studies. Preceding that, she was a Youth and Community Worker. Her main interests are race and gender inequalities, anti-oppressive practice, social care and the law, and ethics in social work. She has researched, taught and published extensively on these subjects, including the highly commended *Anti-oppressive Practice: Social Care and the Law*, which she co-authored with Jane Dalrymple.

Paul Cambridge is a Senior Lecturer in Learning Disability at the Tizard Centre, University of Kent. He has worked as a researcher in a number of social services departments. Key research undertaken includes a Department of Health funded study on the long-term outcomes and costs of care in the community for people with learning disabilities and mental health problems, the sexuality of men with learning disabilities, intimate and personal care and gender and caring roles. His wider interests include inter-agency working, care management and adult protection.

Jim Campbell is a senior lecturer in the School of Sociology, Social Policy and Social Work, Queens University, Belfast. His teaching and research interests include mental health social work and the law, and the impact of political violence on social work practice. He was joint author of *Bloody Sunday: Trauma, Pain and Politics*, an in-depth research into the psychological and political consequences of one of the gravest crises in Northern Ireland's history.

Derek Clifford is Reader in Social Work at Liverpool John Moores University. He has published widely on issues of the theory and practice of social assessment and is currently writing and researching on anti-oppressive ethics in social work. He is co-editor with Professor Sarah Banks of a new international peer-reviewed academic journal, *Ethics and Social Welfare*.

Joe Duffy is a lecturer in the School of Sociology, Social Policy and Social Work, Queen's University, Belfast. Prior to his involvement in social work education, he was a team leader specialising in services for child protection. He has research interests in the areas of human rights and social welfare, citizenship and social work, user involvement and bullying. He also specialises in the teaching of law to undergraduate and postgraduate social workers.

Margaret Fawcett is an independent social worker. She is also a trained mediator and counsellor. She was previously a lecturer and researcher at Queen's University, Belfast from 1988 to 2004, where she undertook a major government study on needs and services for young people from divorcing families. In her current role she continues to practice with Family Mediation (NI) and to undertake training and consultancy work in this area.

John Gibson is an independent trainer and consultant working mostly in the area of residential child care. He is a faculty member of the Residential Child Care Project (RCCP), Cornell University, NY, where is he also consultant to the South Carolina Association of Children's Homes and

Families, Curriculum Development Group. On behalf of RCCP, he has recently taken the lead role in production of a training manual to assist care workers to engage constructively with young people who, at times, resort to proactive aggression. He is currently undertaking a doctoral research project using grounded theory to understand team leadership in residential child care.

Gerry Heery has been a professional social worker and practice teacher since 1981. He has worked mainly within the child care and justice systems across the voluntary, statutory and private sectors. He is currently an independent social worker offering support to families experiencing difficulties related to violence, aggression and abusive behaviour. He continues to write extensively on these subjects. He is co-ordinator of the NI Practice Teachers Training Programme, and an external tutor on the Degree in Social Work Course at Queens University, Belfast.

Stan Houston is a senior lecturer in the School of Sociology, Social Policy and Social Work, Queen's University Belfast. Prior to entering higher education, he spent 20 years in social services fulfilling a number of roles in child and family social work. His academic interests lie in the theorisation of social work practice, particularly in the area of children's services. He has also published on the interface between moral philosophy and social work.

Dorota Iwaniec is Emeritus Professor of Social Work, and founder and former Director of the Institute of Child Care Research at Queen's University, Belfast. She has had extensive clinical and research experience in child care and child protection, and has written wide-ranging studies on these subjects. She is internationally known for her work on emotional abuse and neglect, and on children who fail to thrive. She is co-Chair of the International Residential Care Group.

Greg Kelly is a senior lecturer in social work at Queen's University, Belfast. In recent years he has had lead responsibility for developing the University's undergraduate social work programme. Currently his main research interest is in adoption. He is a research Fellow at Trinity College Dublin, working on a major study of inter-country adoption in Ireland.

John McLaughlin is a lecturer in social work at Queen's University, Belfast and co-ordinator of the adult services module on the BSW programme. He teaches and researches in the areas of health care social work, health and disability, community care and ethics in social work practice. He is currently President of the Northern Ireland Ethics Forum in Medicine and Health Care and a member of the policy development group with Age Concern (NI). Before joining Queen's, he was a hospital social worker (team leader) and staff development and training officer with social services in Belfast.

Kieran O'Hagan was Reader in Social Work at the Queen's University Belfast. Preceding that, he spent 20 years in front-line childcare and child protection work in UK social services departments. This included a four year spell as Principal Case Worker (Child Abuse) in Leeds. He has published many commended books and articles for national and international journals, including *Cultural Competence in the Caring Professions*. His principal interests are child development, emotional and psychological abuse.

Raymond Taylor is a registered social worker and a Senior Research Fellow with the Glasgow School of Social Work, a joint School of the Universities of Glasgow and Strathclyde. He is currently seconded to the School from the Scottish Social Services Council. He has over 20 years of practice, training and management experience in social work in both the statutory and voluntary sector.

Subject Index

Author Index

Bainham, A. 235
Banks, S. 75, 76, 85, 139
Bannister, D. 60
Barnett, M. 95
Bisman, C. 19, 21
Bradley, G. 39, 221
Braye, S. 21, 23
Brearley, C.P. 152
Bronfenbrenner, U. 193, 237
Brown, A. 55, 56

Cambridge, P. 120, 121, 122, 123, 124, 125, 128, 129, 130, 132
Care Council for Wales 14, 15, 17
Central Council for Education and Training in Social Work (CCETSW) 11, 14, 16
Challis, D. 120, 122, 131
Chand, A. 239
Clough, R. 55, 56
Commission for Social Care Inspection (CSCC) 13, 121, 130
Committee for Social Work Education and Policy 11
Corbett, S.S. 207
Corby, B.C. 158, 234
Coulshed, V. 67–8, 181, 241

Davies, B. 120, 122, 131
Department for Education and Skills 12, 234–5, 236–7
Department of Health 13, 14, 96, 97, 102, 106, 107, 111, 112, 114, 117, 120, 121, 122, 125, 131, 132, 158–9, 176, 177, 214, 233, 237, 239, 242
Department of Health, Social Services and Public Safety 191, 233
Department of Health and Social Services (NI) 172–3
Dillenburger, K. 98, 101, 115, 212
Dolan, P. 244–5
Dolgoff, R. 86, 88
Douglas, T. 55
Dutt, R. 107

Evans, P. 38

Fawcett, M. 35, 45
Fox, D. 136
Furness, S. 107

Gilligan, P. 107
Golightly, M. 214, 223

Halpern, D. 141
Hayes, D. 234
Hekman, S. 78
Henly, A. 107
Henricson, C. 235
Hill, M. 237, 242, 243
Howe, D. 21, 22

Iwaniec, D. 192, 198, 200, 201, 202, 203, 204, 205, 207, 208

Jones, J. 23

Kahan, B. 53, 60, 61

Laming, H. 13, 232, 234
Levin, E. 12, 233
Levy, A. 53, 60
Liebmann, M. 37
Loewenberg, F.M. 85–6, 88
Lymbery, M. 173, 178

Macdonald, G. 235
McCarney, W. 136
McPhatter, A.R. 239–40
McPherson, L. 95
Middleton, L. 158
Mitchell, G.D. 17
Montgomery, A. 32
Moorman, M. 16
Muncie, J. 36

NCVQ 16

O'Hagan, K.P. 21, 23, 97–8, 101, 103, 108, 113, 115, 212, 236
Orme, J. 181, 241
Osmond, J. 103

Parker, J. 39, 221
Parker, R.A. 53
Parkes, T. 125, 128, 129, 132

Pattinson, S. 84, 85
Phillips, M. 107
Pilgrim, D. 216, 217
Preston-Shoot, M. 21, 23
Prior, J. 21, 24–5

Roberts, M. 37, 50
Rogers, A. 216, 217

Sapsford, R. 36
Schon, D. 24–5, 78
Smale, G. 241
Smalley, R.E. 14
Social Care Institute for Excellence (SCIE) 18
Statham, R. 136, 145

Taylor, C. 25, 78
Thompson, N. 42, 60, 138, 242
Thorburn, J. 239
Training Organisation for Personal Social Services (TOPSS) 12, 13, 14, 17, 19, 60, 86, 101, 119, 153, 179, 232, 233
Trevithick, P. 13, 17, 18, 19, 21, 23, 24, 97, 115, 232

UK College of Family Mediators 31
Utting, W. 53, 54

Wallcraft, J. 217
Ward, A. 55, 60, 61–2
Warner, N. 54
White, S. 78
Whitehead, P. 136, 145
Winnicott, C. 54, 60